CYBER WAR

CONQUEST OVER AN ELUSIVE ENEMY

Group Captain **A K Gupta**

Introduction by

Air Marshal Vinod Patney SYSM PVSM AVSM VrC (Retd)

KNOWLEDGE WORLD

KW Publishers Pvt Ltd
New Delhi

in association with

Centre for Air Power Studies
New Delhi

The Centre for Air Power Studies is an independent, non-profit, academic research institution established in 2002 under a registered Trust to undertake and promote policy-related research, study and discussion on the trends and developments in defence and military issues, especially air power and the aerospace arena, for civil and military purposes. Its publications seek to expand and deepen the understanding of defence, military power, air power and aerospace issues without necessarily reflecting the views of any institution or individuals except those of the authors.

Centre for Air Power Studies
P-284, Arjan Path
Subroto Park
New Delhi 110010

Tele: (91-11) 25699131

E-mail: capsnetdroff@gmail.com
website: www.capsindia.org

ISBN 978-93-86288-40-0 Hardback
ISBN 978-93-86288-41-7 ebook

Published in India by Kalpana Shukla

KNOWLEDGE WORLD
KW Publishers Pvt Ltd
4676/21, First Floor, Ansari Road
Daryaganj, New Delhi 110002
Phone: +91 11 23263498/43528107
Marketing: kw@kwpub.com
Editorial: jose@kwpub.com
Website: www.kwpub.com

Printed in India by Gopsons Papers Ltd

2011 FPBA BEST PUBLISHERS AWARD (ENGLISH)

CENTRE FOR AIR POWER STUDIES

VISION

To be an independent **centre of excellence on national security** contributing informed and considered research and analyses on relevant issues.

MISSION

To encourage independent and informed research and analyses on issues of relevance to national security and to create a pool of domain experts to provide considered inputs to decision-makers. Also, to foster informed public debate and opinion on relevant issues and to engage with other think-tanks and stakeholders within India and abroad to provide an Indian perspective.

Contents

Dedicated to My Father

Late Sh. Prem Narain Gupta, who introduced me to the wonderful world of books and imbibed in me the spirit of literary exploration, to whom I owe my values and vision.

Acknowledgements

I owe a debt of gratitude to those individuals who guided, corrected and chided me, reined in my impetuousness and supported me in my journey from literary *dilettantism to* professionalism. I am immensely grateful to Air Mshl Vinod Patney SYSM PVSM AVSM VrC (Retd), Director General, Centre for Air Power Studies (CAPS) for believing in me more than I do myself, peering into the text with his characteristic brilliance, clarity of thought and ineffable experience and offering perspicacious insights and observations towards my sometimes juvenile innuendos, inchoate arguments and repetitive articulations. I am also greatly indebted to Air Mshl K K Nohwar PVSM VM (Retd), Additional Director General, CAPS for his generous advice, support and contribution, culminating in the successful fruition of this book.

I am grateful to the Indian Air Force (IAF) – an organisation, par excellence, with focus on seeking insightful and innovative ideas on eclectic subjects within the context of national security – for providing me with the opportunity to undertake this research programme at CAPS. I would like to thank all my colleagues for engaging in stimulating, thought provoking and, at times, enlightening discussions, and offering a perspective, which, at times, challenged the premises and beliefs that are taken for granted. Special thanks to all colleagues who painstakingly checked the etymological integrity, grammatical impeccability and content cogency of my work and, at times, forced me to abandon my cacodoxical views.

I would like to thank all the staff at CAPS for their unstinting help that was crucial to the successful fruition of the book. The administrative and Information Technology (IT) support and a steady supply of coffee kept my focus doggedly on the research. I would also like to thank Mrs. Sushma Zutshi, Ms. Surbhi Sareen and the library staff for helping me in getting hold of varied research material.

My sincere thanks to Ms Kalpana Shukla and Mr Jose Mathew at KW Publishers for publication of this book. I owe my deepest gratitude to Ms Rehana Mishra who took painstaking efforts in editing the script over sleepless nights.

Last, but not the least, my deep and heartfelt thanks to my immensely supportive and patient family: my wife Bhawana and son Achint and my mother Sarla. Their unflinching faith in me has always been an inspiration and the inalienable source of support, encouragement and self-belief.

Preface

Most of us are either too intimidated or too enamoured with the internet and other cyber infrastructure and tend to take extreme views, declaring it the panacea for all ills or the mother of all evils. Cyber crime, cyber warfare and cyber terrorism have been so intricately embedded in the current 'security zeitgeist' that any discourse, technology integration and capability assimilation without multi-faceted foci on these, remains diffused and inchoate. Strategists, decision-makers, practitioners and scholars study cyber warfare, and each group is saddled with its own peculiar and intractable problems. Strategists and decision-makers, despite their many insights, struggle with neologism coined to describe new developments in cyber space. And practitioners and scholars, despite their cyber skills and proficiency in quick understanding of complex technical concepts, are incapable of providing a disciplined framework for policy enunciation. The study of cyber warfare suffers from too many unsubstantiated assertions and unwarranted assumptions which tend to be subjective and heterogeneous. The unique characteristics of this new domain warrant conceptualisation of new expositions, fresh interpretations of traditional concepts and studies of events that contributed to the current cyber zeitgeist.

Most of the government agencies, military organisations and corporations, individually or collectively, are faced with the challenge of managing cyber space so as to maximise the accrued benefits and minimise the risks and vulnerabilities. In cyber space, the implementation and effectiveness of risk and vulnerability reduction strategies largely depend on the ability to understand the broader issues of cyber conflicts and cooperation, and the unique intricacies associated with each challenge. The challenge of finding an appropriate balance between the compelling need for efficiency and innovation in order to foster growth and ensuring that cyber space remains secure, resilient and trustworthy, remains a concern.

Information Technology (IT) has played a significant role in transforming India's image to that of a global player in providing IT solutions of the highest standards. The great strides made over the past years in IT have not only brought economic well-being, enhanced employment opportunities, and increased productivity, but have also underpinned the importance of securing, defending and protecting the cyber space. Slowly but surely, collective and conscious efforts are being made to strengthen cyber security and to prevent cyber misuse in its various forms and manifestations. The cyber challenges are getting more complex, multifarious and unpredictable. This has created a completely new paradigm for national security, economic risk and individual privacy.

The ubiquitous dependence of a nation on cyber space makes the disruption of cyber space a cause of grave concern. The conventional rules and legal norms associated with crime control and criminal justice struggle to keep pace with the changing dynamics of the challenges of policing, regulating and enforcing the provisions of statutory laws in cyber space. The laws newly enacted or amendments made to existing laws are still lagging behind when it comes to governing and regulating the cyber realm.

It is in this context that I have tried to provide an overview of the myriad aspects of cyber security, with special focus on military policies, programmes, and practices. While steering clear of technical terms unless absolutely critical for an understanding of the subject, I have tried to keep things simple for easy assimilation and yet paid adequate attention to the didactic dimension of the narrative. This book draws heavily from the research articles published during the course of my research work with the Centre for Air Power Studies.

Ashish Gupta

Introduction

The very term 'cyber war' has excited the imagination of military practitioners for some years now. The influence of technology on warfare is increasing and cyber capabilities only emphasise the fact. The importance of the subject is implicit in the title of this book. Cyber warriors are indeed an elusive enemy and it is essential that we are able to keep them at bay. It is often mooted that Information Technology (IT) could well determine the victor in a future war. The combination of IT and cyber is the fifth domain of warfare (after land, air, sea and space). The electro-magnetic spectrum is now the sixth domain of warfare but cyber probably impinges on all the others. In an 'interneted' environment, the cyber world promises many distinct advantages, from intelligence accretion and analysis to faster and more reasoned decision-making. As we become more and more reliant on cyber facilities, the vulnerability also increases and proper safeguards are essential.

Cyber warfare is still in its infancy and it is a moot point as to the shape(s) that this form of warfare will take. There have been many cyber attacks in the recent past and the frequency and impact is increasing, but there has not been a cyber conflict involving two or more adversaries in simultaneous offensive and defensive roles. It is certain that complexities in this form of conflict will increase and so will their impact. This underscores the need to stay a few steps ahead of the opposition and that involves good intelligence and the use of intelligent probes to test the waters periodically and, may be, even unobtrusively. More importantly, as cyber war is indeed the fifth domain of conflict, it behoves us to recognise the need for special and specific formal training and adequate funding for research and development. The more adept we become, the more successful we will be in the prosecution of this new type of warfare.

Present-day military practitioners need to establish the likely impact of adverse cyber activity on our plans and what we can realistically expect will be the outcome of our actions on the adversary. As secrecy is ingrained in such activities, some educated guesswork is necessary. It will be obvious that as a feedback loop is not yet possible, the success of a cyber attack can seldom be forecast, and yet any help we can get will be a bonus. At times, the bonus could be significant although at current expertise levels, it cannot be averred that cyber attacks alone can be war-winning. Yet cyber activity must now form part of the planning process. Cyber instruments of war can work independently but will be more effective if dovetailed into operational plans. Deniability is a defining characteristic of cyber attacks and we should have a national cyber control and planning organisation that works alongside the military planners.

Successful cyber attacks at the tactical level could have strategic connotations. Even limited success will have a significant impact on the other domains of warfare. It can be stated with a fair degree of confidence that in time cyber superiority could well take the place of air superiority or aerospace superiority as the essential requirement in war. The first shots in a future conflict could take place in the cyber domain. The book gives some examples of successful cyber attacks but these should be viewed as merely indicative. We should be able to establish as to whether, given the state-of-the-art in the field, cyber attacks can cause impediments in the smooth flow of planned operations, or be a mere nuisance or inconvenience. More importantly, what will make cyber attacks war-winning? Such estimates have to be attempted periodically.

It has been mooted that the primary requirement of the armed forces is to deter the adversary. This is certainly true in the Indian context. But is cyber deterrence a valid thought, a workable concept? If it is, indeed, a valid concept, then the approach must form part of our operational planning and preparedness. How do we effect cyber deterrence? Deterrence is based on the perception in the mind of the adversary that a cyber attack will result in losses much greater than any possible gains. That demands signalling our intent and capabilities but how do we signal without showing our hand? Such issues require deeper deliberations. The flip side is whether we can successfully mount preemptive cyber attacks. It is possible to do so but we have to consider the impact of only a partial success or even a failure. Also, can we afford to advertise an impending military operation? Again, serious deliberations are needed to determine a preferred course of action.

The impact of cyber attacks also needs examination. Can cyber attacks be merely debilitating or could the result of such attacks cause fatalities? If it is the latter and the fatalities are in large numbers, we would have introduced a new form of warfare. As cyber attacks will not be the preserve of the powerful, they could become a weapon for the weak to, at least partially, overcome asymmetries. Brain power and cyber expertise could equalise, in some measure, the advantages enjoyed by the rich and militarily more powerful. It is possible that as the impact of cyber attacks becomes more and more severe, international opinion may seek to outlaw such activities. However, it is a moot point if the international community can formulate rules and laws that permit universal application, verification and action against the offenders. Fortunately, it will be some time before such a requirement becomes urgent and we have time to fashion the required initiatives or defences.

It will be instructive to examine as to what constitutes cyber war. An attempt to define it could leave the reader with a straitjacketed understanding. In fact, cyber espionage, intervention, deception, manipulation, misinformation and probes to disable or deceive are all ingredients of cyber war. The list is incomplete. Cyber war will most likely be a game of thrust and parry played at high stakes, with little surety of success or means of knowing the extent of success achieved. If this is true, our reliance on our probes has to be circumspect. The perpetrator of the attack should be conscious that his actions will invite retribution and the nature of the retribution will remain unknown. Hence, the 'target' has to be carefully selected and in a cyber war, the targets have to be selected to serve the overall requirements. Overconfidence and overreliance on cyber activities could also prove to be counter-productive.

Cyber war is a zero day weapon that should be well-tuned to the overall military plan. It will be worthwhile for allies to pool their knowledge and resources but it is unlikely that this will happen as trust deficits will always remain.

Cyber activities will remain classified but conventional wisdom suggests that we should seek intelligence information on the expertise available worldwide. Cyber plans will always be a function of need, technology base, capability and trained manpower. More importantly they will be highly classified and a degree of prescience may be necessary. China, Russia and the USA are the leaders in the field. China is of continued and increasing interest to the world at large. The book gives some inputs into the Chinese cyber world in some detail. This should interest the readers who are used to China's obfuscation of its capabilities. Similarly, the cyber capabilities of Russia and the USA are also discussed.

Our world is now highly dependent on space assets, the cyber world, communication systems and the media, with special reference to the impact of the social media. As the importance increases, interference in our plants, commerce, and media could become debilitating. It is essential that we protect our critical infrastructure and India has taken steps to ensure this. No such 'protection' programme can be fool-proof and some prioritisation and provision of redundancies will be needed. Also, there is considerable interrelationship and interdependence amongst the facilities to be protected and the task is complex and complicated. Our approach has to be evolving and evolutionary.

Once a threat is discovered, finding a counter is relatively easy. The critical aspect is to forecast, prepare and be ready. The objective must be that cyber attacks on us do not succeed even partially. We have to discern tell-tale signs, and continued practice is called for. Contingency planning is equally essential. The importance of cyber defence cannot be overemphasised.

Cyber war may not be a succession of disassociated events but it will more likely be a continuous process of attack, deception, thrust and parry. Offensive and defensive means have to operate in conjunction. Intelligence on the adversary's cyber intent, design and execution plans will be useful as from such information his operational plans could be discerned.

Warfare is becoming increasingly cerebral. The astounding progress made in technology impinges on operational capabilities and support functions, both as standalone capabilities and in synergy as well. Such synergy now forms the basis for planning and conduct of future conflicts. The 'Internet of Things' has greater applicability, resulting in better efficiency and effectiveness but cyber war has also increased the threat of only partial availability when it is most needed.

The book covers many aspects of this very important area. Cyber terrorism is a new form of warfare that is still evolving. Protection of critical infrastructure is gaining significance as our reliance on cyber increases. There are questions that only time can answer. For instance how can we measure the success of a cyber attack with confidence? Again, can cyber security be automated? Many new ideas will emerge, problems will surface and solutions will be pursued. Like in any other field, the offence and defence will, vie and challenge each other.

In writing this book, Gp Capt Gupta has performed a signal service to inform and educate the layman and the yet to be expert on the cyber world. It is a well written book that should interest many readers. Above all, for Gp Capt Gupta, this book has been a labour of love; for his readers, the book represents a start of getting acquainted with a subject whose importance will immeasurably increase with time.

Air Marshal **Vinod Patney** SYSM PVSM AVSM VrC (Retd)
Director General
Centre for Air Power Studies, New Delhi

1

Cyber War: Quantum of Problem

> *.. attaining one hundred victories in one hundred battles is not the pinnacle of excellence. Subjugating the enemy's army without fighting is the true pinnacle of excellence.*
>
> — Sun Tzu, *The Art of War*

Since the evolution of mankind, recourse to war has been viewed as a rational alternative for the preservation or furtherance of the state's interests. Justification or condemnation of war and its characterisation as just or unjust, depends on the success or failure of achievement of anticipated objectives. Defending or waging war requires aggrandisement of resources and power. The confronting belligerents leave no stone unturned in their efforts to secure favourable outcomes concomitant with anticipated objectives, in spite of expected damage to property and life. With such high stakes involved, a nation commits a sizeable amount of resources to defend its national interests from a number of present, potential and perceived threats. The breakthroughs in technology may come from unexpected fields, largely disconnected from traditional warfare domains. However, depending on their potential in furtherance of existing and aspirational military capabilities, the new technology and its spinoffs are adopted, assimilated and integrated in one or the other domains of warfare. In the face of profound and powerful breakthroughs, capabilities are developed, refined and used in creating a domain without intersecting and overlapping linkages with existing domains. The "domain approach" is an important and often defining aspect of military thinking and the underlying rationale for accruing strategic, operational and tactical advantages over potential adversaries.

Two decades ago, juxtaposition of the two seemingly incongruous terms 'cyber' and 'warfare' would have appeared esoteric and arcane. Back then, the acquired computational power by using computers was viewed as an instrument in furtherance of peripheral efforts and not as a force enabler or multiplier for shaping the operational environment. The development and adoption of an entirely new paradigm that emanated, as a result of the all-pervasive use of the Internet and cyber space, with its tentacles encompassing and entwining almost all the facets of the world's commercial, military and political activities, has turned cyber space into a potential venue for warfare. In military culture, technology is viewed as a panacea for dealing with a myriad challenges and technological solutions as a logical extension of strategic planning. To gain and maintain qualitative superiority by leveraging new technologies to develop new systems to counter a potential adversary, is one of the cardinal principles of military planning. The defence systems of most of the nations are being woven into the fabric of 'system of systems', thereby emerging as a new centre of gravity. It is paradoxical, yet true, that the more critical cyber space becomes to a nation's economy and defence, the more vulnerable it becomes. Even a nation possessing formidable military might, may find the exploitation of cyber space, as its Achilles had especially by non-state players. Cyber space has joined air and outer space as a new medium of conflict.[1]

The term "cyber space" was coined by William Gibson, who used it in his book, *Neuromancer*, written in 1984. The main protagonist in the book, Henry Dorsett Case, a low-level computer hacker in the dystopian underworld of Chiba City, Japan, was caught stealing from his employer and was punitively barred from accessing the global computer network in cyber space; a virtual reality data space, the "Matrix", by the administration of a drug damaging his central nervous system. Gibson defines cyber space as "a consensual hallucination experienced daily by billions of legitimate operators" and "a graphic representation of data abstracted from the banks of every computer in the human system."[2]. Gibson's fictitious character and apocryphal plot presciently described the present cyber ecosystem comprising millions of millions of computers networked on fibre-optical cables, wireless links and the ubiquitous Internet. It gained further currency due to its conceptualisation in compelling detail in Neal Stephenson's *Snow Crash*.

Cyber Space, Cyber Warfare, and Cyber Attacks

Exchange of information in cyber space facilitated through information technology, computers, networks and telecommunications is considered as the ontological keystone of war in any domain. The dynamism, sustainability, survivability and mission accomplishment of a functioning war-fighting entity is directly linked with reliable, secure, resilient and survivable cyber space. As of now, there is only a loose consensus on what constitutes an act of war in cyber space. As a precursor to understanding cyber war, it is worth dwelling over the concept of cyber or cyber space in the context of the military environment. According to the International Telecommunications Union (ITU)of the United Nations, cyber space is "the physical and non-physical terrain created by, and/or composed of, some or all of the following: computers, computer systems, networks and their computer programs, computer data, content data, traffic data, and users."[3]The US National Military Strategy for Cyber Space Operations defines cyber space as the domain "characterised by the use of electronics and the electromagnetic spectrum to store, modify, and exchange data via networked systems and associated physical infrastructures."[4]

The US Department of Defence (DoD) defines cyber space as the "notional environment in which digitised information is communicated over computer networks, consisting of an interdependent network of information technology infrastructures, including the Internet, telecommunications networks, computer systems, and embedded processors and controllers."[5]Cyber operations employ cyber space capabilities primarily to achieve objectives in or through cyber space. The United Nations (UN) defines cyber as "the global system of systems of Internetted computers, communications infrastructures, online conferencing entities, databases and information utilities generally known as the Net." This mostly means the Internet; but the definition can aptly be applied in the context of a digitally interconnected network of computers and other devices, operating in the bounded electronic information environment of an organisation, either the military, government or public/private owned corporations.

An attempt to capture the essence of an activity as complex and exponentially evolving as cyber warfare within the confines of a definition will fail to capture its essence and distinct nuances. A better elucidation of cyber warfare needs much more than encapsulation in a definition. By invoking the work of seminal figures that shaped both antiquated and modern warfare, it may be possible to get an insightful view into the domain of cyber warfare. In the 6th century B.C., the great military expert of ancient China, Sun Tzu, succinctly summed up that "the best form of warfare is to take down the enemy without fighting with him". The eloquence, relevance and importance of these words reverberate much more loudly in the realm of cyber space and cyber warfare. The ongoing shifts in discourses and practices of dominant and emergent structures of cyber warfare are shaping the strategic intent and direction, on the one hand, while, on the other, emerging as a definite force multiplier at the tactical level.

Edward Luttwak in his book, *Strategy: The Logic of War and Peace,* makes a convincing argument that equating war and peace is disparagingly flawed. During war, the methods adopted in peace time pursuits such as economy of scale, concentration of equipment and amassing of personnel are often inconsequential — even detrimental to the overall war effort. A favourable outcome in war requires adoption and execution of decisions diametrically opposed to the peace time methods in terms of redundancy, dispersal and surprise. Surprise, a key determinant of success in war,is the consequence of shock and confusion induced by the deliberate or incidental introduction of the unexpected. Cyber warfare tenets fit in snugly with these conceptual patterns. The deliberate infiltration of cyber weapons into the enemy's network and systems may cause disruption, confusion, and chaos, resulting in degeneration of its war-waging potential. Carl von Clausewitz[6], the Prussian military theorist, while articulating his version of warfare, stated: "Wars in every period have independent forms and independent conditions, and, therefore, every period must have its independent theory of war". With the advent of the information age, cyber space has evolved as a domain of war. Clausewitz provides a timeless framework for reasoning about war, independent of temporal, spatial and technological imperatives. Clausewitz said that he "intended to provide a thinking man with a frame of reference . . . rather than to serve as a guide, which at the moment of action lays down precisely the path he must take"[7]. Thus, for better understanding of cyber warfare, each tenet associated with it needs to be within territorial, technological or temporal boundaries. Clausewitz, while formulating the 'trinity', an interactive set of three elements that shape the events of war, declared that these three dominant tendencies hold the key to success in war. These are "primordial violence, hatred, and enmity; the play of chance and probability within which the creative spirit is free to roam; and its element of subordination, as an instrument of policy, which makes it subject to reason....." The interactive and dynamic interplay of these three elements will sustain the efforts to address even the most severe and debilitating threats. If we provide an analogous framework to these abstractions, it broadly translates into "the will to fight a war in terms of resources, finances and manpower; the means in term of military prowess across the full spectrum of conflict; and the able leadership with a sense of purpose and direction."All of these components have inherent resilience and capability to mutually revive each other in case of individual destruction or degradation. However, in case they are simultaneously attacked and destroyed, a resulting strategic paralytic effect will derail all the war-fighting efforts and make victory an elusive allegory. Initiation of attacks in cyber space with the intent to simultaneously degrade or destroy all the three tendencies will facilitate accomplishment of strategic objectives.

The interpretation of these indelible and inalienable concepts in the digital dimension and in the context of the virtual world will provide a framework for multi-disciplinary and multi-organisational engagements and participations in planning, developing and implementing policies and procedures to operate in cyber space. In the present conflicts, one foresees a battle space characterised by 'hide-and-seek' warfare rather than a 'force-on-force' experience.[8] Alvin Toffler explicitly stated: "The wars of the future will increasingly be prevented, won or lost based on information superiority and dominance."[9] Christopher Coker proclaims that the ultimate manifestation of post-modern war is "humane warfare", in which the mission is to neutralise rather than kill.[10]This implicit reduction of friction and violence perhaps reinforces the beliefs in cyber war operations in the future.

While defining the virtual world, it is crucial to accommodate the views emerging from current discourses and to explore the technological underpinnings. Accordingly, the virtual world can be defined as, "A persistent, simulated and immersive environment, facilitated by networked computers, providing multiple users with *avatars* and communication tools with which to act and interact in-world and in real-time."[11]New technologies of communication and information exchange have built up a scenario, in which all the existential entities are not only to be thought of in terms of their physical forms, geographical locations, demographic influences and socio-economic underpinnings, but also in terms of their cyber footprints, cyber resilience and cyber criticality. While the physical world has become much more fragmented and more differentiated, the virtual world, enmeshed by a network of computers, has become one congruent, virtually connected entity, permitting unhindered flow and exchange of information.

Boundaries in Cyber Battlefield

The boundaries of the battlefield in the real world are usually well defined and could be a geographical feature separating the two battle ready opponents. The clear distinction and demarcation of boundaries in the battlefield is a prerequisite for active combat among two nations likely to engage in a war. In the war on terrorism, the battlefronts are accidental or contingent upon the presence of some specific armed groups with certain ideological differences with established religious, political, social or military institutions. Still, even in this kind of war, there is physical use of weapons and possible exchange of ammunition between warring groups. In cyber space, the traditional boundaries akin to terrestrial boundaries just do not exist.[12]

The chief challenge in dealing with this new paradigm is the difficulty in attributing induced activities within a particular geographical confine. In cyber space, reconnaissance can be carried out by using systems and networks distributed across the world. Planning can be done by group of individuals who do not bear any possible resemblance in relation to typical combatants. The Internet can be both: a resource repository and an attack vector. The potential of the uncharted territories of cyber space are being exploited to create new opportunities and capabilities for preserving and strengthening national security in all its dimensions. For better elucidation, a closer look at this new battle space-in terms of its differentiated structure and shared commonality with antiquated and modern war-fighting domains, the intent and motivation of enemy forces and the most effective weaponry to win on this virtual front-is required. In all the modern war-fighting domains, computers and communication networks are now ubiquitous. The domains in war have evolved commensurate with technological advancements as well as in consonance with the immutable principle of war for establishing a comparative strategic advantage over an adversary. For example, from the initial war-fighting domains of land and sea, the evolution of airplanes brought air within the folds of warfare domain. Commensurate with the operating limitation of aircraft, the air domain encompassed activities undertaken within the Earth's atmosphere: beginning at the Earth's surface and extending to an altitude at which aircraft could operate. The advent of technology breakthrough saw spectacular growth of military activities in this domain. Air power emerged as a game changer and established itself as a force multiplier expertly augmenting, complementing and reinforcing the activities in other domains. Similarly, cyber power owes its genesis, growth and proliferation to technological advancements and it was not long before it gained currency as a valuable military and political tool in the 'internetted' world of interconnected, interdependent and highly interactive resources. While all the domains have different capabilities, strengths and limitations, for eliciting maximum effect, collaborative, collective and comprehensive cooperation of all these domains is a prerequisite for combat operations.

Raising of a New Crop of Warriors

When asked to imagine warriors of modern times, we generally conjure up an image of stern looking, combat hardened and gun brandishing men in camouflage uniforms. This image,in appearance and stature, may not live up to the expectation in the context of cyber warriors. The success of military operations in the cyber realm depends profoundly upon the versatile skills of 'cyber warriors' whose ingenious, coordinated and determined cyber operation activities are central to both offensive and defensive mission accomplishment. Though cyber warriors may not fight along linear geographic boundaries, they clearly operate in an adverse environment which is fraught with unpredictability and uncertainty, with high stakes accountability and consequences. Those involved in cyber operations have to function within the militarily conceptualised policies and strategies. One of the five major initiatives of the cyber strategy of the US Department of Defence (DoD) is to "leverage the nation's ingenuity through an exceptional cyber workforce and rapid technological innovation." According to this strategy document, "The development and retention of an exceptional cyber workforce is central to DoD's strategic success."[13]

The importance of building a cyber warrior workforce with requisite expertise and competencies and the need for identifying, recruiting and training individuals to support cyber warfare operations cannot be overemphasised. At present, many of those involved in cyber operations have not been trained in a formal sense and have acquired various levels of competency based on their ingenuity, aptitude and resourcefulness. The proliferation of cyber threats has made it imperative to holistically formulate training objectives, develop an all-encompassing curriculum,foster attitudes and specific skills to meet the needs of a highly competent cyber warrior workforce. Other related aspects of workforce management, including special skills development, placement and retention, also require to be paid due attention. The potential candidates for cyber warfare operations may not be able to meet the suitability criteria in their present form as laid down for traditional fighting forces the world over. Some qualities and qualification, which may or may not be significant for conducting cyber warfare such as age, military demeanour and specific credentials, may be dispensed with.

Strategic Dimension of Cyber Warfare[14]

In the context of cyber warfare, *complexities exacerbated by a rapidly evolving paradigm* have strengthened the case for 'cyber' to be recognised as a fundamentally distinct and physically unique operating domain. Before analysing the potential strategic potency of Strategic Cyber Warfare (SCW), it will be prudent to examine its characteristics. The deliberate offensive acts and acts of espionage, sabotage, terrorism, sedition and other economic/military violations perpetrated through cyber space by present and potential adversaries, terrorist groups, criminal organisations and rogue states, and their consequential ramifications on national security, make cyber warfare a strategic concern. It was emphatically articulated by Molander, "With new strategic threats, as new strategic vulnerabilities surface, it is increasingly clear ...that the evolution in strategic warfare will include a dimension of cyber space threats and vulnerabilities worthy of the label 'strategic information warfare'."[15]Adm Michael S. Rogers, as the head of the United States Cyber Command (USCYBERCOM) said: "The US possesses superior military might across all war-fighting domains, cyber space included. In truth, however, there has been no large scale cyber conflict yet in history and the state of strategy and execution of cyber warfare is evolving as we speak."[16]

In a war, strategic assets have been used to undermine the morale and political will of the enemy rather than taking recourse to its total annihilation. Strategic bombing, for example, entails systematic attacks from the air using strategic bombers or long- or medium-range missiles to attack targets vital to enemy's war-making capacity. Like strategic bombing, strategic cyber warfare can achieve consequences of strategic value comparable to those of actions induced kinetically, even if the war's arena happens to be cyber space. SCW, like any strategically oriented operation, seeks to bypass enemy surface forces to strike directly at the perceived centre of gravity. However, contrary to the use of destructive firepower and physical force, SCW primarily uses non-kinetic but potent means in the form of 'malicious software' and 'electromagnetic pulses'. Although SCW does not constitute an act of physical violence, its effective use may culminate in possible physical destruction. The objective of SCW is to create strategic effect via disruption rather than destruction.[17]The underlying goal is the same: the end is the purpose, and the end justifies the means. However, merely identifying vulnerabilities and exploiting these is not enough to achieve the intended objectives. For SCW to be strategically effective, it needs to prove its worth, when used in isolation without being supported or buttressed by other strategic assets. A parallel can be drawn between SCW and coercive air campaigns wherein measuring success "is not about assessing combat effectiveness but *strategic* effectiveness".[18]If SCW does not achieve strategic decisiveness independently, then, invariably, the onus will fall back on other more conventional forms of warfare.

When assessing the strategic efficacy of SCW, our understanding becomes blinkered and parochial, unless and until more challenging questions are raised and historical evidence is examined from a more critical standpoint. Even if there is the threat of physical destruction, the cyber vulnerability exploitation does not necessarily translate into strategic success. If argued that 'strategic' refers to all military instruments that serve as means to a favourable end, in the context of SCW, 'strategic' is used to imply a direct and independent relationship between the means and ends.

Operational and Tactical Reasons for Cyber War

The motivation for war, whether for individuals or nations, emanates from the calculation of the decision-makers; such that the anticipated gains in terms of resources, power, glory, territory, and so forth, exceed the expected costs of conflict, including expected damage to property and life. Thus, for war to occur with rational actors, at least one of the sides involved has to expect that the costs incurred will be outweighed by the anticipated gains from the conflict.[19]

At the operational level, cyber war-waging capabilities can be employed in a theatre of war to obtain advantage, leading to attainment of strategic goals through the conduct of campaigns. In war, a campaign involves employment of military resources in a series of related military operations to accomplish an objective with temporal and spatial relevance. Cyber war-waging capabilities need to be designed, orchestrated and coordinated in support of overall campaign objectives. Traditionally, it was about controlling and optimising resources, but today, there is a shift in the way cyber operations are conducted from the resource-specific system towards domination in information resources.

Because of their omniscience and ubiquity, today's critical infrastructure networks are key targets for cyber attacks. Their ubiquitous presence and their ascendancy in the role of running the 'command and control' systems, managing resources, planning operations and gathering intelligence have placed them as vital centres of gravity. During air operations, aircraft act as airborne routers exchanging targeting information constantly. Air Defence (AD) missiles and artillery are equipped with computer systems for initial launch and mid-course corrections. The Intelligence, Surveillance and Reconnaissance (ISR) systems gather information in such unimaginable quantities that the real challenge lies in differentiating between trivial and critical information and translating it into actionable decisions. Just a decade ago, a soldier of any modern army in his full ensemble with Global Positioning System (GPS) tracking devices, night vision goggles, communication gear and infrared camera would have conjured up an image akin to that of a super hero who jumped out from the pages of a comic book and took human form. Today, soldiers are increasingly relying on networked personal devices for interactive instructions and technology-assisted responses for mission accomplishment, survival and protection.

There is a military maxim, "Amateurs study tactics; professionals study logistics," (though the genesis of this saying is loosely attributed to Gen Omar Bradley, we are not contesting its origin, rather focussing on its context-specific applicability). Successful deployment of troops in a theatre of operations is the sum total of success achieved in moving the forces, weapons, equipment and supplies to the right place, at the right time. Logistics operations are conceived, planned, organised and executed by leveraging the computing power of thousands of networked computers. The execution of processes of forecasting, fore-procurement, warehousing, supplying, replenishing and replacing in a proactive and efficient manner are hallmarks of good logistics support that keeps the war-fighting juggernaut well-oiled and ramped up. The intent elucidation and capabilities evaluation of an adversary is possible by monitoring the activities in the logistics system. Disruption in logistics operations by compromising, destroying or disrupting the networks on which these operations ride on, and reside in, can interdict or at least impact capabilities. As was succinctly put by Saydjari, "Cyber-warfare relies on: sensors and exploitation; situational awareness; defensive mechanisms; command and control; strategies and tactics; and then finally, technology and engineering".[20]

Principles of Warfare in the Age of Cyber War

There are some general principles elicited from the understanding of traditional war, which can be transmuted, albeit with some modifications, when applied in the context of cyber space. When deciding on military strategies, we work within the precincts of cardinal 'Principles of War' and when evaluating plans, we factor in ends, ways and means. When we analyse sources of national power, we weigh diplomatic, information, military and economic imperatives. The joint doctrine of the Indian armed forces gives out the following Principles of War for the Indian armed forces:[21]

- **Selection and Maintenance of Aim:** The *raison d'etre* of armed force is to successfully wage a war, destroying the enemy's armed forces and will to fight. Strategic, operational and tactical objectives, once identified, need to be pursued with unwavering resolution till the attainment of desired results.
- **Maintenance of Morale:** Morale is nurtured through good leadership, sound discipline, realistic training, confidence in equipment and sense of purpose. It is a condition, attitude or sense of spirit that is maintained.
- **Offensive Action:** The purpose of an offensive action is to seize, retain and exploit the initiative.
- **Surprise:** To strike the enemy at a time or place or in a manner for which he is unprepared.
- **Concentration of Force:** Concentration implies the massing of the effects of all pertinent capabilities at the decisive place and time.
- **Economy of Effort:** Economy of effort requires allocation of minimum essential combat power to secondary efforts.
- **Security:** This means never permitting the enemy to acquire an unexpected advantage.
- **Flexibility:** To place the enemy in a disadvantageous position through the flexible application of combat power.
- **Cooperation:** To ensure unity of effort.
- **Simplicity:** In term of preparing clear, uncomplicated plans and concise orders for better and unfragmented understanding.

- **Administration:** Successful conduct of military operations requires effective and efficient logistics and administrative support.
- **Intelligence:** Even small forces can achieve significant victory by using intelligence based on painstaking reconnaissance and good information.

Cyber warfare, on the one hand, can transform the virtual world into a battlefield and, on the other, cyber capabilities can be enmeshed with physical war assets. These Principles of War, distilled from the experience and knowledge of great military leaders and from the studies of war campaigns and studies, are free from the temporal and spatial imperatives. Even in the face of evolving objectives and tactics, weapon technology, changing geopolitical landscape, these principles comprise the cornerstone of military decisions and actions. The scope,extent and consequences of applicability of all these principles,when applied in the virtual battlefield, may diverge from ensuing expectations. For their application to elucidate maximum effectiveness, some modifications and extensions may be required to adapt to emerging paradigm shifts in the cyber realm.

Having a clear objective is still the key to success. The objectives in a cyber conflict are the same as in a terrestrial, aerial or naval conflict. In the cyber space context, the number of potential targets with strategic underpinnings extends beyond the immediate combat area. The possible impact of cyber warfare, direct and indirect consequences of cyber warfare and application of cyber capability to enable or enhance ground, sea, air, and space operations — these are morale boosters for military commanders and troops. Defensive actions in cyber warfare call for resource intensive and timely solutions, while cyber attacks — carried out as part of the offensive strategy or active defence measures – are used for accomplishment of objectives with the requisite degree of severity. In other warfare domains, both defensive and offensive components add up and synergistically combine to strengthen overall security goals. The principle conventional military doctrinal exposition primarily focusses on the offence-defence balance that determines the relative efficacy of offensive and defensive security strategies.

In cyber space, the anonymity of the perpetrators, unpredictability associated with consequential damages and potential cascading effects of attacks adds elements of surprise and deception to the overall operational plans. Massing of cyber resources to perpetuate cyber attacks enhances their credibility, potency, and lethality. Concentration does not mean monolithic and unchanging orchestration of war-fighting; rather, it requires careful and organised distribution of cyber resources and capabilities. The principle of economy of force in the context of cyber warfare may be defined as "the employment of all resources available in the digital domain in the most effective way possible; and allocate the minimum essential to secondary effects."Outwitting the adversary by striking at its most vulnerable area with optimal cyber resources may be a significant factor in deciding the outcome of a military operation.

Cyber attacks are increasingly being used as instruments and agents of conflict enunciation, resolution and reconciliation, both as independent entities and in conjunction with broader military operations. The effects and implications of such attacks on variegated targets may be large or small, ephemeral or permanent; cyber attacks have shut down networks, cut off access to essential information and services, damaged industrial infrastructure and disrupted banking services.

The great strides made over the past years in Information Technology (IT) have not only brought economic well-being, enhanced employment opportunities and increased productivity, but also have underpinned the importance of securing the cyber space. Slowly but surely, collective and conscious efforts have been made to strengthen cyber security and to prevent cyber misuse in its forms and manifestations. The ionic Moore's Law of 1965, with unusual clairvoyance, predicted the Information and Communication

Technologies' (ICTs') exponential pace and growth.[23] This growth has proportionally increased the cyber security challenges. The security policies need to evolve at a pace commensurate with the growing processing power, technical sophistication, widespread proliferation of ICT devices and strategic implications of cyber security breaches. Unfortunately, the untethered and explosive growth of new ICTs and the ubiquitous presence and penetration of the Internet saw the emergence of threats — far more insidious, far more formidable and often hiding under a shroud of anonymity — which, at times, outpace the security responses of the military, governmental agencies and public and private users.

Cyber attacks can manifest in various forms and manner and often are stealthy and imperceptibly unnoticeable, catching the defenders by surprise. As the build-up for cyber attacks does not entail physical positioning and mobility of cyber resources, the consequential severity of the attacks remains unpredictable and in many cases, they build-up under the radar of conventional intelligence systems. Because of the element of surprise, anonymity and attributability, cyber attacks are weapons of stealth and silent insinuation.

In the context of cyber operations, the challenge is to find an appropriate balance between complexity and simplicity at each level. Cyber operations are inherently complex as cyber space is a common pool used by citizens, businesses, the military and governments, and demarcating boundaries among different groups is impossible. There are cross-linkages between different entities with cross-disciplinary interactions. To seek advantage over the enemy and to obviate collateral damage to non-military objects, we may need to develop plans that remain simple in objective but increasingly complex in execution. The principles of flexibility, cooperation, administration and intelligence are equally profound and have a bearing on every dimension of cyber warfare, from technology to training, from tactics to strategy, etc. These will be dealt in greater detail in the subsequent chapters.

Cyber Weapons[24]

For successful conduct of operations across the whole spectrum of conflict, weapons commensurate to the threat encountered, with requisite firepower, calibre and effectiveness are essential. In the context of cyber warfare, the requirement, development and acquisition activities related to cyber weapons need to be based on the consideration of a wide range of factors. The *neologistic character of* the term "cyber weapon" encompasses a variety of cyber instruments capable of inflicting effects of varying intensities — from defacing websites to destroying nuclear power facilities. A comparison between the weapons used in the cyber domain and other domains shows many shared commonalities as well as specific distinctiveness. In the physical form, the method of deliverance and the extent of expected physical damage, the cyber weapons may differ from conventional weapons, but at the conceptual level, there is a clear overlap of objectives as both can be used to degrade, disrupt, or destroy the enemy's war potential. There is a growing impression that something is *amiss* with the regulatory and legal framework, when it comes to branding generic software or malware as a cyber weapon, if it can be, or has the potential to be, used for a cyber attack. The lethality quotient of a cyber weapon needs to be evaluated based on its threat level, possible consequences and the malicious intent of the perpetrators. Even the *Dictionary of Military and Associated Terms*[25] of the US Department of Defence, in spite of a voluminous commentary on military terms and definitions, is silent about a generic definition of a cyber weapon. It defines non-lethal weapons and other specific types of weapons (or weapon systems) except cyber weapons. In cyber space, the consequential effect of a military operation will govern whether it would constitute an attack or use of force, even if there is nothing meeting the classical definition of the "weapon" involved.[26]This unnatural dichotomy in cyber space activities leads to uncertainty in identifying cyber weapons. The "cyber attack" or "cyber warfare" can be perpetuated by the employment of cyber weapons. But the uncertainty in the term "cyber warfare" leads to equal uncertainty in identifying cyber weapons and great confusion about when the use of a "cyber weapon" is a "cyber attack" that creates a state of "cyber warfare."[27]

The capabilities of the cyber domain are being inextricably intertwined with the tenets of other war-fighting domains and embedded in all aspects of military operations. The integration of the cyber domain in other domains allows capitalisation on inherent synergies specific to each domain. The evolving scale and character of cyber space has succeeded in altering the scope of cyber threats of multifarious dimensions and manifestations, differentiated in terms of the kind of destruction, disruption or loss caused as well as the required level of defence.[28] Defending against cyber threats demands collective efforts and resources guided by policy guidelines not from a disjointed variety of ad hoc sources. The integration of military, economic and political instruments at each level within the national security framework can only ensure that cyber defence matters remain central to national security determinations in the future. For guarding national security and protecting national interests against cyber attacks, cyber defence strategies and defensive capabilities are being developed, refined and consolidated by almost all nations. However, the existing cyber security measures appear to be always in "catch up mode" to challenges and ubiquitous reliance on cyber space. Capability argumentation and consolidation across the whole spectrum of cyber defence strategies is an inalienable imperative rather than a conceptual presumption. To bolster defence against cyber attacks, improvement and consolidation of existing capabilities and dynamic development of new capabilities through empirical observations, technology innovations and enumeration of threat vectors and actors are mandatory prerequisites. The evolution of cyber warfare strategies, like strategies in other domains of warfare, have in their roots, the cardinal imperative of hindering or disabling military forces, inflicting unacceptable damage, severely denting the morale of the security forces and disrupting economic activities in order to greatly undermine the will of an aggressor or a target country. A deeper understanding in the context of cyber warfare over a wide range of interrelated and independent issues can be best achieved and some intricate nuances of this unique domain can be captured, if we study the evolution of this domain, the prevailing "cyber zeitgeist", existing empirical evidence and proposed directions for the future.

Notes

1. Martin C. Libicki ,*Conquest in Cyberspace* (New York :Cambridge University Press 2007), p. 32
2. William Gibson, *Neuromancer* (New York : Ace Science Fiction Books, 1984), p.37.
3. International Telecommunication Union, Cybercrime Legislation Resources, *ITU Toolkit for Cybercrime Legislation* (Geneva : ICT Applications and Cybersecurity Division, 2009), p. 12.
4. United States Department of Defence, *National Military Strategy for Cyberspace Operation* (Washington D.C.: United States Government Printing Office, 2009), p.12.
5. United States Department of Defence, *Joint Publication 3-0 Joint Operations,* (Washington D.C.: United States Government Printing Office, 2010).
6. Michael Howard and Peter Paret, *Carl von Clausewitz, On War* (New Jersey:PrincetonUniversity Press, 1989)
7. Ibid., p. 141.
8. Martin C.Libicki, "Illuminating Tomorrow's War", *McNair Paper 61,* Institute For National Strategic Studies, October 1999, p.1.
9. Alvin Toffler, "Looking at the Future with Alvin Toffler", www.usatoday.com/ news/comment/columnists/ toffler/toff05.htm. Accessed March 12, 2016.
10. Christopher Coker, "Post-Modern -War", *RUSI Journal,* 143, no. 3, , p. 14.
11. Carina Girvan, "What is a Virtual World? Definition and Classification,"*Technical Reports,* School of Computer Science and Statistics, Trinity College, Dublin, https:// www.scss.tcd.ie/publications/tech-reports/reports.13/TCD-CS-2013-10.pdf. Accessed March 12, 2016.
12. Jason Andress and Steve Winterfeld, *Cyber Warfare Techniques, Tactics and Tools for Security Practitioners* (Massachusetts: Elsevier, 2014), p.35.
13. United States Department of Defense, *Strategy for Operating in Cyberspace* (Washington D.C.: United States Government Printing Office, 2011), p.12.
14. Roger C. Molander, Andrew S. Riddile and Peter A. Wilson,*The Nature of War in the Information Age* (Santa Monica : RAND's National Defence Research Institute, 1996), p.5.
15. Ibid., p.2
16. Kenneth A.Minihan, "Defending the Nation Against Cyber Attack: Information Assurance in the Global Environment", *USIA Electronic Journal,* 3, 1998, http://usinfo. state.gov/journals/itps/ 1198/iipe/toc.htm. Accessed March 12, 2016.
17. Greg Rattray, *Strategic Warfare in Cyberspace* (Cambridge, MA: MIT Press, 2001), p. 19.

18. Robert A.Pape, "The Limits of Precision-Guided Air Power", *Security Studies,* vol 7 , no. 2, 1997–98, p. 95.
19. Christopher J. Coyne and Rachel L. Mathers,*The Handbook on the Political Economy of War* (Cheltenham: Edward Elgar Publishing Ltd, 2011), p. 34.
20. S. Saydjari, "Cyber Defense: Art to Science," *Communications of the ACM,* vol. 47, March 2004, p. 53.
21. P K Mallick , "Principles of War: Time for Relook ", *Manekshaw Paper No. 12,* Centre for Land Warfare Studies, 2009, pp. 9-10.
22. Sai Felicia Krishna-Hensel, *Order and Disorder in the International System* (Surrey : Ashgate, 2010), p.13.
23. Moore's Law, "How Overall Computing Power of Computers Will Double Every Two Years," http://www.mooreslaw.org/. Accessed July 30, 2015
24. Andress and Winterfeld, n. 12, p. 83.
25 United States Department of Defence, "Military and Associated Terms", http://www.dtic.mil/doctrine/new_pubs/jp1_02.pdf. Accessed July 30, 2015
26. Gary D. Brown and Andrew O. Metcalf, "Easier Said Than Done:Legal Reviews of Cyber Weapons", *Journal of National Security Law &Policy,* vol. 7:115, p. 137.
27. Ibid., p. 115.
28. Krishna-Hensel, n. 22, p.13.

2

Coming of Age of Cyber War

There are but two powers in the world, the sword and the mind. In the long run, the sword is always beaten by the mind.

— Napoleon Bonaparte

Reliance on Cyber Space as a Vulnerability

About a decade ago, many analysts were reluctant to accept cyber warfare as a potent threat. This belief stemmed from their conditioning anchored deeply in the principles of conventional warfare. In 2003, James Lewis of the Centre of Strategic and International Studies (CSIS) dismissed cyber warfare as a serious threat—referring to cyber weapons as "weapons of mass annoyance" rather than weapons of mass destruction. [1]In 2004, noted security expert Marcus J. Ranum branded the whole concept of cyber warfare as "hype", propagated by war-mongers and sabre-rattlers to ensure continual funding after the end of the Cold War.[2] These thoughts echoed the general perception prevalent at a time when cyber warfare techniques were in their nascent state of evolution and were considered as innocuous endeavours rather than pernicious enterprises. Back then, actual acts of cyber warfare were insignificant or inconsequential insofar as economic or physical losses were concerned. Without major, publicly known incidents of cyber attacks, there was not even a loose consensus among various strategists and practitioners over their recognition as a potent threat.

The development, adoption, deployment of new technologies and an overreaching reliance on these, adds a new dimension to the legitimacy vs. *modus vivendi* debate in the context of interstate conduct and conflict. These new technologies create new capabilities and vulnerabilities. With almost clairvoyant vividness, the International Institute for Strategic Studies has highlighted that in future conflicts "the use of cyber warfare to disable a country's infrastructure, meddle with the integrity of another country's internal military data, try to confuse its financial transactions or to accomplish any number of other possibly crippling aims"[3]would feature prominently. The dynamic and interdependent interplay of technology and strategy—technology drives reappraisal and revision of strategy, while strategy itself propels improvements and innovations in technology —is a major determinant of political-military manoeuvring among rival states for securing and safeguarding their respective national interests.

While testifying before the Senate Committee prior to his nomination to head the US Cyber Command, Lt Gen Keith Alexander stated that "there is no international consensus on a precise definition of a use of force, in or out of cyber space. Consequently, individual nations may assert different definitions, and may apply different thresholds for what constitutes a use of force." He also added that "if the President determines a cyber event does meet the threshold of a use of force/armed attack, he may determine that the activity is of such scope, duration, or intensity that it warrants exercising our right to self-defense and/or the initiation of hostilities as an appropriate response."[4]

Today, in spite of structure, composition and spatial heterogeneity, the world is more integrated than ever before. This ethnically, culturally, economically and geographically diverse world has a common thread which creates a wonderful tapestry of shared beliefs and common values that amalgamate to create a homogeneous and coherent entity. Much of it may be attributable to technology breakthroughs and communications technology enhancements and deployments. Nation-state boundaries are being routinely traversed by individuals, organisations, groups and corporations over the digital highway in one form or another.[5]This increased world integration has raised the prospect of exacerbating the digital threat even further.

The weapons of cyber warfare have already been conceptualised, designed, used and refined, and manifested in the forms of denial of service attacks, computer viruses, worms, Trojans and a range of hacking tools and technologies. The technology is in place and the expertise is in abundance and it only takes ingenuity, intent and resources to unleash cyber attacks against an unsuspecting and unprepared adversary.

The evolution of our species is probably concomitant with the evolution of kinetic warfare. The archaeological evidence points out a systematic annihilation of the Neanderthals by Homo sapiens. The innate trait of aggression of our species was, and is, a primary determinant to our survival and dominance as a species. Despite the loss of countless human lives, unimaginable suffering and widespread destabilisation, war continues to be a key human interaction. Despite the moral, ethical, social and economic implications, the art of war is studied, taught and refined with intense earnestness and practised with unflagging vigour. For a student and practitioner of warfare, the study of the evolution of kinetic warfare with historical footings and technological development factors, is central to an understanding of war holistically in its multifaceted and dynamic *avatar*. With the emergence of diametrically different methods, processes and doctrines contemporaneous with the evolution of cyber warfare, a better understanding can be garnered from the study of acts of warfare and/or activities below the threshold of war but intentionally destructive or disruptive,which were spurred, supported and perpetuated by cyber attacks.

Since the coining of the phrase "weapons of mass annoyance", history has been replete with examples of cyber attacks of varying degrees of severity, scale, duration, for different objectives or enunciation of strategic intents. Some of these have made us to revisit existing beliefs about cyber war and reinvent a new set of guiding principles governing cyber war. Some of these are:

- Cyber attacks against Estonia as a manifestation of outrage over the relocation of a memorial : Year 2007.

- "Operation Orchard": Preemptive strikes which destroyed Syria's Al Kibar nuclear reactor[6] : Year 2007.
- Hijacking of Internet Protocol (IP) addresses by Hezbollah to circumvent Israel shutting down its web page during the July War : Year 2006.
- Russian cyber attacks against Georgia during the initial phases of its conventional operation :Year 2008.
- Successful stealing of the video feeds of Predator drones by the Iraqi militant group Kata'ib Hezbollah : Year 2008.
- Hacking and monitoring of the Tibetan government-in-exile computer systems: Year 2009.
- Discovery of the Stuxnet worm which caused debilitating damage to Iran's uranium enrichment facilities :Year 2010.
- Activist hackers vs. the Islamic state in Syria (ISIS) : Battling the proverbial Frankenstein monster in cyber space.
- Coordinated and protracted cyber attacks campaign against Ukraine

Cyber Attacks Against Estonia as a Manifestation of Outrage Over Relocation of Memorial

In April 2007, the Estonian government's decision to relocate a memorial,originally installed by the USSR in the year 1944, to commemorate the sacrifices made by Soviet soldiers during World War II, met with strong opposition by the ethnic Russian population of Estonia.[7] The monument at Tallinn, the capital of Estonia, was viewed as a symbol of Russian sacrifices and its relocation triggered violent protests by the Russian speaking minorities. Though by April 29 relative calm prevailed on the streets of Tallinn, Estonia's electronic infrastructure came under attack, result of a campaign of disruption and denial instigated on the Internet. A flood of messages overwhelmed the e-mail servers of the Estonian Parliament and rendered it dysfunctional. The security of the web servers of Estonian political parties was also compromised. With unrestricted access to these servers, the hackers replaced the legitimate content with a fabricated one. The Distributed

Denial-of-Service (DDoS) cyber attacks shut down the websites of all government ministries and two major banks.

Once the Estonian Computer Emergency Response Team(CERT) realised that a cyber attack was underway, it sought help from other national CERTs in Europe, such as the German,Finnish, and Slovenian CERTs. Collectively, the experts were able to identify the nature of the attack as well as the general locations in the networks generating the traffic for the attack and directed network operators to block those systems to arrest the flow of traffic before it reached Estonia. Following this, the DDoS attacks lessened over time and eventually stopped. With the diminishing of anger from the incident, the severity and staying power of the attack also diminished.

About two years after the attacks, a leader from a pro-Kremlin youth group known as the"Nashi" (translated "ours"), named Konstantin Goloskokov, claimed that he and other members of the youth group orchestrated the cyber attacks against Estonia.[8]On the surface,the Nashi appeared to be a Russian youth movement with patriotic overtones, while behind the facade of patriotic fervour it was reported that it thrived due to patronage by the Russian leadership. Its members routinely attended political youth rallies and participated in protests in support of Russian political objectives. More recently, a group referring to itself as the "Russian Wing of Anonymous" posted e-mails that, it claimed, belong to those who lead the Russian youth movements—specifically the head of the Federal Youth Agency Vassily Yakemenko and its spokeswoman Kristina Potupchik.[9] The e-mails revealed that the youth groups were often used as a tool for pro-Putin propaganda. The Nashi is believed to be involved in the 2008 cyber campaign against Georgia as well as cyber attacks against independent media outlets in Russia. Even if the claims made by Nashi are legitimate, some questions remain unanswered. It is believed that the group leveraged the computing resources at its disposal to generate the traffic against Estonia—which caused the DDoS. However, in general, DDoS attacks resulting from incitement of a large number of people who generate massive amounts of traffic toward specific websites are difficult to sustain over time. Eventually, either the participants in the attack lose interest or exhaust themselves or the compromised or subverted systems participating in the attacks are discovered and walled off or shut down.

'Operation Orchard': Preemptive Strikes which Destroyed Syria's Al Kibar Nuclear Reactor[10]

Since the founding of the Jewish state of Israel, relations between the Israel and its neighbour Syria have been characterised by periods of hostility, ceasefire talks and disengagement agreements. Unlike its other neighbours, Egypt and Jordan, that were able to forge normalised relations with Israel, the *impasse* in *Syrian-Israeli* peace negotiations was preventing progress towards peace in the Middle East. Israel's invasion of Syria in June 1967 resulted in the capture of the Golan Heights which continues to be under its occupation. In July 2000, Bashar Assad, a dilettante in politics and an ophthalmologist by profession, succeeded his deceased father Hafez Assad. Bashar Assad, in efforts to consolidate his power, espoused radical and controversial positions, including supply of massive amounts of weapons to the Iranian-backed Hezbollah in Lebanon and receiving high-ranking delegations from North Korea. It was widely believed that Damascus was engaging with Pyongyang for developing a Syrian nuclear programme. Mossad's suspicion turned to apprehension and later to conviction, when the American National Security Agency (NSA) shared the intelligence on the detection of a high number of telephone calls between Syria and North Korea, originating from a place in the northern Syrian desert called Al Kibar, to the North Korean capital, Pyongyang.

While still in contemplation on how to deal with this development, a window of opportunity opened in Israel's favour. In 2006, a senior official in the Syrian government, while visiting London, brought his computer with him. In an act of sheer carelessness, he left the hotel, leaving his laptop behind. In his absence, Mossad agents clandestinely entered his room and installed a Trojan to monitor the electronic communications traffic. While rummaging through the computer files, a photo caught their attention. A man of Asian origin in the company of an Arab in the middle of the desert was identified as Chon Chibu, a leader of North Korea's nuclear programme and Ibrahim Othman, director of the Syrian Atomic Energy Commission. While collaborating this explosive piece of information with other documents such as construction plans, the Israelis concluded that with aid from North Korea, the Syrians were secretly constructing a facility at Al Kibar to process plutonium. The Israeli apprehension was later confirmed by an International Atomic Energy Agency (IAEA) investigation. These damning revelations were enough for Israel to undertake drastic steps against its openly hostile neighbour. This culminated in the mounting of 'Operation Orchard'.

Just after midnight on September 6, 2007, seven Israeli F-15I fighter jets flew into enemy territory and dropped several bombs, levelling the Al Kibar complex to the ground.[11] The Syrian air defence response was almost non-existent and not a single shot was fired. This happened because the Israelis were able to compromise the Syrian military's computer network and were able to feed their own data streams in the Syrian system. Once inside, a false image of a radar screen was introduced which misled the Syrians into believing that all was well, even when Israeli planes were deep inside Syrian territory. The Israelis gave the world a front seat view of the effectiveness and efficacy of cyber war.

Hijacking of IP Addresses by Hezbollah to Circumvent Israel Shutting Down its Web Page During the July War[12]

Hezbollah, a Shi'ite militant Iranian-supported group, came into existence in Lebanon following the Israeli invasion in 1982. Since its inception, its primary objective was to offer resistance to the Israeli occupation. In February 2005, after the withdrawal of Syrian troops, a result of mass Lebanese protests after the assassination of former Prime Minister Rafiq al-Hariri, all warring factions, barring Hezbollah, agreed to disarm. Hezbollah continued with its objective of waging an armed conflict against Israel. In July 2006, in a preemptive action against Israel, its members killed three and kidnapped two Israeli soldiers in cross-border raids. This was followed by a series of short-range rocket attacks against Israel. The Jewish state was quick to ,retaliate causing significant damage to the Lebanese infrastructure and the death of over 1,000 civilians, but failed in its prime objective of decimating Hezbollah. The conflict came to an end after the United Nations Security Council unanimously approved UN Security Council Resolution 1701, which was accepted by the Lebanese government and Hezbollah on August 12, 2006, and by the Israeli government on August 13, 2006.

Both sides used cyber war operations to leverage the power of the media and propaganda as an adjunct to the ground operations. The Israelis conducted a denial-of-service attack on the website of Hezbollah's television station, Al Manar. The members of the World Union of Jewish Students (WUJS) used a piece of software called 'Megaphone' that directed the users to anti-Israeli chat rooms or opinion polls to encourage them to post supportive messages for the furtherance of the Israeli cause. On the other side, Hezbollah hackers were able to gain access to the networks of the Israeli Defence Force (IDF) units stationed on the Lebanese border.

In the context of Israel vs Hezbollah, cyber warfare emerged as an extension of the asymmetrical war leveraged by the convergence of bloggers, gadgetry and populist journalism. Hezbollah probably exploited the "information battlefield" better than its Israeli counterparts. Hezbollah showcased the plight of the Lebanese victims in an effort to garner support for its cause, branding Israel as an aggressor. In response to Hezbollah's Cyber Psychological Operations (CYOPs), many of Israel's allies in the West banned Hezbollah websites such as Al-Manar. There were also reports of the IDF launching unspecified cyber attacks against Al Manar and other Hezbollah sites. On being denied the use of legitimate IP addresses, Hezbollah resorted to the highjacking of IP addresses from corporations worldwide—including the United States, Canada and India. In support of the Israeli cause, a group called "Society for Internet Research" monitored Hezbollah's Internet traffic in order to identify the highjacked addresses and alert the target company in order to shut down Hezbollah's Information Operations (IO). However, once detected, Hezbollah quickly hijacked new IP addresses.

Russian Cyber Attacks Against Georgia During the Initial Phases of its Conventional Operation[13]

In August 2008,hostilities between Georgia and Russia commenced as a result of Russian support to South Ossetia, officially part of Georgia but which unilaterally declared itself as an independent state. Georgian troops engaged with local separatist fighters, as well as with Russian forces that had crossed the border with the stated intent to defend Russian citizens and peace-keeping troops already in the region. Prior to the commencement of the ground campaign, Russian hackers targeted Georgian news and government websites. The Russians claimed the commencement of attacks as a retaliatory response to the Georgians' hacking of South Ossetian media sites earlier in the week. The date of commencement of the Russian cyber attack i.e. one day prior to the actual ground attack, is also significant and is suggestive of the fact that the hackers knew the date of the invasion beforehand. Initially, the cyber attacks launched by the Russian hackers were primarily DDoS attacks by botnets. The Georgian media and government websites were knocked out due to the DDoS attacks followed by the targeting of financial institutions, businesses and educational institutions. To spread disinformation and propaganda, hackers infiltrated official Georgian government sites and made the Georgian president look like Hitler.

The attackers targeted Georgia's banking system, overwhelming financial sites with numerous fraudulent transaction attempts. Sensing this, international banks shut down banking services, resulting in almost zero monetary transactions inside Georgia for several days. The cell phone service also went down the day after the banking system crashed. The origins of the cyber attack on Georgia were traced to the Russian Business Network (RBN), a shadowy group of sophisticated cyber criminals, which gained notoriety in the wake of the massive spamming and phishing attacks in 2004.

If we calibrate the Russian Georgian War on the scale of forces involved and duration, it neither involved a large military force nor lasted a long time. However, in the context of cyber domain operations, it was watershed event, setting a precedent for examining and evaluating the effects of cyber warfare across a broad spectrum of national security issues. This was the first case in the annals of cyber warfare when this domain was integrated with other war-fighting domains. The Russian cyber attacks upon Georgia's military and government networks were highly successful. "It seems that 54 websites in Georgia related to communications, finance, and the government were attacked by rogue elements within Russia ... So as tanks and troops were crossing the border and bombers were flying sorties, Georgian citizens could not access websites for information and instructions."[14] Unlike the Russian cyber attack upon Estonia in 2007, the Russian cyber attack on Georgia was accompanied by physical combat between Russian and Georgian military forces. The cyber operations had shown their potential as a worthy adjunct to military operations at the strategic, operational, and tactical levels.

At the strategic level, the Russian cyber space reconnaissance and probing attacks began weeks prior to the actual commencement of combat. The Georgia president's website came under DDoS attack from Russian hackers. The attacks against Georgia's Internet infrastructure began as early as July 20, 2007, with a coordinated onslaught of spurious traffic that overloaded and effectively shut down Georgian servers. The July attack may be viewed as of preparatory nature for an all-out cyber war after the firing of the first salvo of ammunition. Another important strategic consideration was that the cyber operations were in sync with the overall strategic objectives of the Russian government. It was pointed out in a study conducted by John Bumgarner and Scott Borg,[15] "They didn't attempt to cripple sites that could have caused chaos or injury, such as those linked to power stations or oil-delivery facilities, but merely those that could trigger comparative inconvenience. There was a political decision not to attack those critical infrastructures directly. They made the point that they could launch these attacks. They showed they have the capability to do more"[16] This was exactly what Russia did against Georgia's most important strategic installation with kinetic weapons. Russia bombed all around the pipeline without actually hitting it -- a clear message that it could do so. Indeed, the cyber attacks fit into an overall Russian strategy against Georgia.

Successful Stealing of the Video Feeds of Predator Drones by Iraqi Militant Group Kata'ib Hezbollah[17]

In late 2008, US military personnel in Iraq arrested a Shi'ite militant in possession of a laptop that contained video footage of feeds from Predator Unmanned Aerial Vehicles (UAVs), the mainstay of the US Air Force. In July 2009, laptops of other insurgents were also found to be having recordings of Predator feeds. One particular group, the Kata'ib Hezbollah, which was known to have been supported by Iran, was also found to be in possession of feeds and the necessary equipment to obtain them. Reports of Predator intercepts in Afghanistan also emerged. The story first appeared in *Wall Street Journal*[18], which reported that militants in Iraq had used $26 US dollar off-the-shelf software programmes such as Sky Grabber to intercept live video feeds from US Predator drones, potentially providing them with information they needed to evade or monitor US military operations.

The Predator has become the UAV of choice for strike operations owing to on-board availability of a variety of high-end reconnaissance and targeting tools, including the Synthetic Aperture Radar (SAR) with 1-foot resolution, laser designators and range finder, a Moving Target Indicator (MTI) and the Multi-Spectral Targeting System (MTS), which provides real-time imagery of the battlefield—complete with features such as zoom and a telescopic spotter. For transmission of information i.e. for line-of-sight communications, the Predator operates in the C band. However, for beyond line-of sight missions, it uses Satellite Communication (SATCOM) in the Ku band. Additionally, it is equipped with Ultra High Frequency (UHF) and Very High Frequency (VHF) radio relay links. For SATCOM, the

Predator relies on commercial communication satellite infrastructure to transmit its data. The use of the Ku band SATCOM proved to be its Achilles' heel which resulted in compromise of the intelligence data collected on the aerial platform. The data transmission was taking place in an unencrypted format on a widely understood medium. A key component to the vulnerability of the Predator was the use of the broadcast model. This implies that all devices within the range and tuned to transmitter frequency, receive the transmitter's message. Normally, the devices not specifically programmed to accept these messages discard them. In order to avoid interception of communications, most administrators encrypt such traffic.

Hacking and Monitoring of Tibetan Government-in-Exile Computer Systems[19]

On March 29, 2009, the details of what would become one of the most, if not *the* most, talked about example of Advanced Persistent Threat (APT) activity in recent history were released via a story in *The New York Times*. The history of this particular attack is intriguing and its depth and breadth are impressive to say the very least. The target of interest was the office of the Dalai Lama (the Tibetan government-in-exile), which was, at the time, located in Dharamsala, India. Suspecting that they were the unwitting victims of espionage, the representatives of the Tibetan government engaged a group of third-party investigators, the Info War Monitor (IWM). The team comprised researchers from the Secdev Group, and other consultancies and research bodies. The results were quite shocking and revelatory. Compromised systems were identified in 103 countries the world over, including systems in the Embassies of India, South Korea, Indonesia, Romania, Cyprus, Malta, Thailand, Portugal, Germany, and Pakistan, in addition to the office of the prime minister of Laos. In addition to these national embassies, financial institutions within the region were also compromised, leading to approximately 1,295 hosts having been compromised and identified. Estimates suggested the progression of the attack saw about a dozen computers being attacked on a weekly basis.

Discovery of Stuxnet Worm and its Effectiveness in Causing Debilitating Damage to Iran's Uranium Enrichment Facilities

The year 2009 was a defining year which marked the arrival of the first true cyber weapon, "Stuxnet". On June 17, 2010, security researchers at one of the firms at Belarus came across a piece of virulent and malicious software that infected the USB memory sticks.[20] The discovery was followed by the revelation that a similar kind of infection was discovered in the Fuel Enrichment Plant (FEP) at Natanz, Iran. The severity of the problem was publicly acknowledged by President Mahmoud Ahmadinejad with the admission that a computer worm was the root cause of the problems in some of the Iranian centrifuges. The arrival of Stuxnet on the scene, and the aftermath of the Iranian crisis made the computer security community sit back and take notice of the severity and effectiveness of malware. Some were quick to label the Stuxnet worm as an "evolutionary leap" unprecedented in its functioning, unpredictable in its actions, catastrophic in its effects and unimaginably successful in its ultimate consequences.

Stuxnet was designed to attack and infect a type of industrial equipment known as SCADA (Supervisory Control and Data Acquisition) systems. The SCADA systems are widely used by a large number of industrial plants for data collection in real-time and for controlling and monitoring the vital parameters for the functioning of the plants. The physical components that go into the functioning of the plant SCADA systems are often controlled by the PLCs (Programmable Logic Controllers), a piece of computer hardware. In order to make the PLCs function in a particular fashion within the acceptable tolerance levels, these are pre-programmed by the administrator. The brilliance and ingenuity of Stuxnet lies in its ability to intercept a genuine command by the administrator and instead send its own set of instructions. In an attempt to mislead an unsuspecting operator, it makes the software falsely report back, in a manner and format interpretable as normal.

The serious nature of the Stuxnet worm has led to no end of speculation and conjecture. It was introduced into the facility's computer system with a USB drive and proceeded to infect machines running Microsoft windows. By brandishing a digital certificate showing that it had come from a reliable source, the worm was able to evade the automated-detection system. Stuxnet then checked, if a machine was part of the targeted industrial control system made by Siemens. It then compromised the target system's logic controllers, exploiting zero-day vulnerabilities yet to be identified. In the beginning, it spied on the operations of the targeted system. Then it used the collated information to take control of the centrifuges, making them spin themselves to failure. Meanwhile, it provided false feedback to outside controllers, ensuring that they did know what was going wrong until it was too late to do anything about it. It is believed that the perpetrators used four zero-day security vulnerabilities to spread around Microsoft's Windows operating system. After a detailed study, Microsoft admitted that the attackers initially exploited the old MS08-067 vulnerability which was a remote code execution vulnerability. Successful exploitation of this vulnerability enables the attacker to take complete control of an affected system remotely. A new LNK (Windows Shortcut) flaw was used to launch the exploit code on vulnerable Windows systems and a zero-day bug to exploit the Print Spooler vulnerability (this vulnerability was leveraged to propagate and affect systems connected to the affected machine's network).

Activist Hackers vs. ISIS :Battling the Proverbial Frankenstein Monster in Cyber Space

Terrorism, a scourge that transcends geographical borders and cuts across religious, sectarian and ethnic lines, evolves, propagates and retains its terror potency by permeating the public consciousness and infesting our societies with fear. The degree of success of terrorism in realising its insidious goals is largely determined by the sense of terror which may be infused across all sections of society. Terrorism thrives on publicity, and modern communication technology enables terrorists to penetrate the collective consciousness and to vicariously expose the global community to the pain and suffering of the victims and their families. Besides, by propagating their convoluted ideological discourses with *pseudo-religious fervour*, the terrorist organisations partially succeed in bringing potential fence-sitters, sympathisers and ideologically aligned individuals into their fold. The dreaded and perfidious Islamic State in Syria (ISIS) has transformed the way terrorist groups reach and recruit followers globally and has become an expansive enterprise making unsubstantiated and/or fraudulent claims of religious or political legitimacy. By fanning religious fervour, nurturing hatred, perpetuating violence, committing acts of unprecedented cruelty and taking advantage of ignorance, the ISIS ensures that its ranks are filled with committed recruits.

The transformative power of the new media and social networking platforms has been woven into the terrorist enterprise of the ISIS almost from its inception. In the wake of the ISIS offensive in June 2014, a number of Twitter accounts came up claiming to represent the ISIS in Syria and Iraq. During the initial days of the offensive, the various Twitter accounts were giving live updates and images of its advances in Syria and northern Iraq. The ISIS' digital footprint on social media kept pace with its advances made in Syria and Iraq. The images of captured Iraqi security personnel went viral, garnering an even wider online audience. In an attempt to fan the religious jingoism, the information, including of the number of bombings, suicide missions and assassinations it has carried out, was shared on the growing number of Twitter accounts having large followings. In an attempt to expand its digital reach on social media, the ISIS branched out to other platforms like YouTube, Facebook and Instagram. The ISIS shocked and enraged the whole world when it posted the video of the beheading of American and British journalists and other innocent individuals. The deliberate attempt of the ISIS to take its social media strategy to a whole new level probably stemmed from its belief that the overly shocking and terrifying events posted online would attract maximum viewership and may accomplish the objectives of its propagandic campaign.

The war against the ISIS is being fought by many nations — at times, in a wary collaboration, at times, in an open alliance — in many forms, at various locations. Opening another front against the ISIS in the virtual world, the cyber warriors – some government affiliates, others driven by a sense of outrage at the ISIS' brutal reign of terror — in an effort to deprive the group of the opportunity to use cyber space for online propaganda, are trying to shut down the ISIS supporters' media accounts, and portray the group in its true evil and demonic form. The hackers and cyber experts on government payrolls – for the most part being in a cat and mouse relationship — have joined hands to fight a common enemy.

One day after the attacks in Paris on November 13, 2015 a video was released online, supposedly by the hacking group Anonymous, proclaiming, "We are uniting humanity, expect us." In the days that followed, the members of the group took out the Twitter accounts believed to be those of supporters and sympathisers of the ISIS and some directly handled by ISIS operatives.[21] Behind the Guy Fawkes masks, *'anonymous hacktivists'* have rallied under the banner "#OpParis" and have vowed to oust ISIS operatives from social media. Another group called "Ghost Security", with the self-declared mission of targeting "Islamic extremist content" from "websites, blogs, videos, and social media accounts," claims to have carried out DDoS attacks against ISIS linked websites, resulting in the disruption or the taking down of more than 130 websites by overwhelming their servers with fake traffic from multiple sources. [22] Another group called "CtrlSec", closely related to "Ghost Security", claims to have made elimination of pro-ISIS accounts on Twitter its sole mission.

The intentions of these *hacktivists* are gallant and brave, but the outcome of these operations may not meet the expectations that had initially been perceived. The critics are questioning the effectiveness of these operations as there is no immediate and substantial reduction *in the barbaric dispensation among the ranks and files of the ISIS' cadre.* In a study by Brookings Centre for Middle East Policy titled

"The ISIS Twitter Census", it was brought out that from September 2013 through December 2014, by a conservative estimate, at least 46,000 Twitter accounts were used by ISIS supporters. This figure leapfrogs to 70,000 accounts with the maximum estimate. Much of the ISIS' social media success can be attributed to a relatively small group of hyperactive users, numbering between 500 and 2,000 accounts, which tweet in concentrated bursts of high volume.[23] The Twitter accounts of ISIS supporters far exceed in numbers the accounts that "Anonymous" claims to have helped unplug.

However, some computer security experts opine that the online war against ISIS may prove effective as a counter measure to interrupt or prevent the process of radicalisation before social frustrations and religious sentiments manifest in violence and unbridled cruelty. In addition, the online efforts of the ISIS to lure young recruits with radical learnings into its ranks will also be undermined. Battling the ISIS in cyber space is not limited to just online vigilantes. Various government intelligence officials and cyber security experts have also spurred up their efforts in countering and curtailing the propaganda of extremist groups. The "Think Again Turn Away" campaign on Twitter, launched in English in December 2013, by the US Department of State is an effort to enter the war of ideas and win over the hearts and minds of radicalised individuals on social media. This was broadened with a Facebook account in August 2014.[24]

Despite these efforts, the ISIS is still using the power of social media as a key instrument of coercion, enticement, indoctrination, proselytisation and propaganda for waging its own version of a modern *jihad*. Its operatives have switched to a more sophisticated form of encryption to evade detection. The messaging apps like WhatsApp, Viber and Telegram are increasing being used by the ISIS and other militant organisations. As these messaging apps use sophisticated and end-to-end encryption, the shared messages — despite their dark and insidious contents — cannot be decrypted even by the app's creators, owners and developers. Other ISIS members have switched to the Internet's dark web— its shadowy alter ego populated by illegal sites which enables routing of a user's communication through an unfathomable maze of networks, obliterating the possibility of tracing its source. Some ISIS operatives have even resorted to offensive cyber tactics. A group called Cyber Caliphate urged its followers to use Twitter to spread propaganda. ISIS extremists have posted online the hacked personal details, including mobile phone numbers of the heads of the Central Intelligence Agency (CIA), the Federal Bureau of Investigation (FBI) and National Security Agency (NSA).[25]

The war against the ISIS shows no sign of abating in spite of massive air strikes and the efforts of well-equipped multinational armies. However, the meagre success of various groups in containing the ISIS online activities in cyber space is viewed with subtle optimism and as a minuscule precursor to the overall objective of decimating the ISIS and ridding the world of its brutal and oppressive ideology.

Coordinated and Protracted Cyber Attacks Campaign Against Ukraine

The simmering political unrest in Ukraine flared up in November 2013 after the abandonment of plans by the former Ukrainian president to sign a trade agreement with the European Union (EU). This was constructed as a sign of leaning towards Moscow, and culminated in mass protests and unrest that were met with an iron-fisted crackdown. These violent protests created a schism between those who endorsed close ties with Russia and those who opposed this and favoured ties with the EU instead. In the wake of this development, the Russian hacker groups sprang into action and executed DDoS attacks on websites opposed to the Yanukovych government's pro-Russia posturing. During the Ukrainian crisis,the prodigious leveraging of cyber space drew on most of the chief tenets of cyber warfare raging from tampering with the phones of the Ukrainian parliamentarians to the use of classical malicious cyber tools such as DDoS attacks and defacement of some of the websites.

In low-level hacking attacks, the highly visible sites, voicing their displeasure on the government decision, were either rendered inaccessible or started displaying modified and fabricated contents. The Ukrainian government, on its part, also used the national telecommunication infrastructure in an effort to intimidate protesters. Under mounting pressure, Yanukovych eventually fled the country and Moscow became more involved. The covert support gave way to Russian troops brazenly entering Ukraine and after seizing the military airfield in Sevastopol and the Simferopol international airport, raided the Ukrainian telecom firm Ukrtelecom. The principle Ukrainian government website became non-functional for three days coinciding with the Russian troops' arrival at Crimea on March 2, 2014. In a retaliatory cyber strike, Ukrainian hacker groups such as "Cyber Hundred" and "Null Sector" carried out DDoS attacks against the websites of the Kremlin and the Central Bank of Russia. In efforts to discredit Ukrainian officials and garner support in Russia's favour for the March 16 referendum on the fate of Crimea, the intensity and severity of attacks by Russian hackers increased. James Lewis of the Centre for Strategic and International Studies befittingly described the Russian strategy as, "[to] control the narrative, discredit opponents and coerce." In fact, the day before the presidential election in Ukraine, a virus in the systems of the Central Election Commission, designed to tamper with data on the results of the election, was detected. This audacious attempt, if not thwarted in time, would have derailed the whole political process. A hacker group, Cyber Berkut, claimed responsibility for the attack.

As the Ukrainian issue remained unresolved, there was no diminishing of the severity and frequency of the cyber attacks. In January 2015, Ukrainian Prime Minister Arseny Yatseniuk blamed Russia for cyber attacks against German government websites, ostensibly to discourage Berlin from supporting the Ukrainian government. The attack came in the wake of the scheduled meeting between Ukrainian Prime Minister Arseny Yatseniuk and German Chancellor Angela Merkel a couple of days later. The attack targeted the web pages of the German chancellor and of the German Parliament, leaving the sites inaccessible for some time. Again, the proverbial cyber warriors, Cyber Berkut claimed responsibility.

In October 2014, detailed technical reports from the security companies iSight and Fire Eye, made a series of more substantial allegations of Russian state-sponsored hacking. The iSight reported details of activities of a group it nicknamed Sand Worm and after profiling the organisations targeted by Sand Worm and the attacks' technical underpinning, attributed its origin to Russian intelligence agencies. The intent and technical sophistication of the group can be gauged by the fact that it used 'zero-day' attack, a preferred and effective tool used by resource endowed threat actors. The Sand Worm group used its zero-day attack to target several Ukrainian regional governments, an act not consistent with normal cyber criminal activities and is suggestive of state sponsored targeting.[26]

Conclusion

These examples are just a few of the innumerable cyber attacks against sovereign states, economic institutions, critical infrastructures, state agencies, individual targets, etc. Unlike other attacks perpetrated by the use of a specific weapon system or pervasive technology, for cyber attacks, the list of potential targets is only limited by the ingenuity, resourcefulness, technical sophistication and motivation of the perpetrators. Nation-states, cyber criminal groups, phishers, terrorist groups, disgruntled insiders, foreign intelligence services, phishers, spammers, espionages, spies, etc. – the list of possible threat actors and vectors has been expanding as a result of the enormous *increase* in potential targets, consummate results, asymmetric and attributional advantage and low entry cost. In comparison to the conventional domains of war, the diametrically different cyber domain calls for different competencies and skills that are not usually acquired in the course of the study and practice of conventional warfare. Different methodologies associated with the processes of cyber capability development and doctrinal framework contemporaneous with the evolution of cyber warfare can be garnered, refined and consolidated from the study of the above acts of warfare and/or activities below the threshold of war but intentionally destructive or disruptive, which were spurred, supported and perpetuated by cyber attacks.

Notes

1. PBS's flagship investigative journalism series, " Interview James Lewis,"*Frontline*, February 2003, http:// www.pbs.org /wgbh /pages/ frontline/shows /cyberwar / interviews /lewis.html. Accessed June 1, 2015.
2. Marcus J. Ranum, "Cyber War: Reality or Hype?," http://www.ranum.com/ security/computer_security/archives /myth-of-cyberwar.pdf. Accessed June 1, 2015.
3. John Chipman, "Military Balance 2010", International Institute for Strategic Studies Press Statement, February 2014, http://www.iiss.org/publications/military-balance/the-military-balance-2010/military-balance-2014-press-statement/. Accessed June 1, 2015.
4. CBS News , "Military Asserts Right To Return Cyber Attacks", *News Division of CBS*, April 14, 2010, http://www.cbsnews.com/news/military-asserts-right-to-return-cyber-attacks/. Accessed June 1, 2015.
5. Lech J. Janczewski ,*Cyber Warfare and Cyber Terrorism* (Auckland : University of Auckland, New Zealand, 2008), p.13.
6. Erich Follath and Holger Stark, "The Story of 'Operation Orchard': How Israel Destroyed Syria's Al Kibar Nuclear Reactor", *Spiegel Online International*, http:// www.spiegel.de/international/world/the-story-of-operation-orchard-how-israel-destroyed-syria-s-al-kibar-nuclear-reactor-a-658663.html. Accessed June 20, 2015.
7. Karsten Brüggemann and Andres Kasekamp, "The Politics of History and the 'War of Monuments' in Estonia," *The Journal of Nationalism and Ethnicity*, Nationalities Papers, July 2008.
8. Paulo Shakarian, Jana Shakarian, and Andrew Ruef, *Introduction to Cyber-Warfare: A Multidisciplinary Approach* (Massachusetts: Elsevier, 2013), p.19.
9. Ilya Mouzykantskii, "Polishing Putin: Hacked Emails Suggest Dirty Tricks by Russian Youth Group," *The Guardian*, February 7, 2012, https://www.theguardian.com/ world/2012/feb/07/putin-hacked-emails-russian-nashi. Accessed June 20, 2015.
10. Follath and Stark, n. 6.
11. Ibid.
12. Shakarian , et. al., n.8, p.23.
13. Jeffrey Carr, *Inside Cyber Warfare: Mapping the Cyber Underworld* (Sebastopol, *CA* : O'Reilly, 2012), p.183.
14. Jon Oltsik "Russian Cyber Attack on Georgia: Lessons Learned?", *Network World*, August 17, 2009, http://www.networkworld.com/community/node/44448. Accessed June 20, 2015.
15. John Bumgarner and Scott Borg, "The US-CCU Report on the Georgian Cyber

Campaign", *US Cyber Consequences Unit*, August 2009, at http://www.registan.net/wp-content/uploads/2009/08/US-CCU-Georgia-Cyber-Campaign-Overview.pdf . Accessed June 20, 2015.

16. Steve Levin, "Cyber-Attack Strategy: Part of Russian Attack on Georgian Pipelines, Report Finds", oilandglory.com, August 20, 2009, at http://www.oilandglory.com/2009/08/cyber-attack-strategy-part-of-russian_20. Accessed June 20, 2015.
17. Thomas Strouse, "Kata'ib Hezbollah and the Intricate Web of Iranian Military Involvement in Iraq", *The Jamestown Foundation*, March 4, 2010 , at http://www.jamestown.org/single/?tx_ttnews%5Bt t_news%5D=36109#.VrhRJVQrLIU. Accessed June 20, 2015.
18. Siobhan Gorman,YochiJ. Dreazen and August Cole, "Insurgents Hack US Drones $26 Software Is Used to Breach Key Weapons in Iraq; Iranian Backing Suspected", *The Wall Street Journal*, December 17, 2009, http://online.wsj.com/news/articles/SB126102247889095011?mg=reno64-wsj&url=http%3A%2F%2Fonline.wsj.com%2Farticle%2FSB126102247889095011.html. Accessed June 20, 2015.
19. Luppicini, Rocci, *Moral, Ethical, and Social Dilemmas in the Age of Technology*, (Pennsylvania : Information Science Reference, 2013), p. 114.
20. Kupreev Oleg and Ulasen Sergey, "Trojan-Spy.0485 and Malware-Cryptor.Win32.Inject.gen.2 Review", VirusBlockAda, July 2010.
21. Mirren Gidda, "Cracking the Caliphate :Can Hackers and Western Security Services Win the Online War Against ISIS?", *Newsweek*, December 4, 2015.
22. Simon Cottee, "The Cyber Activists Who Want to Shut Down ISIS," *The Atlantic*, October 8, 2015, http://www.theatlantic.com/international/archive/2015/10/anonymous-activists-isis-twitter/409312//. Accessed December 3, 2015.
23. J.M. Berger and Jonathon Morga, "The ISIS Twitter Census," *The Brookings Project on US Relations with the Islamic World Analysis Paper*, No. 20, March 2015, p.2.
24. Rita Katz, "The State Department's Twitter War With ISIS Is Embarrassing," *Time*, September 16, 2015, http://time.com/3387065/isis-twitter-war-state-department/. Accessed on December 3, 2015.
25. Ian Gallagher "ISIS 'Cyber Caliphate' Hacks 54,000 Twitter Accounts and Posts Phone Numbers of Heads of the CIA and FBI in Revenge for the Drone Attack that Killed a British Extremist," *The Mail*, November 8, 2015, http://www.dailymail.co.uk/news/article-3308734/ISIS-cyber-caliphate-takes-54-000-Twitter-accounts-Terrorists-hack-social-media-site-spread-vile-propaganda.html. Accessed on December 3, 2015.
26. "West Accuses Russia of Cyber Warfare", *IHS Jane's Intelligence Review*, December 28, 2014. http://www. janes.com/article/47299/west-accuses-russia-of-cyber-warfare. Accessed June 20, 2015.

3

Enunciation of the Principles of Cyber Deterrence

Nuclear deterrence, in the era of the Cold War, was the single, most important determinant in preventing the destruction of our planet from the scourge of nuclear weapons. During the Cold War, the deterrence theory was the lynchpin of the US strategy for containment of the former Soviet Union, protection against nuclear attacks and preservation from nuclear blackmail. Deterrence is a broad phenomenon that involves using threats of harm, usually to be inflicted by force to convince others not to do designated harmful things.[1] For a credible deterrence posturing, the inalienable requirement is development of commensurate capabilities, their overt visibility and frequent deployment as a way of issuing and resurrecting threats, particularly in the wake of a crisis/ confrontation. Deterrence is used to manipulate the perceptions and actions of others and in altering or reinforcing behavioural responses or containing belligerent posturing, and in case of its ineffectiveness, use of coercion or threat of use of force or overt use of force emanating from acquired deterrence capabilities.

Drawing parallels with nuclear deterrence and contextually applying these concepts for evaluating the veracity and effectiveness of 'cyber deterrence' might turn out to be futile and counter-intuitive due to varying nuances of intent, applicability, participants and consequences. In the context of nuclear deterrence, the potential enemy is clearly identifiable in form and intent, and the deterrent will remain convincing and credible as long as the survivability of weapon systems and delivery vehicles is ensured. A nuclear threat emanating from a non-state actor is almost non-existential. Adm Michael Rogers, commander of the US Cyber Command, while appearing before the House Select Intelligence Committee on November 20, 2014, commented, "I often will hear people use the nuclear analogy in terms of how we were able to develop the concepts of deterrence, norms and behaviour. I try to remind people to remember that the challenge of the nuclear analogy is... that [nuclear weapons] were controlled by a very small number of nation-states -- two really."[2]The main assumption underlying nuclear deterrence is to contain the threat of nuclear annihilation by stemming the motivation of states with nuclear arsenals to cross the nuclear threshold. In cyber space, the enemy may employ disguises, masquerade or hide behind the 'digital veils' without a verifiable or discernible objective or motivation. The primary perpetrator may be an individual, an organisation, a non-state actor or a nation-state. In the cyber domain, the lack of clear lines of demarcation — in terms of intent, motivation and geographical location — makes the task of identifying the true perpetrators, apportioning responsibility and undertaking reprisals a herculean one. The problem of deterrence in cyber space is exacerbated due to several reasons: its inherent asymmetric nature, difficulties in accurate and timely attribution of hostile activities, level of threshold above which an inimical act warrants punitive reprisals, overarching dependence on technological prowess and a plethora of potential adversaries having the requisite intent and capabilities.

The strategy of using deterrence is meant to maintain a frozen status quo. As per William Kauffman[3], "Deterrence consists of essentially two basic components: first, the expressed intention to defend a certain interest; secondly, the demonstrated capability actually to achieve the defence of the interest in question, or to inflict such a cost on the attacker that, even if he should be able to gain his end, it would not seem worth the effort to him." The potentiality and potency of a deterrent declaration is directly proportional to its credibility. The overt demonstrations of intentions to leverage the innate, acquired or developed deterrent capabilities in order to thwart threats against targets and interests, as enumerated in the deterrent declaration, are the hallmarks of effective and preponderant deterrent posturing.

In the present times, deterrence as the cornerstone to strategy has been pushed down to a lower rung on the hierarchical ladder. After all, the Cold War of more than forty years ended rather unspectacularly, without the usual march of great armies, unfurling of victory flags and roars of cheerful crowds, with expectant jubilation. Nuclear deterrence which was the mainstay of the Cold War era and the nuclear arsenal that supposedly saved the world from nuclear war because of the certainty of Mutual Assured Destruction (MAD), suddenly were stigmatised as liabilities rather than strategic assets. Nuclear deterrence today appears to be an antiquated solution to a dominant problem of the past. With changing times, strategic considerations have also changed and contextual solutions are emerging from ideas best suited for the present. Although, deterrence is conceived and executed as part of the coercive strategy to deter unfriendly behaviour, its effectiveness is totally dependent on the consent and intent of the deterree. The efforts to shape that consent by deterrence are vastly inferior in quality in comparison to the control secured by military action which effectively deprives the enemy of the power to make a wrong move.[4] In addition, the possibility of potential foes rejecting the perceived rational behaviour paradigm and functioning irrationally from the stand-point of strategic logic, is high. The whole premise of deterrence is based on mapping the enemy's rational intent. Besides, if the intended deterree is either unwilling or unable to be deterred, then deterrence cannot work. [5] In addition, deterrence has its limitations against asymmetrical threats which cannot be consistently and tangibly fitted into any threat evaluation model.

The classical deterrence doctrine is based on the basic premise that abidance or violation of established rules or conventions stems from the rational calculation of the risk of reprisal or punishment versus potential advantages accrued from an act. A deterrence doctrine, which is capricious, uncertain and is not leveraged by commensurate capabilities,fails to be amenable to rational actors. For the deterrence doctrine to be effective and credible, it essentially requires an amalgam of three individual components in equal measure: **severity, certainty, and celerity**.[6] The 'severity' of a punitive action will deter a rational state committing an act of perceived wantonness or malice against another state. Punishment should be calibrated based on the extent of the crime at the appropriate severity level. 'Certainty of punishment' is the expression of inalienable resolve to punish the offenders irrespective of the cost. Infliction of punishment closer to the commission of an offence will reinforce the veracity of the deterrence posture. Deterrence works most efficaciously when it can rely, not upon the potency of explicit threats but rather upon the fears of deterrees — who are discouraged from taking action by their anticipation of the threats that adventurous behaviour would bring down upon their heads.[7]Deterrence,for the manipulation of cost/benefit calculation and for generation of fear, is a form of coercion requiring two essential elements: the credible capability to harm and the credible intent to carry out this harm.[8]Deterrence in cyber space aims to dissuade or discourage potential enemies from carrying out activities detrimental to perceived interest. If an adversary intends to wage war in the cyber domain, he will have to weigh his options and decide what will yield commensurate dividends: a daring cyber attack with proportionate returns or exercise of restraint to avoid the retaliatory wrath of a deterrer.

Closely associated with the theory of deterrence is the 'theory of preemption'. It is widely believed that if an adversary cannot be deterred, poses 'clear and present' danger and if its threat instruments can be neutralised by the available capabilities, pre-emption will be a better suited option. The centrality of the theory of deterrence is somewhat limited in its unambiguous applicability across the broad spectrum of present, perceived and potential adversaries. It somewhat relies on absorbing the consequences of a hostile act, identifying the perpetrators and then undertaking punitive actions proportionally weighted or exemplarily applied. Against irrational actors, such as terrorist groups, preemption may be more appropriate as terrorist organisations have very little to lose, cannot be trusted with a rational disposition or checked by the threat of retaliation and their nefarious intent needs to be nipped in the bud before it culminates into terrorist attacks.[9]Preemptive options, once exercised,are likely to stir up geopolitical and strategic tensions. Preemption, as an instrument of policy, an adjunct to force posture and an occasional subterfuge against rogue actors is essential. However, the policy of preemption cannot be a central strategic deterrence posture.

The applicability of traditional concepts of deterrence in an unmodified form to the realities of cyber threats has its own challenges and limitations. Cyber space does not comply with the classic definition of sovereignty as propagated by the dominant 'Westphalian conceptions'. In the realm of cyber space, the relative anonymity of an attacker makes the issue of attributability an arduous and contentious process. Cyber attacks can occur without any warning or without any obvious or subtle indications. Cyber attacks can remain undetected even when they stealthily cause intended damage - as perceptible physical manifestation of the consequences of an attack, in quantifiable attributes, takes time. The possibility and potentiality of a cyber attack remains the same in war-time as well as in peace-time, without any apparent period of crisis or strained relations. Since an attacker can use the infrastructures of a third party — either in connivance with it or under a tacit agreement or without its knowledge — it limits the possibility of attribution and proportionate response against the true perpetrators. For credible deterrence, cyber weapons need to be developed, evaluated and checked for efficacy and factored into the overall deterrence policy. In response to a question, while appearing before the Senate Armed Services Committee (SASC), to head the US Cyber Command (USCYBERCOM) Adm Michael S. Rogers responded by stating,

"The establishment of the US Cyber Command is an element of a deterrence strategy, but more work and planning will be required to evolve a solid national strategy. Classic deterrence theory is based on the concepts of threat and cost; either there is a fear of reprisal or a belief that an attack is too hard or too expensive. Cyber warfare is still evolving and much work remains to establish agreed upon norms of behavior, thresholds for action, and other dynamics." Adm Rogers further stated, "A broad understanding of cyber capability, both defensive and offensive, along with an understanding of thresholds and intentions would seem to be logical elements of a deterrence strategy, both for our allies and our adversaries, and as they are in other war-fighting domains."[10] The uncertain causal evidence and ambiguous consequences of cyber attacks tend to undermine deterrent postures in cyber space. Despite these challenges, a deficient or inadequate deterrent in cyber space creates vulnerabilities that could be exploited by a determined adversary.

The national interests, which a nation intends to defend,if threatened have potentially debilitating ramifications and devastating consequences. A nation's interests consist of the physical and cyber assets of public and private institutions in several sectors: agriculture, food, water, public health, emergency services, government, defence industrial base, information and telecommunications, energy, transportation, banking and finance, and shipping. Inimical actors, ranging from mischievous hackers, to criminals, terrorists, non-state actors as also nation-states, are ready to exploit the cyber space for notoriety, power, money, state secrets or just for the thrill of it. A fraction of such attacks are reported, investigated and recorded. The origin of some may be traced behind the physical boundaries of a hostile state, thwarting even the investigative efforts, let alone concluding those with convictions. Some of them may be individual and isolated enterprises by disgruntled employees, cyber criminals, cyber terrorist groups, professional hackers, etc., while others may be closely coordinated acts of more sinister intent perpetrated by nation-states. It is difficult to discern the quantum of evidence which qualifies for retaliation. Investigating every breach in cyber space is not possible as it is a resource and effort intensive exercise. There has to be some discernible correlation between the magnitude of retaliation and the magnitude of damage. Loss of life makes a tractable threshold but cyber attacks have yet to claim the first casualty. If benchmarking a figure based on some monetary considerations justifies a retaliatory attack, how would it be communicated to the attacker that crossing a certain threshold would result in retaliation? The evolution of deterrence theory/ strategy in cyber space cannot be equated with conventional deterrence strategy, as cyber space is unique in its physical characteristic, functionality, scope and context. The unique character of cyber space presents new challenges.

Problem of Attributability

The anonymity and impunity, with which acts of cyber terrorism and espionage are being carried out has made the process of fixing accountability and subsequent prosecution extremely difficult. Cyber space, being a common entity shared by governments, institutions, companies and individuals, does not offer a sense of security as physical/ geographical boundaries do. The perpetrators with nefarious intentions do not have to undertake the arduous task of breaching the security over physical boundaries to carry out a cyber attack. Unlike in the case of conventional attacks, where the source of attack can be conclusively and irrevocably established, in the realm of cyber warfare, the question of attributability and accountability becomes controversial. In a hypothetical situation, let us examine a scenario in which a group in State A assimilates computers located in State B into its botnet. The group then uses the botnet to overload computer systems in State C based on instructions received from State D. Though by the conventions of the laws of natural justice, the attributability of the conduct rests with State D, it will take a long legal battle to exonerate State B and State C of the responsibility for the conduct of the attack.

Problem of Credible Response

Almost all forms of retaliation are directed towards the vulnerability of the target. The quantum of retaliation will depend on near-accurate prediction of vulnerabilities. Through assiduous exploration and by investigating key systems vulnerable in specific ways, potential adversaries may be identified, tagged, documented and mapped in the overall orchestration of the deterrence policy. While such actionable information may be reassuring to a certain degree in one's ability to respond credibly on a given day, a consistent deterrence posture requires the ability to respond as long as the deterrence policy is operative. Vulnerabilities can be discovered and patched, rendering the effectiveness of response initiated as punitive action ineffective. The quantifiable measure of the outcomes of such attacks may also be speculative. It has been postulated that the use of many kinetic weapons will have the comparable problem when used against a large variety of targets. The damage assessment after cyber attacks on information systems will only be speculative based on its resilience and patching up of vulnerabilities. Furthermore, the extent of damage to any information system is strongly related to the reaction of its human operators: for example, how quickly faults can be found and fixed; how easily damage can be routed around; how frequently the data is backed up; or the availability of extant contingency plans. Besides, complacency of the targets, stemming from the belief that their systems face no serious threats, apart from those that have been anticipated and dealt with, may prove their Achilles' heel. Once such targets are put at obvious risk, operators may no longer be so complacent and, thus, targets may not be so vulnerable. The more the complacency on the part of human operators, the more vulnerable the targets become.

Reestablishment of Deterrence Posture After Attack

After an attack in cyber space, the threats designed as part of deterrence need to be realised. This will jolt the defender from its stupour and will energise it to protect its cyber assets with much more rigour and strength. An alert defender will carry out a critical review of existing systems and plug in the associated vulnerabilities. In the wake of this, reestablishing the deterrence posture will require designing new threats with the potential to dissuade the adversary from undertaking another misadventure. Now the task will be much more gruelling as the vulnerabilities which were exploited and exposed previously would have been plugged in, the targets hardened, and the associated complacency would have vanished.

Cyber Deterrence in Limiting the Number of Contests

In general, conventional conflict takes place between two warring groups. The ideological, economic, political or allegiance imperatives may bring in third party interventions or associations. However, as cyber space is so intricately interwoven, an unsuspecting and innocent party may get affected by an act of retaliation against an adversary in cyber space. It may inadvertently draw the affected party into the conflict, thereby expanding the quantum and dimension of the conflict. This may prove counter-effective as a deterrence posturing is normally aimed at controlling escalation.

Effectiveness of Cyber Deterrence in Safeguarding Privately Owned Critical Infrastructures

Critical infrastructures consist of assets in the physical and cyber domains. Many of the infrastructures important for the subsistence, sustenance and security of the population, are privately owned and operated. It is the responsibility of system operators to ensure operations of critical infrastructures without disruption and corruption. Formulation of a deterrence posture in the wake of this puts the spotlight on the attackers rather than the system owners who have an obligation to protect their critical infrastructure. System owners may take the recourse of absolving themselves of any wrongdoing by arguing that cyber attacks are acts of war and may invoke the *force majeure* clause.

Escalation Avoidance

The ensuing crisis following a cyber attack may force the aggrieved opponent to respond with kinetic weapons, thereby escalating the level of conflict. As a part of the deterrence policy or strategy, in response to a cyber attack, if a retaliatory action is initiated in cyber space, there is no assurance of restrained behaviour from the other side. Article 5, which is a fundamental principle of the North Atlantic Treaty Organisation (NATO), stipulates that if a NATO ally is the victim of an armed attack, each and every other member of the alliance would consider this act of violence as an armed attack against all members and would take the actions it deems necessary to assist the ally attacked. In a policy endorsement, the principle that a cyber attack can constitute an armed attack was approved by NATO defence ministers in September 2013. Similarly, Russia, without mincing words, has made it clear that it may respond with strategic means at its disposal if a cyber attack directed against it crosses the strategic threshold. While retaliating as part of the deterrence policy in cyber space could logically be construed as a natural progression of events, the possibility of crossing a threshold and exacerbating the escalation potential of violence is real.

Sanctions as Part of Overall Deterrent Posture

Sanctions – predominately economic and peripherally political and military – constitute an important element of the deterrent policy. Sanctions against a state or an entity are employed as coercive instruments to elicit a behavioural change or to diminish belligerent posturing. In the post-Cold War era, the waning reliance on armed conflicts and wars, within and among states, for resolution of belligerent, contentious and complex problems has resulted in widespread use of economic sanctions. Sanctions have been used in support of foreign policy goals: to discourage armed aggression, cap the aspirations of potential nuclear states, rein in drug trafficking, expedite political change, discourage proliferation of weapons of mass destruction and dissuade support for terrorism.

Some political observers and decision-makers think of sanctions as a measured and proportionate response to a challenge considered below the threshold of perceived national interests at stake. In addition, sanctions can be considered as a form of expression or message-sending to communicate disapprobation of a particular action or behaviour. It was appropriately observed by America's Catholic bishops, "Sanctions can offer a non-military alternative to the terrible options of war or indifference when confronted with aggression or injustice."[11]

In order to gauge the efficacy of economic sanctions and ascertain the underlying rationale, an analysis of the sanctions against Iran provides some perspectives. In the case of Iran, in order to cap its supposedly illicit nuclear activities, the US, the member states of the European Union and others put in place a strong, interlocking matrix of sanctions measures relating to Iran's nuclear, missile, energy, shipping, transportation, and financial sectors.[12] The EU embargo and the US sanctions played havoc with the Iranian national economy. Iran's oil exports fell drastically and in January 2013, Iran's oil minister acknowledged that the fall in oil exports was costing the country between US $ 4 billion and US $ 8 billion each month. Iran is believed to have suffered a loss of about US $ 26 billion in oil revenue in 2012, down from a total of US $ 95 billion in 2011. In April 2013, the International Monetary Fund (IMF) forecast that Iran's Gross Domestic Product (GDP) would shrink by 1.3 percent in 2013 after contracting by 1.9 percent the previous year.

In exchange for Iran's commitment to limit its nuclear capabilities and its pledge to limit its nuclear energy activities for purely peaceful purposes, the United Nations Security Council, on July 20, 2015, unanimously approved a resolution that created the basis for international economic sanctions against Iran to be lifted.[13]

Buoyed by the degree of success, albeit still speculative, as a result of the sanctions measures against Iran, the US tried to buttress similar tenets in an entirely different domain. The US, wary of cyber-economic espionage initiated by Chinese hackers – perhaps with the tacit approval and support of the Chinese government – has suffered enormous monetary losses as well as loss of intellectual property and prestige. For the US, securing cyber space represents the Holy Grail of "National Security." In response to the rising wave of cyber attacks growing exponentially in numbers and the potential severity of subsequent consequences, the US tried to put in place a framework intended to subject Chinese companies and individuals, who have been direct or incidental beneficiaries of US trade secrets through cyber theft,to unprecedented economic sanctions.[14]

The provision of sanctions against the Chinese companies and individuals, once enacted and established as expedient, would mark the far-reaching use of the Executive Order (EO) signed by President Barack Obama in April 2015. The EO, "Blocking the Property of Certain Persons Engaging in Significant Malicious Cyber-Enabled Activities", identifies the increasing prevalence and severity of malicious cyber-enabled activities originating from, or directed by, persons located, in whole or in substantial part, outside the United States as an unusual and extraordinary threat to the national security, foreign policy, and economy of the United States.[15] The EO explicitly specifies blockage of all property and interests in property in the US of persons responsible for, or engaged in, either directly or indirectly, in cyber-enabled activities.

This US move is being described as the second serious and important shot at deterring China on the issue of cyber espionage. In May 2014, in a first-of-its-kind case, the US Justice Department indicted five Chinese military officers on charges of stealing data from six US companies. The US formally accused the Chinese officers and sought their extradition to face charges under US laws for infiltrating the computer networks of six US companies and for stealing data, which could be leveraged for benefits by their trade competitors. The FBI had gone to the extent of putting the faces of the five officials on "Wanted" posters.[16]

However, some US officials within the government cautioned against such moves and questioned their overall efficacy in the long run, arguing that sanctions might not act as a deterrent and would exacerbate tensions in the already tumultuous diplomatic relations between the United States and China. Besides, the US taking the moral high ground appeared to be dichotomous, when the US itself is accused of perpetrating cyber espionage, mass surveillance and other forms of information gathering directed at its allies and adversaries. The whole exercise orchestrated by the US appeared to be an attempt to "send a strong message" to Beijing, probably as an attempt to bolster its cyber deterrent posture.

Sanctions alone cannot bring a paradigm change in the sinister and belligerent cyber behaviour of a determined adversary. A nation's resolve to deter cyber attacks needs to be part of its overarching defence strategy, encompassing all instruments of national power: diplomatic, economic, informational and military. The shroud of anonymity behind which cyber criminals operate has made the process of establishing the identity of transgressors an arduous one. Attribution is the first step in assigning responsibilities and seeking appropriate recourse against transgressors. The economic linkages in this global era have become much more interdependent and entwined, and economic prudence does not justify such mutually incriminatory measures. On the other hand, it may adversely impact the mutually beneficial economic ties between two countries as reprisals frequently lead to counter-reprisals and further escalation in already tense bilateral relations.

Conclusion

The fruition of a credible deterrence strategy built on traditional threat evaluation is in itself a complex process and the complexities are further exacerbated when ambiguities associated with operations in cyber space are factored in. Historically, the measures of the successful conduct of war manifest in territorial gains or attrition or annihilation of enemy forces. Deterrence, by contrast, is an exercise in shaping the mindset of adversaries and fanning the fear of retaliatory actions far exceeding the cost of a potential misadventure. The process involves formulation of policy, proportionate capacity building, overt display of capabilities and convincing the adversary of one's intent. With nuclear deterrence, the deterrence posturing involves exploiting the primordial element of fear.

While gauging the impact of cyber weaponry and overall threat of cyber war looming large in the near future, it is worth the effort to try to ascertain its footprint on the global geopolitical landscape. Cyber weapons have yet to prove themselves as capable of altering the strategic military balance among states engaged in military conflict. Some critics point out that a cursory comparison between cyber and nuclear weapons is enough to prove the vanity and vexation of cyber weapons. In the context of nuclear weapons, James Chadwick discovered the neutron in 1932 for which he was awarded the Nobel Prize,and in 1945, the world witnessed the devastation and destruction caused by the first atomic bomb. Its use ended World War II, followed by shaping the strategic relations between the superpowers over the next five decades. Possession of, and the ability to launch, nuclear weapons within the available temporal window is central to interstate power relationships as lucidly illustrated by the Iranian and North Korean examples. In comparison, close to fifteen years have passed since the tenets of cyber warfare started intriguing the strategists and practitioners of warfare and the world has yet to witness a state being forced into subliminal subjugation exclusively or even primarily by cyber attacks, let alone being overthrown.

The argument does not in any way question the validity of deterrence in cyber space. Establishing deterrence in cyber space is not an easy task owing to the lack of clear delineation of a cyber attack from technical glitches, cyber crimes or a blatant act of war. The detection, categorisation and initiation of the response commensurate to the severity of the attack will require technical scaffolding and a policy framework. The existential chasm between the deterrence theory in cyber space and its practice is broad and needs to be bridged with clearly stated – and substantiated by – policy, procedures and guidelines.

Notes

1. Emanuel Adler and Vincent Pouliot, *International Practices: Cambridge Studies in International Relations* (Cambridge: Cambridge University Press, 2011), p.141.
2. *Cybersecurity Threats: The Way Forward,* Hearing of the House (Select) Intelligence Committee National Security Agency, November 20, 2014 (statement of Adm Michael Rogers, commander, US Cyber Command and director, National Security Agency), https://www.nsa.gov/public_info/_files/ speeches_testimonies/ ADM.ROGERS. Hill.20.Nov.pdf. Accessed January 12, 2016.
3. William W. Kaufmann, *The Requirements of Deterrence* (Princeton: Centre of International Studies Princeton University, 1954), p.4.
4. Colin S. Gray, *Maintaining Effective Deterrence* (Carlisle, PA: US Army War College, Strategic Studies Institute, 2003).
5. Colin S. Gray, *Explorations in Strategy* (Connecticut: Greenwood Press, 1996), p.32.
6. Ronald L. Akers, *Criminological Theories: Introduction and Evaluation* (New York: Roxbury Publishing Company, 1999), p.15.
7. Gray, n.4.
8. Austin Long, *Deterrence From Cold War to Long War: Lessons from Six Decades of RAND Research* (Santa Clara CA: RAND Corporation, 2008), p.8.
9. Alan M. Dershowitz,*Preemption: A Knife That Cuts Both Ways* (London: W.W. Norton & Company Ltd, 2006), p.10.
10. David E. Sanger, "N.S.A. Nominee Promotes Cyber War Units", *The Washington Times,* March 11 2014, http://www.washingtontimes.com. Accessed January 10, 2016.
11. National Conference of Catholic Bishops, "The Harvest of Justice is Sown in Peace: A Reflection of the National Conference of Bishops on the Tenth Anniversary of the Challenge to Peace" (Washington, DC: United States Catholic Conference, 1994).
12. US Department of State, "Diplomacy in Action: Tran Sanctions", http://www.state.gov/e/eb/tfs/spi/iran/ index.htm. Accessed September 10, 2015.
13. Somini Sengupta, "UN Moves to Lift Iran Sanctions After Nuclear Deal, Setting Up a Clash in Congress", *New York Times,* July 20, 2015, http://www.nytimes.com/2015/07/21/world/middleeast/security-council-following-iran-nuclear-pact-votes-to-lift-sanctions.html?_r=0. Accessed January 10, 2016.
14. David Nakamura, "US Developing Sanctions Against China Over Cyberthefts", *The Washington Post,* August 30, 2015, https://www.washingtonpost.com/world/national-security/administration-developing-sanctions-against-china-over-cyberespionage/2015/08/30/9b2910aa-480b-11e5-8ab4-c73967a143d3_story.html. Accessed January 10, 2016.

15. The White House: Office of the Press Secretary, "Executive Order – "Blocking the Property of Certain Persons Engaging in Significant Malicious Cyber-Enabled Activities", April 1, 2015, https://www.whitehouse.gov/the-press-office/2015/04/01/executive-order-blocking-property-certain-persons-engaging-significant-m. Accessed January 10, 2016.
16. Eric Holder, "Chinese Military Officials Charged with Stealing US Data as Tensions Escalate", *The Guardian*, May 20, 2014, http://www.theguardian.com/technology/2014/may/19/us-chinese-military-officials-cyber-espionage, 20 May 14. Accessed January 10, 2016.

4

Cyber-Military Doctrinal and Functional Convergence

The armed forces of a nation-state are an assertion of its ability and capability to effectively counter present, perceived and potential threats to its sovereignty, territorial integrity, and vital interests and to maintain the credibility of its deterrence posture. The measure of the credibility and potency of the armed forces of a nation is the sum total of capabilities derived from its strategic vision, political-military leadership structure and cutting edge technology assimilation. The qualitative and quantitative strength of troops, weapons and equipment impetus on training are other equally important factors that add up to determine the capability and preparedness of the armed forces. In the military context, capacity building is a dynamic and progressive process in which existing capabilities are continually enhanced and upgraded. All available assets, resources and strengths are integrated and amalgamated for developing robust capabilities, to be used in the furtherance of national interests and protection of national security. Within a coherent doctrinal framework, the acquisition, assimilation and exploitation of such capabilities are guided by existing and future threat perceptions, cutting edge technology assimilation and strategic innovation. The 'doctrinal expositions' and 'strategic exhortations' offer directions and interventions on how to act/ react in a given situation. Based on archival understanding, past experiences, present circumstances and future expectations, the guiding principles are distilled down to easily *assimilable and actionable* operational statements.

Technology is a major driver that influences the conduct of war.

Technological advancements have kept pace with the evolving lethality and complexity of the modern battlefield, at times even enhancing these. Technology plays a significant role in shaping and reshaping the national strategy and doctrinal contours at all levels. Its continual integration into capacity building initiatives accrues strategic leverage, tactical advantage and operational effectiveness. The technology-driven dynamics entails commensurate organisational reorientations and operational realignments. The industrial revolution ushered in an era of military dominance by Western Europe and its offshoots in global affairs.[1] Similarly, the information revolution ushered in a whole new age of technological innovation comparable to the industrial revolution.[2] A natural progression of this revolution is the emergence of information as a militarily important asset. Advances in technology have transformed the way the information is acquired, disseminated and utilised. With an ever-growing reliance on network-centric operations, the corresponding doctrinal changes are required to meet the demands of the changing nature of military operations. Most of the nations, conscious of this paradigm, have embarked on the mission to add a cyber dimension to their doctrines for both defence and offence. Some of these doctrines may be in the nascent stage of development; however, with experience and better understanding, their respective doctrines will act as roadmaps for leveraging cyber capabilities.

China in the Fifth Domain of Warfare

The People's Republic of China (PRC), at a pace commensurate with its economic growth and its emergence as a key aspirational player in global affairs, embarked on a wide-ranging and sweeping programme of military modernisation at the end of the Eighties. China's leaders unequivocally chose to fully utilise and exploit the opportunities presented by the global Information Technology (IT) revolution for high technology industries, global competitiveness, tapping global market opportunities and technical innovations. They have also focussed on the need to pay equal attention to the associated innovations in international security, especially in the development of the armed forces and diplomacy.[3]

The vision of cyber dominance across the full range of military operations has propelled the People's Liberation Army (PLA) to fundamentally transform its ability to fight high-tech wars, pushing beyond its traditional sphere of interest focussed on regional dominance and towards more globally relevant and significant roles. The sustained modernisation of its conventional forces, assimilation of new concepts into existing doctrinal propositions, adoption of new technology for the development of new capabilities and enhancement of existing capabilities has brought a transformative change in the PLA's force structure and the echelons of 'command and control'. The new strategic framework of the PLA focusses on the broadening and deepening of efforts to create a modern Command, Control, Communications, Computers, Intelligence, Surveillance, and Reconnaissance (C4ISR) infrastructure. This drive has fuelled the efforts to develop cyber warfare capabilities at all levels for defending the Chinese networks from cyber attacks. Achieving outcomes propitious to the Chinese national interests during a hostile situation – in both the physical and cyber space – is the keystone of Chinese strategic thinking. The PLA leadership views control of cyber space as an important tenet of war-fighting. Chinese strategists are mostly consistent in their assessment of the critical role of cyber operations in modern warfare.

China's military organisational and doctrinal exposition on 'informatisation' began as early as 2004. In December 2006, then Chinese Premier Jiang Zemin, while speaking in public, stressed on the need to create an 'information deterrent' to strengthen national defence and for complementing its nuclear deterrent.[4]In a White Paper, "China's National Defense in 2004," it was made amply clear that the PLA considers "informationalization" as a focal point for strategic competence and operational orientation. The operational information support by incorporating IT elements into the main battle weapon systems – for enhanced leadership and combat efficiency, overall planning and development of new operational theories – would be the mainstay of the PLA in the new stage of the 21st century. [5]China fully recognises and realises that the development and proliferation of information technology has entailed unprecedented challenges to the security of individual states and of the international community as a whole.[6] While diligently working on an informationalised force structure, China has adopted comprehensive and sophisticated measures to protect its cyber assets and resources.

In China, informatisation has become a central and deeply entrenched belief and practice. This has entailed leadership reorientation, structural realignments, capability aggregation and reworking of training processes and needs. The year 2010 witnessed the setting up of the "Information Warfare Base" by the General Staff Department (GSD).[7] With robust and integrated cyber warfare capabilities and their potential use in the pursuit of strategic objectives, China has the capability to identify an adversary's cyber vulnerabilities and exploit these. Besides, cyber operations targeted against the adversary's military, logistical, communication and commercial networks will limit the adversary's actions or capabilities. During times of crisis or conflict, these will slow the response time of the adversary and will act as force multipliers, when used in conjunction with, or as an adjunct to, kinetic attacks.

To date, the Chinese network operations have largely been used for political and economic espionage. But a study of various Chinese doctrinal expositions and analysis of the tacitly assigned role of various Chinese establishments unequivocally reveal China's unremitting intent to use cyber capabilities as an integral appendage to war-fighting and as a coercive instrument. Some analysts view Chinese cyber warfare capabilities as a culmination of efforts to develop an asymmetric advantage to compensate for the relative inferiority of its military strength in comparison to that of the US. It is also a low risk option likely to accrue comparable results as with kinetic attacks. Besides, cyber warfare capabilities can also be used as instruments for industrial espionage and political intimidation.

The Chinese cyber strategy is often termed, both in China and by the Western analysts, as a "network strategy,"[8] because of the contextual differences between the use of the term 'cyber' in the West and its semantic understanding in China. While the term "cyber security" is used for the protection and defence of a plethora of widely used electronic and communications information, in China, the use of the term "network security" is specifically associated with the protection of digital information networks. The term 'information security' is used to encompass the other information and communication systems. Computer Network Operations (CNO), called 'network warfare' by the Chinese military, are defined in the PLA's military dictionary as: "Also known as network confrontation. The destruction of the adversary's network of information systems and network information, the undermining of effectiveness of the adversary's use of its capabilities, while protecting one's own network of information systems and information in cyber space."[9] In addition, the same dictionary defines 'information offense' as: "Information attacks: the utilisation of information warfare technology to interfere with, and sabotage, enemy information operations and information systems. Important tactics include electronic attack and network attack. The purpose is to affect and weaken the enemy's information acquisition, transmission, processing and utilisation decisions."[10]

While a formal doctrine for cyber operations has never been publicly issued by China, the PLA has been provided with authoritative directives for military modernisation in the form of "Military Strategic Guidelines" under the authority of the Military Commission of the Central Committee of the Chinese Communist Party.[11] These are in sync with other Chinese policy documents, explicit in their reference of the need to prepare to "fight local wars under high-tech conditions", an irrefutable assertion of the importance of information technology in Chinese operational plans. This directed the PLA to fight and win "local wars under informationalized conditions."[12]

The PRC government actively encourages commercial IT companies and universities to undertake research in the field of CNO, in both offensive and defensive aspects of cyber warfare. This viable programme has significantly contributed in enhancing the information warfare capabilities of China. It has been reported that at least 50 civilian universities, supported by generous government grants, are involved in research work on information security. The spinoffs of these research efforts are being used to make CNOs more effective and result-oriented. The commercial IT sector in China also contributes significantly in this endeavour by undertaking R&D and developing new dual use technology. Since mainstreaming of cyber into its strategic plans, the PLA is expanding its cyber capabilities to coercively dominate or manipulate its military rivals, economic competitors and political dissidents. For the furtherance of this goal, it has acquired capabilities to translate this strategic imperative into operational implementation. Achieving information dominance at the strategic and campaign levels is at the heart of present Chinese strategic thinking.

The Chinese approach towards 'network warfare' is to coordinate and interweave various facets of offensive and defensive operations for accomplishment of campaign objectives. The senior political and military leadership is vested with power to make decisions on employment of CNO as a primary or adjunct approach to conflict management or resolution, or for espionage and subterfuge. The operational control of CNO for military usage rests with the PLA's Third and Fourth Departments of the General Staff Department (GSD). The Third Department (3PLA) – China's primary Signals Intelligence (SIGINT) agency – monitors and analyses communication originating from, or between, actual and potential adversaries to measure the magnitude of their threat indices. It has been reported that the Third Department is responsible for computer network defence as well as for carrying out cyber exploitation activities. The

Fourth Department (4PLA), the electronic warfare arm of the PLA, more likely undertakes network attack missions.[13]

- **The Third Department of the General Staff Department (3PLA):** The General Staff Department's Third Department is primarily a SIGINT collection and analysis entity. It manages at least 12 operational bureaus and three research institutes from its headquarters in Beijing.[14] The 12th Bureau of the Third Department of the PLA GSD is believed to exercise control over the notorious yet elusive PLA Unit 61486.[15] The Third Department is believed to undertake SIGNIT operations by maintaining a system of several ground stations, instrumented ships and airborne platforms. It has on its payroll a sizeable number of trained linguists and technicians. Its tasks include collection, collation, exploitation and analysis of electronic signals originating from outside China involving foreign nationals and overseas Chinese dissidents. Though there is no official published evidence to substantiate this claim,the department is believed to be responsible for information security testing and certification of the PLA's secrecy protection products through the PRC's State Secrecy Bureau.
- **The Fourth Department of the General Staff Department (4PLA):** The GSD Fourth Department, formerly the Electronic Counter-Measures Department (ECM), undertakes Information Warfare (IW) activities with a primary focus on offensive network operations and oversees ECM regiments. Founded as an electronic warfare entity in 1990, the Fourth Department also manages and oversees research projects as well as R&D of electronic counter-measure systems. In sync with the strategic direction of the PLA, it actively undertakes missions aimed at degrading, compromising or controlling the C4ISR infrastructure of an adversary. The Fourth Department has actively encouraged research work on on GPS jamming, Joint Tactical Information Distribution System (JTIDS) counter-measures, jamming of frequency ranges associated with Communication Satellites (SATCOM) commonly used

by Western militaries, and Synthetic Aperture Radar (SAR) jamming. Electronic warfare platforms and capabilities developed by research institutes working under the direct supervision of the Fourth Department are being leveraged to develop cyber attack capabilities for use against the key command and control nodes and networks of an adversary.

- **Technical Reconnaissance Bureaus (TRBs):**[16] The PLA maintains a series of facilities responsible for SIGINT collection known as technical reconnaissance bureaus. At least six technical reconnaissance bureaus are located in the Lanzhou, Jinan, Chengdu, Guangzhou, and Beijing Military Regions (MRs). These facilities, subordinate to the Third Department, carry out tactical and strategic SIGINT collection missions based on the threat perception over demarcated geographic areas.
- **Information Warfare Militia:** The directive of fighting under "informationization conditions" has forced the PLA to relook at the traditional force structure and replace it with a network-centric focussed structure with increasing effect-based capability. By recruiting many tech-savvy civilians in its ranks, the PLA has augmented its capability to exploit an adversary's cyber vulnerabilities. This recruitment strategy by the PLA has paid rich dividends in terms of expansion of militia units proficient in all types of computer network operations.

Chinese Offensive Cyber Capabilities

In 2000, in order to bolster its offensive IW capabilities, the PLA adopted a multi-layered approach to integrate its network operations infrastructure into its operational tactics. The strategy, referred to as the Integrated Network Electronic Warfare (INEW),[17]seeks to leverage the combined effects of CNO and EW to attack an adversary's C4ISR networks and other key information systems. The genesis of this strategy stems from a growing realisation that in combat, denial of access to, or dissemination of, information to the enemy is essential for success. The degree of mission success increases proportionally with the integration of various components of IW under a unitary command and control structure.

In spite of the Chinese's government denial of being involved in cyber espionage activities, there is enough evidential basis to suggest its involvement in directing and executing cyber espionage campaigns against its adversaries. The Second Department of the PLA GSD, which is responsible for military intelligence, also undertakes cyber operations for support or coordination of non-military activities. In spite of the best Chinese efforts to keep the role of its offensive cyber operational units under wraps, an incriminating report by Mandiant,[18] a private US cyber security firm, has established the existence of two units:

- PLA Unit 61398, based in Shanghai, is likely to be the 2nd Bureau of the General Staff Department's Third Department. Unit 61398 has penetrated the networks of at least 141 organisations, including companies, international organisations and foreign governments. At least 20 sectors of 15 countries are the victims of cyber espionage activities by this cyber threat group. According to Mandiant, Unit 61398 is responsible for conducting computer network operations with the objective of gathering strategic and economic intelligence on targets.
- The Shanghai-based PLA Unit 61486 is a part of the 12th Bureau of the Third Department of the PLA GSD. This unit has bolstered attempts to steal trade and military secrets from foreign targets by hacking into their computers and stealing data. According to the CrowdStrike report, this unit is also believed to be involved in 'space surveillance' and 'intercept of satellite communications' preferentially targeting Western companies in the space and imaging/remote sensing sectors. The size and number of satellite dishes within the vicinity of its location area are undeniable assertions of its role in the perpetration of malevolent acts.

In May 2014, in a first-of-its-kind case, the US Justice Department indicted five Chinese military officers on charges of stealing data from six US companies. Though the Chinese government has tacitly undertaken or sponsored the acts of corporate data theft for many years, this was the first time the US had formally accused Chinese officers of involvement. The US even sought extradition of the Chinese officials to face charges under US laws for infiltrating the computer networks of six US companies and for stealing data by their trade competitors. The FBI went to the extent of putting the faces of the five officials on "Wanted" posters. The companies allegedly affected were Alcoa, US Steel, US Steelworkers Union, Westinghouse, Allegheny Technologies Inc and Solar World.[19]

Developments Related to Chinese Information Technology Companies

In October 2012, in a report by the US House Permanent Select Committee on Intelligence (HPSCI), China's two largest telecommunication equipment manufacturers, Huawei and ZTE, were categorised as companies that could pose a risk to US national security. The report stated that these companies could facilitate the Chinese government in its efforts to gather intelligence on its adversary.[20] The report issued an advisory to US companies against using products or services provided by Huawei and ZTE. In an interview in July 2013, former Director of the CIA and NSA, Gen Michael Hayden (Retd.), when asked if it was reasonable to assume that Huawei had engaged in espionage on behalf of the Chinese state, said, "Yes, that's right. At a minimum, Huawei would have shared with the Chinese state intimate and extensive knowledge of the foreign telecommunications systems it is involved with."[21] Indian intelligence agencies have also raised genuine concerns about the alleged collusion of Huawei and ZTE with the Chinese government for intelligence gathering. The Research and Analysis Wing (RAW) had informed the Department of Technology (DoT) that Huawei had links with the Chinese Army. "Huawei Technologies is known to have links with the People's Liberation Army (PLA) and the ministry of state security of China..," RAW wrote to DoT. [22]

Some of the concerns stem from the past affiliations of Huawei's founder, Ren Zhengfei. Although the company is selectively mute about his background, some information garnered from other sources indicates that Ren Zhengfei attended the Chongqing University of Civil Engineering and Architecture and served in the PLA's engineering corps, reportedly in its information-technology research unit. He rose to the position of deputy director but without a military rank. He left the army and moved to Shenzhen, where he set up Huawei in 1987. Though Huawei has projected itself as a company with explicit commercial intent, the former association of its founder with the PLA and Huawei's refusal to provide details on its R&D programmes and other documents undermine its claim of not working in collusion with the Chinese military or intelligence services. The intelligence community is abuzz with speculation that there is more to Huawei's rise than innovation and technology breakthroughs. It is widely believed that its expansion is attributable to heavy subsidy by the Chinese government, eager to use it as a Trojan horse for infiltration into more and more foreign networks.[23]

A Ringside View of US Cyber Security Strategy and Cyber Activities

The US,credited as being the fountainhead for most of the developments in cyber space, knows very well that 'cyber security' has acquired the character of the *proverbial Frankenstein's* monster, beyond the control of its creator. Driven by real and imagined concerns and wary of consequences of terrifyingly dangerous uncertainties of 'cyber attacks', the US' strategic approach unwaveringly focusses on the cyber means, methods and techniques to defend US interests. With the greater awareness and knowledge gained in the development process of cyber technologies, standards and equipment, the US – with almost clairvoyant vision – embarked on the formulation of a strategy for cyber operations when other countries were still in the process of understanding the nuances of cyber warfare. But this disparity was shortlived and quickly narrowed, once cyber tools and techniques quickly proliferated and were widely acquired, improved upon and used by friends and foes alike.

In the "National Strategy to Secure Cyber Space", issued by the White House in February 2003, President George W. Bush laid down the framework by stating: "The way business is transacted, government operates, and national defense is conducted have changed. These activities now rely on an interdependent network of information technology infrastructures called cyber space." The document is an assertion of the acceptance of a dramatic increase in cyber space threats as envisaged by the US. In mid-2009, President Barack Obama, without circumlocution, stated that the threats emanating in cyber space are "one of the most serious economic and security challenges we face as a nation." According to Obama, "The digital infrastructure we depend on every day is a strategic national asset, so keeping it secure must be a top national priority. Cyber space is real and so are the risks that come with it."[24] The president did not rule out the possibility that the United States would come under cyber space attack. Similarly, the US National Security Strategy, published in May 2010 by the White House, highlights the cyber space threat against the United States and determines: "The space and cyber space capabilities that power our daily lives and military operations are vulnerable to disruption and attack." In order to meet its strategic objectives in cyber space, the American military evolved the GIG (Global Information Grid), an intricate and interdependent grid of various communications means (including satellites) deployed globally. This capability allows the US to be in constant contact with deployed troops, guide smart bombs to targets using GPS, and control UAVs across the globe. Any damage or degradation to this network will result in loss of the dominance presently enjoyed by the US in its response to various terrorist groups and militants. In 2011, Deputy Secretary of Defence William Lynn articulated three types of cyber space threats: network exploitation, network disruption (e.g., denial of service), and sabotage.[25] According to Lynn: "It is possible to imagine attacks on military networks or critical infrastructure – like our transportation system and energy sector – that cause severe economic damage, physical destruction, or even loss of life."[26]He further added that the US "stands at an important juncture in the development of cyber threats. More destructive tools are being developed, but have not yet been used. And the most malicious actors have not yet laid their hands on the most harmful capabilities. But this situation will not hold forever. For this reason, we must have the capability to defend against the full range of cyber threats."[27]

American Establishments for Cyber Space Security

The White House is at the helm of the inter-agency development of national cyber security strategies and policies. To facilitate this, the presidential appointee, the "cyber security coordinator", oversees implementation of cyber security policies as well as ensures effective coordination and partnership among the federal government, private sector, non-governmental organisations, and other nations.[28]

The National Cyber Security Division (NCSD)is the Department of Homeland Security's (DHS') lead agency for securing cyber space, US cyber assets and networks. The NCSD has been mandated to explore and develop cyber security strategies to protect the nation's critical cyber infrastructure on 24x7 basis. The NCDS defines the goal of cyber security as: "The prevention of damage to, unauthorised use of, or exploitation of, and, if needed, the restoration of electronic information and communications systems and the information contained therein to ensure the information's confidentiality, integrity, and availability."[29] It is also entrusted with the responsibility of implementing the National Cyber Space Response System. The division also monitors government networks to identify and respond to cyber threats and attacks, improve network security, increase the resiliency of critical e-government services, and enhance the survivability of the Internet.[30]

The Department of Defence (DoD) has been mandated to possess the necessary capabilities to operate effectively in all domains. The DoD organises, trains and equips for the complex challenges and vast opportunities of cyber space at all levels. The cyber space mission responsibilities have been assigned to the United States Strategic Command (USSTRATCOM). As a sub-unified command of the

USSTRATCOM, the US Cyber Command was established in May 2010, and became fully operational in October 2010, with the following mission statement: "USCYBERCOM plans, coordinates, integrates, synchronises and conducts activities to direct the operations and defense of specified Department of Defense information networks and prepare to, when directed, conduct full spectrum military cyber space operations in order to enable actions in all domains, ensuring US/Allied freedom of action in cyber space and deny the same to our adversaries."

The establishment of the USCYBERCOM is a manifestation of the US strategy to treat cyber space as an operational domain. Broadly, the USCYBERCOM is responsible for:

- Managing cyber space risks through efforts such as increased training, information assurance, greater situational awareness, and creating secure and resilient network environments.
- Assuring integrity and availability by engaging in smart partnerships, building collective self-defences and maintaining a common operating picture.
- Ensuring the development of integrated capabilities by working closely with the Combatant Commands, Services, agencies, and the acquisition community to rapidly deliver and deploy innovative capabilities where they are needed the most.

The Department of Defence has laid down a strategic framework for operating in cyber space:

- To develop capabilities to operate effectively in cyber space as has been achieved in other domains – air, land, maritime and space – with an aim to take full advantage of cyber space's potential.
- To employ new defence operating concepts to protect DoD networks and systems.
- To establish partnerships with other US government departments and agencies and the private sector to enable a whole-of-government cyber security strategy.

- To build robust relationships with US allies and international partners to strengthen collective cyber security.
- To leverage the nation's ingenuity through an exceptional cyber workforce and rapid technological innovation.

Adm Michael S. Rogers, President Obama's nominee to run the National Security Agency (NSA), as well as the head of the USCYBERCOM, appearing before the Senate Armed Services Committee (SASC) in March 2014, responded in writing to a set of questions raised outlining the mission statement, vision and functioning of the USCYBERCOM. "The US possesses superior military might across all war-fighting domains, cyber space included," Adm Rogers wrote. "In truth, however, there has been no large scale cyber conflict yet in history, and the state of strategy and execution of cyber warfare is evolving as we speak." He envisioned, "All of the major combat commands in the United States military will soon have dedicated forces to conduct cyber attacks alongside their air, naval and ground capabilities The activation of these combat units would help counter the perception around the world that the United States is 'an easier mark' for cyber attacks because it did not 'have the will to respond'". Adm Rogers took over the reins at a tumultuous time, an offshoot of grave concerns in the intelligence community, a result of the release of thousands of documents on Wikileaks by former NSA contractor Edward Snowden, related to highly classified NSA surveillance operations. Adm Rogers reiterated that the key to success in the future would be synergetic partnerships between the USCYBERCOM and NSA, FBI, Homeland Security and Justice Departments. From the inception of the USCYBERCOM, there are certain issues which are still ambiguous. This ambiguity stems not from the lack of clarity of mission or thought, but due to the unconventional nature of the expected warfare in cyber space. These are:

- Use of offensive tools after commencement of an identified/ perceived attack. Both Gen Alexander and Adm Rogers were guarded in their response on the use of offensive tools against an attacker after the commencement of an attack. In defence parlance, any such activity by its nature is defensive.

- Use of "offensive cyber weapons" in response to an attack without conclusively establishing the identity of the true perpetrators. In response to this, Adm Rogers wrote, "If the 'attack' met the criteria approved by the President in our Standing Rules of Engagement, the military would exercise its obligation of self-defence. However, operationally, it is difficult to develop an effective response when we do not know who is responsible for an 'attack'."
- Initiation of mitigating actions when the responsibility of an 'attack' cannot be attributed to a particular nation, group or individual.
- Development of a direct cyber deterrence policy. There is an inherent dichotomy deeply embedded in this approach. For being effective, cyber weapons need to be secretly developed, evaluated and checked for efficacy. In response, Adm Rogers wrote, "The establishment of the US Cyber Command is an element of a deterrence strategy, but more work and planning will be required to evolve a solid national strategy. Classic deterrence theory is based on the concepts of threat and cost; either there is a fear of reprisal or a belief that an attack is too hard or too expensive. Cyber warfare is still evolving and much work remains to establish agreed upon norms of behavior, thresholds for action, and other dynamics." Adm Rogers further wrote, "A broad understanding of the cyber capability, both defensive and offensive, along with an understanding of thresholds and intentions would seem to be logical elements of a deterrence strategy, both for our allies and our adversaries, and as they are in other war-fighting domains."

Adm Rogers' answers to the Senate Armed Services Committee brought to the fore one of the most detailed public revelations of US efforts to develop offensive cyber capability. As per the statement of Adm Rogers, the US Cyber Command priorities include:

- **Secure, "Cyber Robust" and "Defensible" Telecommunications Architecture:** The limited capability of legacy information systems and some weapon systems to withstand a dedicated and determined cyber attack from an adversary determined to undertake operations detrimental to US interests, is still a matter of concern. There is a need to upgrade and incorporate "cyber robust" technologies in these systems.
- **Training Cyber Warfare Personnel:** US military personnel are not fully geared up to confront advance cyber threats. This is attributable to the lack of requisite training and confidence in waging cyber war across its full spectrum. They also are not able to comprehend the levels of risk acceptable in the cyber domain and lack "reliable cyber situational awareness".
- **Intelligence on Global Cyber Threats:** Admittance in the cyber domain is easy, costing only a pittance as compared to other war-fighting domains. This has led to the emanation of cyber threats from state-sponsored military operations and espionage activities, to extremist organisations, to cyber criminals and recreational hackers seeking financial gain and notoriety. Though it would be a herculean task to compile and collate data of all the individuals and groups capable of compromising US interest by acts committed in cyber space, the availability of such data would ensure monitoring, tagging and confronting potential perpetrators.
- **Delegation of Authority for Conducting Cyber Attacks:** The authority for defending networks and conducting cyber attacks is vested with many military and government entities, having different origins, objectives and orientations. This may result in failure to undertake concerted and collaborative efforts. Additionally, cyber warfare operating concepts are "undefined and not wholly realistic."

- **Defending Government and Private Networks:** In the recent past, cyber threats have transformed in their severity, complexity and rationality, shifting from temporarily disruptive attacks to extremely damaging cyber strikes capable of destroying data, threatening the economy and possibly endangering lives. The Cyber Command also needs to proactively defend the networks from adversaries intending to steal data, money, and other property.

In addition, in the National Defence Authorisation Act for Fiscal Year 2012 (H.R. 1540, sec. 954, "Military Activities in Cyber Space"), Congress affirmed the policy principles and legal regimes applicable to conflicts in cyber space.[31] It states, "Congress affirms that the Department of Defense has the capability, and upon direction by the President, may conduct offensive operations in cyber space to defend our nation, Allies and interests, subject to the policy principles and legal regimes that the Department follows for kinetic capabilities, including the law of armed conflict."[32]

US Offensive Cyber War Policy

Despite the US public declaration of exercising only its legitimate rights for protecting US national objectives in cyber space by both offensive and defensive means, the US behaviour in cyber space blurs the dichotomies of *legitimate–illegitimate*. Presidential Policy Directive-20 on the subject of US Cyber Operations Policy, made public by Edward Snowden, lays equal emphasis on Offensive Cyber Effects Operations (OCEO). Under the paragraph Offensive Cyber Effects Operations, it states:

- Offensive Cyber Effects Operations can offer unique and unconventional capabilities to advance US national objectives around the world with little or no warning to the adversary or target and with potential effects ranging from subtle to severely damaging. The development and sustainment of OCEO capabilities, however, may require considerable time and effort if access and tools for a specific target do not already exist.

- The United States government shall identify potential targets of national importance where OCEO can offer a favourable balance of effectiveness and risk as compared with other instruments of national power, establish and maintain OCEO capabilities integrated as appropriate with other US offensive capabilities, and execute those capabilities in a manner consistent with the provisions of this directive.

This directive reeks of Cold War paranoia, when the nuclear missiles were ready to be launched at the slightest provocation on targets of strategic importance on enemy territory. Today, a similar strategy has evolved in cyber space with identification of potential targets based on threat severity. The strategy also directs the use of offensive cyber attacks in response to overtly aggressive cyber posturing or hostile rhetoric from an adversary.

National Security Agency (NSA) in Cyber Space

The NSA, which undertakes both Signals Intelligence (SIGINT) and Information Assurance (IA) operations as well as Computer Network Operations (CNOs) for the US, has hogged the limelight since mid-2013 for its infamous PRISM programme. Attempts by the NSA to undertake a mass surveillance programme of the magnitude never undertaken in the annals of espionage history exposes the intent and capabilities of the US in the cyber domain. PRISM stands for"Planning Tool for Resource Integration, Synchronization, and Management" and can be categorised as a programme leveraging on the cyber tools and techniques to record and analyse communications, including the identification of the source. From a 41 slides PowerPoint presentation probably designed to train intelligence operatives on the capabilities of the Prism programme, the NSA could access the systems being used by Internet giants such as of Google, Facebook, Apple and other US Internet companies. Under the US laws, the companies are legally obliged to comply with the request of providing details of users' communications under US laws. The PRISM programme allows the analysts of the NSA to obtain targeted communications covertly without formally requesting the concerned companies for it and without legitimate court orders. Some of the largest Internet giants have been roped in to be part of the information sharing programme. [33] This was followed by the 'Boundless Informant'[34] programme, under which the NSA has developed capabilities to record and analyse communication, including the identification of the source from where the communication has been generated. As per the *Guardian*, this tool allows the NSA to count and categorise the records of communications, known as metadata, rather than the content of an e-mail or instant message. Under this programme, the NSA has collected close to three billion pieces of intelligence from US computer networks over a 30-day period ending in March 2013. The tool even allows a user to select a country on the map, view the metadata volume and select details about the collections against that country.

The Russian Federation and Cyber Dominance

"The Military Doctrine of the Russian Federation"[35] which, after approval was published in 2010, is one of the fundamental documents envisioning its strategic direction and preparedness for armed defence and armed protection of the Russian Federation. The doctrine lays emphasis on the integration of all instruments of national power for the protection and pursuance of national interests. The document, while characterising the modern military conflict, is unequivocal in its proclamation that information warfare is a potent and cost-effective means to accomplish political objectives. The fourth paragraph of the doctrine is an assertion of Russia's undeniable intent to "implement measures of information warfare in order to achieve political objectives without the utilisation of military force and, subsequently, in the interest of shaping a favourable response from the world community to the utilisation of military force." In order to achieve this objective, it is imperative to "develop forces and resources for information warfare". The development of cyber defence systems and capabilities has become the mainstay of Russian strategic thinking. In order to provide a strategic impetus to cyber security and information systems, the Russian Ministry of Defence has made organisational changes, creating new positions for policy decisions, governance, administration and policy implementation. In 2010, for example, a new official post with the designation Deputy Defence Minister for Information, was created.[36]

Russia is an enthusiastic proponent and practitioner of cyber warfare and its checkered past of using cyber attacks for political and military dominance has been widely reported. The Russian bear bared its cyber fangs and viciously attacked its adversaries using cyber weapons, while being engaged militarily with Georgia in 2008 and on being alienated with Estonia in the year 2007. The latest manifestation of Russian predilection for 'cyber aggression' was in the year 2014 in Ukraine.Russia has covertly leveraged a network of cyber criminals to undertake highly effective cyber espionage operations such as 'Snake' and 'Red October' using groups such as 'Energetic Bear', 'Russian Business Network' and 'Nashi'. It is a symbiotic paradox, in which the Russian state offers resources to the cyber mercenaries to design, develop and launch cyber operations for furtherance of its political and military strategy, while the hackers community is profited either monetarily or supposedly provided with patriotic gratification. The Ukrainian crisis saw the group CyberBerkut as the principle cyber proxy, working in consonance with Russian interests. The group shot into prominence when it carried out a high profile DDoS attack against NATO websites. Since becoming operational in March 2014, CyberBerkut's meteoric rise is an assertion of Russian intent and covert support to the group.

The Russian penchant to use proxy cyber groups was noticeably observed when the members of the Nashi youth group carried out cyber attacks against Estonia in 2007. The Nashi was ostensibly created in 2005 as a reaction to counter Ukraine's Orange Revolution, in which youth-led street protests facilitated smooth sailing for pro-Western candidate Viktor Yushchenko to become the president. Tacit financial and ideological support from the Kremlin and some of the Nashi activities have led some critics to conclude that "Nashi's true function was as a personality cult for Putin whose job was to intimidate, bully and harass his opponents."[37] As cyber security measures adopted by various nations become more sophisticated and effective, the Kremlin required groups with more experience and potent cyber capacities. The Nashi, in contemporary times, was considered a less capable cyber group and the loss of its favoured position coincided with the rise of CyberBerkut. Groups such as Nashi and CyberBerkut have been used as instruments of Russia's proxy wars against its adversaries in cyber space.

The Russian dichotomous behaviour in cyber space has come to the fore on multiple occasions. Russia has refused to sign the "European Convention on Cyber Crime" which is a collective effort to curb cyber crimes through appropriate legislation and international cooperation.[38] On other hand, Russia has joined China and a few other states to regulate the free flow of information on the Internet. On September 12, 2011, along with China, Tajikistan and Uzbekistan, Russia submitted a proposal in the United Nations General Assembly for discussions on "an International Code of Conduct for Information Security in the Framework of the United Nations". The proposed code mandated the member states to pledge "not to use information and communications technologies, including networks, to carry out hostile activities or acts of aggression, and pose threats to international peace and security or to proliferate information weapons and related technologies."[39]

The "Doctrine of Information Security of the Russian Federation" of September 2000, tries to cover a myriad issues related to information security, such as data protection, personal privacy, copyright and computer misuse, access to information and control of the media.[40] Part I of the doctrine ("Information Security of the Russian Federation") describes the importance of protection of the interests of individuals those of the state in securing the environment for information. Part II describes the "Methods of Ensuring

Information Security of the Russian Federation". Part III sets out – at a high level of generality – the policy of the government. This ranges from observing the Constitution to supporting the development of new technologies. Part IV maps the broad contributions of different constitutional actors to the policy.[41] In summary, the doctrine is a document that tries to address various aspects of information security. It fails, however, to offer viable and workable specific solutions to the problems and shortcomings that it identifies.

The release of "The Military Doctrine of the Russian Federation",[42] just eight months into Putin's presidency, lays emphasis on the Russian Federation's adherence to the utilisation of information along with other instruments for the protection of its national interests. It also recognises disruption of the functioning of the informational infrastructure as one of the main internal military dangers. The intensification of the role of information warfare as well as prior implementation of measures of information warfare without the utilisation of military force has been recognised as a characteristic feature of contemporary military conflicts. To improve the system of information support for the armed forces and to equip forces and develop resources for information warfare is one of the main tasks for the development of the military organisation. Russia is in overdrive recruiting for new cyber forces at an estimated cost of some US$ 500 million.[43] To counter cyber threats, the Russian Army is setting up a new division to monitor and process information especially originating from overseas to effective identify and neutralise cyber threats and attacks.

In order to bolster the capability and potency of the Russian military, the Ministry of Defence, in collaboration with Russian universities is trying to identify young programmers and IT experts with a penchant for this kind of work. The functional and hierarchical structure of such units has not yet been disclosed but a number of inferences point to the establishment of a special Cyber Defence Centre in the General Staff and similar centres for each military district and fleet of the country. In order to provide impetus, the

Russian government plans to accelerate training of programmers, engineers, cryptographers, communicators, interpreters and other staff under contractual obligation to serve in the Russian Army.

If we were to metaphorically transform Russian cyber war capabilities into a soccer match, the score would read as *"Russia Now 3 and 0 in Cyber Warfare."*[44] The Russian cyber juggernaut is on the roll and its wrath was unleashed against Estonia, Georgia, apparently Kyrgyzstan, in January 2009 and Ukraine. Russia has shown its intent, willingness and capabilities in conducting effective cyber warfare operations to achieve military and national objectives in cyber space. Russia now, and in the foreseeable future, will be treated as a potential and worthy adversary with the tools, expertise and experience to successfully wage serious cyber war.

Conclusion

During the Cold War era, the two superpowers were always the focus of criticisms, expositions and comparisons of any debate or doctrinal dialogue. The historical and ontological origins of concepts such as nuclear arms race, Mutual Assured Destruction (MAD) and military alliances of gargantuan proportions can be traced back to the rivalry between the two nuclear superpowers.

The other nations, based on their national security concerns and external threat perceptions, also acquired sizeable nuclear and non-nuclear arsenals, with matching force structures. The overlying intent of stockpiling of the military arsenal was to defend, deter, subjugate, defeat and even annihilate present, perceived and future adversaries. The regional security concerns of the 'middle powers' were much greater than global concerns. The superpowers orchestrated and drummed up the regional insecurity scenarios by allying with, or opposing, regional players based on their perceived ideological–political outlook, geostrategic analysis and economic considerations. With the end of the Cold War and emergence of cyber as a domain in which military, political, economic, social stakes are high enough,the nations are aggressively pursuing the acquisition of cyber capabilities across the full range of military operations. The wherewithal or instrument for domination in cyber space is power, taken in the widest sense of the term. The power, which a nation is capable of projecting and sustaining in cyber space, is measured in terms of its cyber capabilities. The study and observance of behavioural patterns, doctrinal frameworks, geostrategic alignment/ arrangements and technology acquisitions of the so-called 'great powers' in cyber space can be invaluable tools for other nations to review, consolidate, strengthen and possibly restructure the framework and doctrinal formulation for cyber security with matching tools and techniques.

Notes

1. Carl Mosk, *Traps, Embraced or Escaped: Elites in the Economic Development of Modern Japan and China* (Singapore: World Scientific Publishing Co., 2011), p.60.
2. Henry R. Nau, *Perspectives on International Relations: Power, Institutions, and Ideas* (Singapore: SAGE Publication, 2017), p.32.
3. Greg Austin, *Cyber Policy in China* (Cambridge: Polity Press, 2004), p. 129.
4. Jiang Zemin, *On the Development of China's Information Technology Industry* (Burlington Massachusetts: Elsevier, 2009), p.295.
5. White Paper on China's National Defense in 2004, *Revolution in Military Affairs with Chinese Characteristics*, Chapter III, http://english.people.com.cn/whitepaper/defense2004/defense2004.html.Military Affairs with Chinese. Accessed December 30, 2015.
6. UN Docs A/61/161, July 18, 2006, p.4.
7. Austin, n.3, p.211.
8. Amy Chang, *Warring State: China's Cybersecurity Strategy* (Washington, DC: Centre for a New American Security, 2014), p.10.
9. Academy of Military Science, *Chinese People's Liberation Army Military Terminology* (Beijing: Military Science Press, 2011), p.286.
10. Jon R. Lindsay, Tai Ming Cheung and Derek S. Reveron, eds., *China and Cybersecurity: Espionage, Strategy, and Politics in the Digital Domain* (Oxford University Press: Oxford, 2015), p.139.
11. David M. Finkelstein, "China's National Military Strategy: An Overview of the Military Strategic Guidelines", *Asia Policy* 4.1, 2007, p. 82.
12. Andrew Jones and Gerald L. Kovacich, *Global Information Warfare: The New Digital Battlefield* (Boca Raton: CRC Press, 2015), p. 162.
13. Lindsay, et. al., n.10, p.10.
14. Ibid., p. 170.

15. Ibid., p. 172.
16. Ibid., p. 173.
17. James Mulvenon, "PLA Computer Network Operations: Scenarios, Doctrine, Organizations, and Capability: Beyond the Strait: PLA Missions Other Than Taiwan" (Strategic Studies Institute, US Army War College, 2009), pp. 257-259.
18. Mandiant APT1, "Exposing One of China's Cyber Espionage Units, February 18, 2013", http://intelreport. mandiant.com/Mandiant_APT1_Report.pdf. Accessed April 23, 2016.
19. Spencer Ackerman and Jonathan Kaiman, "Chinese Military Officials Charged With Stealing US Data As Tensions Escalate", *The Guardian*, May 20, 2014, http://www..com/technology/2014/may/19/us-chinese-military-officials-cyber-espionage. Accessed April 23, 2016.
20. US House of Representatives 112th Congress, *Investigative Report on the US National Security Issues Posed by Chinese Telecommunications Companies Huawei and ZTE*, 2012.
21. Amrutha Gayathri, "Former CIA, NSA Chief, Michael Hayden, Accuses Huawei of Spying for China; Huawei Denies Claim", *International Business Times*, July 20, 2013, http://www.ibtimes.com/former-cia-nsa-chief-michael-hayden-accuses-huawei-spying-china-huawei-denies-claim-1354011. Accessed April 23, 2016.
22. Manoj Gairola, "Huawei, ZTE Under Scanner", *Hindustan Times*, http://www.hindustantimes.com/india/huawei-zte-under-scanner/story-SYhgG0xNLNyZHDT8INEFLM.html, May 8, 2013. Accessed April 23, 2016.
23. "Huawei : The Company that Spooked the World," *Economist*, August 4, 2012, http://www.economist.com/node/21559929.
24. Michael Danie, "Strengthening Cyber Risk Management", *White House Profile*, February 2, 2015, http://www.whitehouse.gov/blog/author/Michael%20Daniel. Accessed April 23, 2016.
25. John D. Banusiewicz, "Deputy Secretary Lynn Details Anti-Cyber Threat Strategy", *US DoD News*,June 16, 2011, http://archive.defense.gov/news/newsarticle.aspx?id=64351. Accessed June 10, 2015.
26. Ibid.
27. Ibid.
28. Danie, n.24.
29. US Department of Homeland Security, "National Cyber Security Division Resilient Accord Read Ahead," https://www.fbiic.gov/public/2010/sep/NCSD_Information_for_Resilient_Accord_20100310_v00.pdf. Accessed April 23, 2016.
30. Ibid.
31. Stein Schjolberg, *The History of Cybercrime: 1976-2014* (Norderstedt: BooksOnDemand.com, 2014), p.135.
32. Ibid.
33. Glenn Greenwald and Ewen MacAskill, "NSA Prism Programme Taps in to User Data of Apple, Google and Others", *The Guardian*, June 7, 2013, http://www.theguardian.com/world/2013/jun/06/us-tech-giants-nsa-data. Accessed April 23, 2016.
34. Glenn Greenwald and Ewen MacAskill, "Boundless Informant: The NSA's Secret

Tool to Track Global Surveillance Data," *The Guardian*, June 11, 2013, http://www.theguardian.com/world/2013/jun/08/nsa-boundless-informant-global-datamining. Accessed April 23, 2016.

35. Carnegie Endowment for International Peace, "Text of Newly-Approved Russian Military Doctrine", http://carnegieendowment.org/files/2010russia_ military_doctrine.pdf. Accessed April 23, 2016.

36 Dan Fayutkin, "The American and Russian Approaches to Cyber Challenges", *OMICS International*, vol 2 issue 4, 2012, http://www.omicsgroup.org/journals/the-american-and-russian-approaches-to-cyber-challenges-2167-0374.1000110.pdf. Accessed April 23, 2016.

37. Gavin Knight, "The Alarming Spread of Fascism in Putin's Russia", *Newstatesman,* July 24, 2007 http://www.newstatesman.com/politics/2007/07/putin-russia-nashi-soviet. Accessed April 23, 2016.

38. Susan W. Brenne, *Cybercrime: Criminal Threats from Cyberspace* (California: Praeger, 2010), p. 209.

39. *UN Document A/66/359 Dated September 14, 2011,* General Assembly, Letter Dated 12 September 2011 from Permanent Representatives of China, the Russian Federation, Tajikistan and Uzbekistan to the United Nations addressed to the Secretary-General", p. 4.

40. Ian Leigh, "Information Security Doctrine of the Russian Federation," Geneva Centre for the Democratic Control of Armed Forces (DCAF),www.dcaf.ch/content/download/36442/528101/file/Doctrine_security_LEIGH.pdf. Accessed April 23, 2016.

41. Ibid.

42. Danie, n. 24.

43. Eugene Gerden, "$500 Million for New Russian Cyber Army", *S C Magazine,* November 6, 2014, http://www.scmagazineuk.com/500-million-for-new-russian-cyber-army/article/381720/. Accessed April 23, 2016.

44. Ward Carroll, "Russia Now 3 and 0 in Cyber Warfare", *Defensetech,* January 30, 2009, http://defensetech.org/ 2009/ 01/30/russia-now-3-and-0-in-cyber-warfare/. Accessed April 23, 2016.

5

Cyber Surveillance, Espionage and Exploitation

Kautilya's *Arthasastra,* composed around 321 BCE, is one of the oldest and most comprehensive treatises,[1] which still acts as a signpost and a point of reference, giving pragmatic and empirical solutions to theoreticians and practitioners on complex statecraft issues. The exhaustive and indigenous political theory propounded by Kautilya covers many tenets of statecraft, including diplomacy, peace, intelligence, security, war and political economy. According to Kautilya, *yuddh* or war was of three kinds: *Prakash-yuddha* (open fight) at a place and time *of choosing, Kuta- yuddha* (concealed fighting) involving cunning and *tactical* manoeuvring in the battlefield and *Tusnim-yuddha* (silent fighting) by using secret agents for enticement or neutralisation of the enemy.[2] In today's geopolitical landscape, an open fight or *Prakash-yuddha* continues to be a conceptual possibility, if not an empirical reality in all domains of war. On the other hand, the tenets of *Kuta-yuddha* (concealed fighting) and *Tusnim-yuddha* (silent fighting) as described by Kautilya are still visible and applicable across the broad spectrum of strategic manoeuvring and geopolitical engagement among nations. In the realm of modern warfare, the conceptual expositions as well as practical applications of Kautilya's *Kuta-yuddha* and *Tusnim-Yuddha* still serve as anchoring points for strategic perception management and intelligence and counter-intelligence operations across political, economic and military dimensions.

The relevance of the *Arthasastra* in the present scenario is both insightful and profound. Some of the concepts propagated by

Kautilya have parallels and undeniable resemblance with existing practices of espionage undertaken by several nation-states, either as a pretext for securing national interests or for complying with strategic objectives. For the advancement and achievement of the short and long-term objectives, espionage, in one form or other, has been used—deliberately, relentlessly and unrepentantly—by almost every nation-state. The practitioners of this clandestine craft undertake intelligence gathering against present, potential and perceived adversaries in areas of extreme importance to their security, economy and military. The professionalism and tactical value of the skills of these agent provocateurs are much sought after in peace-time and become almost indispensable in the times leading to, and during, a war. The organisations entrusted with the responsibility of undertaking espionage operations secretly, covertly and clandestinely—depending upon their mandate and expertise—continue with the task of gathering intelligence for various purposes.

The generation and processing of unimaginable quantities of data are manifestations of the 'cyber Zeitgeist'. For almost all the agencies, organisation, institutions or individuals, data from a range of sources, is a resource that can analysed and synthesised for decision-making. Data as a resource must be protected and preserved across its life-cycle. Lost and compromised data can result in financial losses, loss of confidential information and, with that, loss of credibility, loss of functionality and operational effectiveness. The measure of criticality of data determines its ultimate importance to friends and foes alike. The efforts to protect data are matched with incentives to access, steal or manipulate information. In effect, intelligence is the product resulting from the collection, collation, evaluation, analysis, integration, and interpretation of collected information.[3]

Most nations have complied with the demands of the grim imperative of espionage, revamping it as an inalienable necessity and an instrument of state policy. Intelligence in its essence pertains to the ways in which sovereign powers create, exploit, and protect secret advantages against other sovereignties. Sovereignty, of course, need not be a modern state; it also comprises "non-state actors" who have the will and the means to use force to control territory, resources, and other people.[4] There is a subtle difference between intelligence and espionage. However, with multiplicity of meanings reflecting the multifaceted nature of intelligence operations, there is an emerging synonymic convergence between the two. The gathered intelligence facilitates the decision-makers to select a course of action which best serves the nation's interests. The systematic institutionalisation of cyber espionage and associated clandestine activities to garner, analyse and synthesise data have emerged as a new discipline or set of disciplines, combining traditional intelligence methods with a new and sophisticated technical approach.

The Evolution of Information Gathering

In the practice of the craft of intelligence gathering, some tools, techniques and methodologies have remained free from the political, cultural, temporal and spatial imperatives, while some have evolved into a distinctively different form,necessitated by the changed characteristics of the targets, types of information and the evolving intent. All humans are endowed with intelligence and memory along with social, emotional and cognitive vulnerabilities and are likely to, unwittingly or otherwise, succumb to the temptations of power, greed and ambition. The elicitation of intelligence from human sources has been used across the expanse of history. Human intelligence is the most common and highly effective method used for espionage. Human Intelligence (HUMINT) is defined as "a category of intelligence derived from information collected and provided by human sources."[5]Intelligence agencies have refined the art of exploiting people, using cyber space in general and social media in particular, by intimidation, allurement or fraudulent means in garnering critical intelligence. In cyber space, for HUMNIT to be effective, a pre-existent or a newly created relationship in cyber space is exploited either by threats, inducement and enticement or by exploiting human frailties, frustrations and inequities. HUMINT is predicated on identification of the most appropriate targets for exploitation by coercion, deception, enticement or the threat of use of violence.

The intelligence gathering process involving visual clues, pictures and images collected, collated and analysed during the specific time period, is an effective and result-oriented methodology. For a battlefield commander, real-time visual clues provide 'real-time situational awareness'—the holy grail of intelligence. During the American Civil War, the union army used hot air balloons for observation and photography.[6] The Germans experimented with both kites and rockets as platforms in the late 1800s.[7] With the advent of flight, aerial photography became an integral part of the information and intelligence gathering processes. The evolution of some of the finest flying machines such as Lockheed U-2, Lockheed SR-71 "Blackbird" and MiG-25 is largely attributable to the accordance of extreme relevance and importance to Imagery Intelligence (IMINT) during times of both peace and war. With satellites and unmanned aerial vehicles, the aerial intelligence acquisition techniques have transformed to a new level. The basic satellite imagery can now be easily accessed by the click of a mouse using 'Google Maps' and Google World.

In the annals of history, cryptography and espionage may have their genesis in the same time period. From a humble beginning during the Roman period, the renaissance and resurrection of cryptography in the form of complex codes and ciphers is mainly attributable to French and Italian cryptographers in the 1500s.[8] In early 1917, the deciphering of a German encoded telegram, often referred to as the "Zimmerman Telegram", changed the course of the war. The "Zimmerman Telegram" was a secret communication from the Foreign Secretary of the German Empire, Arthur Zimmerman to the German ambassador in Mexico making an offer to Mexico to join the German cause and, in return, to reclaim the territory of New Mexico, Texas, and Arizona from the United States. Until that point, the United States saw the war largely as a European affair and attempted to remain neutral. When being informed about the contents of the telegram, the US officially declared war against Germany and its allies on April 6, 1917. [9]

During World War II, Arthur Scherbius invented the "Enigma", an ingenious electro-mechanical machine for encryption and decryption.[10] The Enigma had several rotors and gears which could be arranged in numerous configurations, making it virtually unbreakable with brute force methods. The claim of 'unbreakability of encryptions' provided by Enigma made German operators overconfident about their ability to encrypt secret messages. To break the innumerable key combinations of Enigma, Alan Turing designed and used the first electronic computer which helped in "deciphering the Enigma code". The German overconfidence and overreliance on Enigma during the course of the war was exploited to the hilt by the Allied cryptographers.[11] For code breaking or cryptanalysis, the signals or messages transiting between people (e.g. COMINT or Communications Intelligence) or between machines or networks (e.g. Electronic Intelligence or ELINT) or a combination of the two need to be intercepted, collated and analysed.

Cryptologic encryption has become almost a standard requirement for the privacy of electronic mail, secured e-commerce transactions and the digital economy. End-to-end encryption ensures that data in any conceivable form are encrypted in transit and in storage, and the key to decrypt these is available only with those mutually communicating. To counter this, the governments of some of the countries, such as the US, are trying to force the tech companies to provide 'back doors' within the encryption schemes to facilitate privileged access to the law enforcement and secret services. After the San Bernardino shooting, on December 9, 2015, FBI Director James B. Comey, while making a statement before the Senate Judiciary Committee, brought out that the ISIS is increasingly using encrypted private messaging platforms. He said, "This real and growing gap, which the FBI refers to as 'Going Dark', we believe it must be addressed, since the resulting risks are grave in traditional criminal matters as well as in national security matters." He further commented that the US government is trying to ensure that the private players who own and operate these platforms— with end-to-end encryption—understand the national security risks that result from the use of their encrypted products and services by malicious actors. Though there is no legislating obligation upon these companies, the companies are being asked to cooperate constructively with the US government. [12]

Research in Open Publications (OSINT)

The publicly accessible information, which can be scouted from a number of myriad sources,is a treasure trove of data capable of producing actionable intelligence. The initial scepticism about acquisition of intelligence from non-classified and open sources has given way to acceptance of this form of intelligence gathering, as a mainstay of intelligence operations. Tools and methodologies are being evolved within the national security apparatus on how to use information *gleaned from open sources.* The evolution of OSINT as a mainstay of intelligence operations can be attributed to three main factors. The first is the paradigm shift in challenges from largely state-centric security considerations of the Cold War era to multiple threats emanating from more diverse individuals, groups or agencies. During the Cold War, the primary focus of the Western intelligence community was on the intentions and capabilities of the Soviet Union and its allies. Similarly, Soviet intelligence agencies were actively involved in intelligence gathering about their adversaries. The disintegration of the erstwhile USSR, the emergence of a new world order and the evolution of contemporary terrorism in a more dangerous and deadlier form, has given rise to many challenges for the intelligence community. The scope and range of issues to be dealt with by the intelligence agencies have spiralled to unprecedented levels. Terrorism, organised crime, state sponsored terrorism, home-grown terrorist organisations, proliferation of illegal weapons, rogue states, illegal immigration, energy security—these are the issues that keep the intelligence agencies on their toes at all times. In the wake of multifarious challenges to national security and widening of the security agenda to non-military threats, intelligence agencies have to trawl through gathered intelligence to identify subtle and specific signatures to determine the magnitude, timing and place of conditioned responses. This, in turn, has seen a greater demand for more information and a natural progression of this is the increased reliance on, and utilisation of, OSINT. A second driver for the growth of OSNIT is technology. The emergence of the collaborative web and the presence of the ubiquitous Internet have provided the security actors a new set of tools and technologies for collecting, collating, analysing, and disseminating information in the span of a very short time.

Web Source Intelligence (WEBINT)

The ability to gather information by leveraging the power of the Internet is termed as WEBINT. By using powerful Web crawlers and indexing systems, it is possible to harvest just about any piece of information stored on publicly available servers. The incentives to undertake acts of cyber crime, espionage, subversion and sabotage are only limited by the ingenuity, dexterity and technological capabilities possessed by hostile malevolent entities. The successful culmination of an espionage activity in cyber space may be a technology and capability demonstrator, a deliberate attempt to garner tangible and intangible results or a premediated design to cause severe *disruption* in the *functioning* of political, financial, social or military entities. An act of espionage in cyber space by a state may also be a manifestation of its deterrence capability. After all, credible deterrence depends on the communication of actions and responses in the wake of the adversaries' attempt to cross the security threshold prescribed by the state in the pursuit of its stated national interests.

Cyber Espionage and Exploitation

Today, use of stealth techniques and exploits with an aim to proliferate computers and networks of various organisations and institutions, has become a menace of unparalleled proportion. Cyber crime and espionage reveals the dark underbelly of cyber space. This has given rise to an increasingly dangerous ecosystem inextricably embedded within the fabric of the global cyber space. This ecosystem is teeming with inimical activities and devious enterprises, not only within existing precincts but foraying into systems beyond immediate reach. The cyber attackers have become more ingenious and opportunistic in their endeavours and attack vectors and techniques have evolved in terms of lethality and consequences. The cyber espionage activities may also be undertaken to keep the dynamic relationship equation consistent between two rival states. The desire of a state to bring parity to the sum total of all capabilities may be the main motivation for the adoption of non-conventional means. The dedicated cyber espionage campaigns launched by China against the US may be one of the drivers for this. China tries to make up for what it lacks in conventional military means by exploiting the cyber space.

Cyber espionage activities may provoke a reaction and intensify latent hostilities. The reaction can be offensive or defensive in nature, based on the perceived tolerance threshold. Defensive actions in response to an espionage activity are generally exhaustive and at times are way out of proportion in terms of resources, time and manpower. In a bid to secure itself from future cyber espionage threats, the target may overreact and overprotect. In the bargain, it may lose out on opportunities the global information age has to offer. This sets in motion the vicious circle in which a substantial amount of money is committed to clean up existing systems malware while even more money is spent for future protection. This may end up being a 'Pyrrhic victory' as the time, money and efforts spent may not result in accruing the intended results.

Cyber Espionage by Non-State Actors

Although nation-states tend to have larger stakes in exploitation of cyber space, non-state actors have equal motivation, though for different reasons. The use of cyber space as a potential venue for undertaking various malevolent, insidious and traitorous activities has become the order of the day. While motives may vary from one hacker to the next, the objective is consistent with the goal of exploiting the cyber space for malicious intent. Financial gains, espionage, ephemeral fame, nefarious notoriety, entertainment, hacktivism, terrorism or misplaced sense of patriotism are some of the drivers which propel hackers into the murky world of cyber crime. Motivation for making money rules the roost, closely followed by corporate espionage activities. The hacking skills acquired by individuals are much sought after and there is an increasing demand for their services for industrial espionage, intellectual property thefts, financial frauds and monetary misappropriation.

Cyber criminals and cyber espionage operators have evolved a myriad attack techniques with ever-increasing lethality and sophistication commensurate with their evolving expertise and experience. A cyber criminal gains currency in a small, exclusive and secretive community based on the success, quantum and frequency of his exploits. The success of such exploits largely depends on an understanding of system architecture, network transmission protocols, exploitation of associated vulnerabilities, malicious codes and content exploits. The understanding of almost every aspect of human fallibility and frailty also assists them in their nefarious endeavours.

Zero-Day Vulnerability Exploitation

In recent times, the vulnerability quotient due to espionage activities in cyber space has gone many notches up. A direct ramification of this is a burgeoning market offering services, tools and technologies facilitating credible and potent espionage activities. The spirit of entrepreneurship has caught up with computer geeks, who, having proven prowess in exploiting cyber vulnerabilities, have no qualms in offering their services to the highest bidder. These espionage activities in cyber space may threaten the economy, national security and well-being of people.

The mother of all malicious programmes and bugs is the "zero-day exploit". In a zero-day exploit, the creation of the exploit is concomitant with the knowledge of vulnerability before, or on the same day. By creating a virus or bug that takes advantage of a vulnerability not known to the vendor and without a security patch, the attacker can inflict debilitating damage on unsuspecting victims. On an average, zero-day vulnerability remains unknown to the affected software vendor and its users for an average of 312 days. [13]

In the recent past, software vendors and security researchers have been caught up in an animated debate on the issue of the ethicality, legality and desirability of disclosing vulnerability information. The dichotomous dilemma of making the information public, on the one hand, may allow all affected parties to carry out risk assessment, while, on the other, the information will also be available for exploitation. The dependence of society on information technology has transformed the knowledge about security vulnerabilities, a highly prized and valuable asset. An ethical security researcher may seek monetary compensation for the time spent in uncovering vulnerabilities. However, reporting vulnerabilities for seeking compensation might be viewed as akin to extortion by the vendor. On the other hand, cyber criminals, with no ethical considerations, are willing to pay substantial amounts for suitable vulnerability information. The market for the sale and purchase of vulnerabilities has evolved from its nascent stage, operating from dark and isolated alleys under the shroud of anonymity, to commercial service offerings with legitimacy.

Vulnerability Purchase Programmes (VPPs)

Traditionally, the primary players in the commercial vulnerability market have been iDefense, which started its Vulnerability Contributor Program (VCP)[14] in 2002 and Tipping Point, which started its Zero Day Initiative (ZDI)[15] in 2005. In a bid to show their ethical intents, both vendors publicly disclosed their vulnerability handling services and policies. The VCP and ZDI programmes typically purchase vulnerability information to protect customers before the vulnerability becomes public knowledge, subsequently informing the vendor of the affected software. The VCP and ZDI programmes entreat security researchers to accept lower compensation with the assurance that the information would not be used with malicious intent. Upon acquiring a vulnerability, both programmes provide detailed technical information on the vulnerability and on the timeline from its initial purchase through publication. Under the VCP and ZDI programmes, the two companies together had purchased 2,392 vulnerabilities till September 23, 2013.

Bug Bounty Programmes

In order to bring resilience into their product, a number of software vendors have embarked on "Bug Bounty Programmes". Under this programme, a finder can directly report a vulnerability to the software vendor and is monetarily compensated by the vendor. This incentive may discourage a finder going public with the vulnerability information or selling it to an unscrupulous person. It was first introduced by Mozilla Foundation and since then Google, Facebook, PayPal and others have followed suit. Microsoft, which vehemently opposed such a system, finally succumbed to commercial and security imperatives and introduced its bug bounty programme.

- Under the bug bounty programme, Google, on January 28, 2016 announced that it had paid more than US $ 2 million to security researchers in the year 2015. Since the launch of the programme in 2010, the company had paid more than US $ 6 million, with the largest single payment of US $ 37,500 to an Android security researcher. [16]
- Mozilla, in the last three years, has paid approximately US $ 570,00 for information on 190 vulnerabilities which were discovered in a Firefox browser.
- Facebook has paid out a whopping US $ 4.3 million since it introduced its bug bounty programme in 2011 to more than 800 researchers around the world.[17]
- Microsoft has paid to the tune of US $ 100,000 from June 2013 onwards, when it decided to became part of the bug bounty

programme. On October 8, 2013, it awarded US $ 100,000 to James Forshaw (head of vulnerability research at Context Information Security) for discovering a new type of mitigation bypass technique that could potentially threaten the security and integrity of its latest version of the Windows operating system.[18]

The cost benefit accrued by the bug bounty programme is much higher than the cost of hiring full-time security researchers to locate bugs internally. The bug bounty programmes helps software vendors to plug in the security loopholes which otherwise have the potential to be exploited offensively. It also hastens up the action towards the remedy of the vulnerabilities reported.

Most nation-states are leveraging cyber warfare techniques either with hostile intent or for protection of their Critical Information Infrastructure (CII). In the recent past, the budget outlays and spending to acquire capabilities for waging cyber war have increased manifold. While unethical hackers and even criminal organisations have limited resources and have to operate within the confines of shoestring budgets, a nation-state's cyber warfare assets have plenteous resources and immunity from prosecution. In order to keep a step ahead of potential adversaries, it is not uncommon for nation-states to purchase vulnerabilities for exploitation. The US government, for example, is an enthusiastic buyer, with the NSA devoting US $ 25.1 million to "covert purchases of software vulnerabilities" from private vendors during fiscal year 2013. This would enable it to acquire an estimated minimum of 100 to 625 exploits based on the present going rate.[19] Other countries are also big spenders when it comes to acquiring exploits.

The year 2009 was a defining year which marked the arrival of the first true cyber weapon, the "Stuxnet'. A complex computer worm was developed with the specific objective to decommission the uranium enrichment facilities in the Natanz reactor in Iran. It is believed that the perpetrators used four zero-day security vulnerabilities to spread around Microsoft's Windows operating system. After detailed study, Microsoft admitted that the attackers initially exploited the old MS08-067 vulnerability which was a remote code execution vulnerability. Successful exploitation of this vulnerability enables the attacker to take complete control of an affected system remotely.[20] A new LNK (Windows Shortcut) flaw was used to launch the exploit code on vulnerable Windows systems and a zero-day bug to exploit the Print Spooler vulnerability (this vulnerability was leveraged to propagate and affect systems connected to the affected machine's network).

Presently, a number of new entrants are offering services ranging from vulnerability feed, penetration testing to vulnerability and security assessment. Among them are Exodus Intelligence and Netragard in the US, Vupen in France, Revuln in Malta and Telus in Canada. In fact, Vupen publicly offers sales of "exclusive and extremely sophisticated zero-days for offensive security". It also advertises that it offers government-grade zero-day exploits which may be used by law enforcement agencies and the intelligence community in furtherance of their offensive cyber missions and operations. These companies are hunting with the hounds and running with the hares with an aim to make money by leveraging the fear factor emanating from concerns among companies and organisations about the security of their systems as well as by selling the zero-day exploits to the highest bidder.

On any given day, a number of vulnerabilities are privately known. Out of these, it can be safely assumed that a substantial number are exploitable. These vulnerabilities and exploits are being purchased with equal gusto by cyber criminals as well as by government agencies. Big software vendors will leave no stone unturned to plug these vulnerabilities either by internal evaluation or by purchasing outrightly from vendors under the bug bounty programme. This has added a new dimension to the already complex issue of cyber espionage and exploitation.

Large-Scale Surveillance Programmes

The *governments of some of powerful nations*, such as the US and China have embarked on an organised, state sponsored but publicly denied surveillance programme, in effect *trampling 'the human right of privacy' with impunity.* Such acts often dichotomise between the government's overt assertion of human rights and covert sponsoring of mass surveillance on its own citizens.

US Surveillance State

In one of the earlier such attempts, under the US-UK security agreement, the five signatory nations namely, Australia, Canada, New Zealand, the UK and the US became part of the SIGINT collection and analysis network, code-named "Echelon". With the objective of monitoring the communications of the erstwhile USSR and its allies in the 1960s, Echelon carried out interception and eavesdropping on voice and data communication over commercial satellites. With the arrival of the ubiquitous Internet, the electronic communication was largely being transmitted through this new medium. In order to monitor the traffic going to and from a suspicious target, in the late 1990s, the US FBI came up with the "Carnivore" programme. The fruition of the program saw the attachment of a device at the Internet Service Provider (ISP) of the target, facilitating filtering and recording of all inbound and outbound traffic.[21] After much public outcry, the programme was abandoned in 2001, only to metamorphose into commercially available devices. Still trying to make strides in the field of mass surveillance,[22] the FBI developed the "Magic Lantern" technology which allowed installation of powerful software on a remote machine, transmitted through an exploit or a Trojan horse via a seemingly innocuous yet extremely malicious e-mail.[23] Once installed, the software would begin to record every keystroke made on the compromised machine. In the year 2002, the existence of the Magic Lantern programme was confirmed by the FBI, however, with the equally implausible statement of denial of its deployment ever.

Tone and Tenor of Mass Surveillance after 9/11

The American psyche, lacerated with hurt, clouded with anger and ripe with distrust, scepticism, alienation and self-criticism in the aftermath of the September 11 attacks in 2001, was malleable to the acceptance of some harsh steps. The resolve to negate the possibility of future attacks of such magnitude paved the way for the enactment of many laws granting sweeping powers to government agencies to undertake mass surveillance such as the Patriot Act, Protect America Act and FISA (Foreign Surveillance Act) Amendments Act. Under the Protect America Act, the mandatory requirement of a warrant for government surveillance of foreign targets was removed.[24] Under the FISA Amendments Act, some of the original FISA court requirements were dispensed with.[25] The NSA and its international collaborative partners went into overdrive to bring every US citizen and all possible foreign nationals, even without any significant interest in US affairs, under the surveillance net. However, some in investigative journalism got wind of what government agencies were up to. In November 2010, WikiLeaks and five major news journals, namely, *El País* of Spain, *Le Monde* of France, *Der Spiegel* of Germany, *The Guardian* of the United Kingdom and *The New York Times* of the United States began publishing leaked US State Department diplomatic "cables" simultaneously.[26] Other documents of classified nature which were leaked to the public domain included the Afghan War documents, Iraq War documents and the Guantanamo Bay files. However, to witness the mother of all leaks, the world had to wait till June 6, 2013, when the British newspaper *The Guardian* began publishing a series of revelations made available by Edward Snowden, an ex-NSA-contracted systems analyst. Snowden, acting as a whistle-blower, came in contact with two journalists, Glenn Greenwald and Laura Poitras, and provided them a cache of around 15,000–20,000 documents.[27] The Snowden revelations made it amply clear that the NSA was operating a complex and intricate network of spying programmes intercepting Internet and telephone conversations from over a billion users around the world.

Snowden's act was criticised and applauded in equal measure from various quarters. NSA Director General Keith Alexander in a swift and acerbic statement, blamed Snowden for causing "irreversible damage" to the US.[28] The Senate Intelligence Committee Chair, Dianne Feinstein, described Snowden's action as treasonous. The process to indict Snowden on charges of espionage and treason was initiated. However, some saw the situation from a different vantage point. Former Vice President Al Gore viewed the NSA surveillance as violation of the Fourth Amendment (Amendment IV) to the United States Constitution.[29]

The Snowden revelations have triggered a dichotomous debate over the issue of accountability and the value of privacy. There is a perceptible shift in opinion in many parts of the world over not succumbing to the '*Orwellian doublespeak*' of the high and mighty. Besides, there is a resurgence of resolve and renewed vigour among mainstream media to sensitise the public on key issues that may have been deliberately kept out of the public domain. However, Snowden's disclosures had almost inconsequential effects over an overwhelming majority of countries to respond in a convincing and assertive way. If we look closely and dissect through the layers of protests in the form of representations, governmental inquiries and media coverage, the collective measures for prevention and mitigation of such occurrences were largely insignificant. The small numbers of reforms that have been adopted by governments appear to lack the necessary drive to set up an institutionalised international system with provisions for prosecution and punitive actions to act as deterrence.

The Snowden disclosures caused a broad-based sense of outrage in the US mostly focussed on the privacy rights of US citizens. The revelations triggered numerous protests and campaigns particularly over the NSA's telephone call detail records collection programme. At least six lawsuits were filed against the NSA's mass surveillance and several legislative proposals were made to modify the NSA surveillance programme. However, none of the recommended surveillance reforms focussed on the bulk collection of communications of non-US persons. On May 22, 2014, the US House of Representatives passed the USA Freedom Act, which offered a series of milder reforms for surveillance which subsequently was approved by the US Senate and signed by the president.[30] In order to quell the outrage sparked by the Snowden revelations, under Presidential Policy Directive 28 (PPD 28), the president instructed the US intelligence community to reexamine its mass surveillance programmes and to make recommendations if these programs could be limited in their scope and application. PPD 28 acknowledged that privacy rights must be respected "regardless of the nationality of the individual to whom the information pertains or where that person resides."[31] However, such protection is neither explicit nor sweeping. Moreover, the US has interpreted the clauses of the International Covenant on Civil and Political Rights(ICCPR)as non-obligatory with respect to extra-territorial surveillance.

Role of US Private Sector

The role and reach of private companies in providing the bulk of the communication infrastructure and facilities makes their explicit or covert participation absolutely necessary for the success of a surveillance programme. The first of a multitude of documents, was a court order to Verizone to furnish an electronic copy of all call details records or "telephony metadata" on a daily basis to the NSA. This was followed by documents accusing companies, including Google, Facebook, and Apple of being hand in glove with the NSA. Before Snowden, the response to the NSA's legal authority to conduct spying activities was almost muted a barring a few known instances of protests. Post-Snowden revelations, either out of commercial compulsions or due to the fear of a backlash from customers, companies have been more assertive in voicing their opposition to the government's surveillance programme. In a bid to bridge the trust deficit, major Internet companies have taken the initiative to provide statistical data and put in place policies to deal with issues related to privacy and the right of expression. The major telecom companies started issuing periodic transparency reports. In November 2013, a coalition was forged among several major Internet companies to create the "Global Reform Government Surveillance"[32]. The coalition seeks legislative initiative, conjoined with issues related to the surveillance of individuals and access to their information supporting five guiding principles: Government's Authority to Collect Users' Information, Oversight and Accountability, Transparency About Government Demands, Respecting the Free Flow of Information and Avoiding Conflicts Among Governments. In November 2014, in an open letter to the Senate, it urged it to vote on the bipartisan USA Freedom Act as reaffirmation of America's commitment to freedom as well as protection of national security.[33]

China's Quest for Mass Surveillance

The Communist Party of China, while being weary of implications of unrestricted online access to information to its legitimacy, has enthusiastically promoted the use of the Internet as an inalienable part of its quest for global hegemony, economic growth and orchestration of its technical prowess. China views the Internet as a fertile ecosystem that germinates, fosters, nurtures, and engenders political dissent, detrimental social activities and societal unrest. To counter this, China has an aggressive and multifaceted online censorship system, commonly known as the Great Firewall. After viewing the contents on the Internet through the prism of its own contentious policies and cultural interests, the censorship apparatus filters or blocks access to online material deemed dangerous to the state.

The Chinese leadership has, for long, had an ambivalent relationship with the Internet. During the Arab Spring in early 2011, China bolstered its censorship bureaucracy, reportedly creating a new office under the State Council Information Office to "regulate every corner of the nation's vast Internet community,"[34] However, confinement within the precincts of the Great Firewall has given an impetus to an evolving and thriving Chinese online ecosystem driven, sustained and perpetuated by indigenous innovation, enterprise and entrepreneurship. Beijing's efforts to alienate its citizens from the global net has paved the way for home-grown companies to cater to the online requirements and needs of 1.3 billion people in their societal interactions, financial transactions, knowledge exploration, online resource exploitation and a myriad other services. The Internet's ubiquitous and totemic icons—Google, Wikipedia, Twitter, YouTube, Facebook, Instagram — are under the censorship of the ruling Communist Party due to fears of fanning the flames of anti-government sentiments. In the absence of a competitive environment, Chinese home grown companies are thriving and have garnered market capitalisation, even exceeding that of their foreign counterparts which they emulate.

At the helm of the Chinese online oppression against free speech and tyrannical censorship is China's new Internet czar, Lu Wei, who took over the State Internet Information Office in 2013 and became the director of a powerful Internet committee headed by President Xi Jinping in 2014.[35] While unrepentantly defending China's need for stronger Internet content control, he issued new regulations restricting sharing on social media sites and increasing censorship of popular online video sites. In response to criticism of such controls, Lu Wei said, "The Internet is like a car. If it has no brakes, it doesn't matter how fast the car is capable of traveling, once it gets on the highway you can imagine what the end result will be." [36]

The home-grown Chinese firms have ensured that, most of the Chinese, incarcerated behind the Great Firewall, are not deprived of online experiences and services unless they want to voice their political dissent online. Adherence to Chinese government regulations and sticking to Chinese sites is rewarded with sufficiently high speeds and reasonable access charges. In the first quarter of 2015, the total transaction value of China e-commerce market exceeded US $567.49 billion, an increase of 10.1 per cent on a year-over-year basis.[37] As of December 31, 2014, top five listed Chinese Internet companies by market value were Alibaba

(US $253.41 billion), Tencent (US $135.50 billion), Baidu (US $80.32 billion), Jingdong (US $31.52 billion) and Netease (US $13.01 billion). In September last year, e-commerce king Alibaba scored the largest Initial Public Offer (IPO) in Wall Street history. Tencent, the designer of a messaging company WeChat, has a market capital more than that of IBM. As a hybrid of Twitter and Facebook, Sina Weibo has emerged as the most popular Chinese microblogging website with a market penetration comparable to that of Twitter.

In its infancy, the Internet shook the very foundation of sovereignty as propagated by the dominant 'Westphalian conceptions'. The belief that the Internet's transcendence of physical boundaries would render it immune to oppressive regulatory regimes has given way to acceptance of the fact that a determined state with technical underpinnings can regulate and control the Internet. The Chinese Internet strategy, aimed at containing the simmering political dissent, has a much more sinister dimension to it. Chinese state-backed hackers have been accused of cyber espionage. In a recent report made public by Fireeye Labs, a company that provides cyber security solutions, examination of malware aimed predominantly at entities in Southeast Asia and India revealed a decade-long operation focussed on targets—government and commercial—that hold key political, economic and military information about the region. The planned development efforts aimed at regional targets, and missions made the lab believe that this activity was state sponsored—most likely by the Chinese government.[38]

China is also determined to extend its oppressive regime beyond its borders. In the cyber lexicon repository, the "Great Cannon" has been added alongside "Great Firewall", christening a new tool for censorship developed by China. When used offensively, that ability can turn a normal Internet user into a vector of an attack. In one such case, the Great Cannon intercepted traffic sent to Baidu infrastructure servers and returned a malicious script, unwittingly enlisting the web surfer in the hacking campaign against foreign websites that have helped the circumventing of Chinese censorship. [39]

Acme of Surveillance Alchemy : Mastering 'Data,Information, Knowledge and Wisdom' (DIKW) Model

The existing surveillance and analytical systems are routinely getting overwhelmed by the sheer volume, complexities and associated processing difficulties of the raw data being collected. The data is being generated in various forms and structures and is often stored in isolation without lateral exchange, as a deliberate measure to arrest its cross-fertilisation and exploitation, in conformity with security imperatives. This acts as a hindrance to view the data coherently and to infer the right approach to deal with this complex issue at the required level.

With the emergence of new challenges to national security, the changing nature of global terrorism and an ever-growing reliance on network-centric operations, the intelligence agencies have to trawl through vast amounts of data to identify subtle and specific signatures to determine the magnitude, timing and place of conditioned responses. For intelligence analysts, the emphasis is switching increasingly to a more immediate response to fleeting signatures and away from the time-consuming monitoring of routine 'pattern of life' in order to find those signatures.[40] The consequences of not dealing effectively with these challenges are potentially profound. Against this backdrop, the evaluation of the **Data-Information-Knowledge-Wisdom (DIKW) Hierarchy** also known as the **'Knowledge Hierarchy'** becomes an operationally useful, functionally utilitarian and intellectually stimulating construct. The acquired raw data moves up the hierarchical ladder to transform into information. This relevant, usable significant, meaningful or processed data offers an answer to an enquiry.

The definition of data is largely contextual based, encapsulating the results produced by a process. For example, information systems define data as unprocessed information. Other processes produce data as a representation of objective facts.[41] Data can be placed in databases or can fill a repository. It is discrete, recordable and can be manipulated,captured and retrieved. Data is a physical entity with an objective existence. Yet, despite this possibility of manipulation, a very limited amount of actions can be performed on data as it lacks an inherent structure or viable relationship. The next category is information. Information is quantifiable,adaptable and measurable. It can be processed and accessed, generated and created, transmitted, produced and consumed.[42] Information can also be of different types with different attributes. Information can be sensitive, contextual, contemporaneous and ephemeral, with or without temporal and spatial relevance.

In the DIKW hierarchy, knowledge is often construed as know-how or skill in a controlling role to transform information into instructions. Knowledge is generally personal, subjective and inherently local. Within the field of knowledge management, there exist two quite distinct and widely accepted types of knowledge: tacit and explicit. Tacit knowledge is knowledge that is hard to encode and communicate. It is ephemeral and transitory and "cannot be resolved into information or itemised in the manner characteristic of information."[43] Further, tacit knowledge is personal, context-specific and hard to formalise. Towards the other end of the scale, explicit knowledge is exactly that kind of knowledge that can be encoded and is transmittable in language.

In this hierarchy, the first three rungs of the hierarchical ladder lead to 'wisdom'. Data needs to be manipulated and supplemented and to be sieved through some processes to elicit tangible meaning. Information needs to be analysed and organised cogently and succinctly to create knowledge. But, whether the sum total of knowledge will lead to attainment of wisdom is a debatable issue. In several scientific communities, there is an explicit distinction made between general knowledge and wisdom-related knowledge. Thus, there might be interconnections of information that create knowledge —but that will not build a foundation for wisdom.[44] Furthermore, the three lower concepts are considered to be storable, transferable and sharable. Wisdom, however, cannot be stored, or transferred from one being to another. It implies deeper understanding and application of the wisdom-based knowledge.[45]

For practitioners of strategic art and science, the collected raw data must traverse through the hierarchical ladder to provide real or at least simulated wisdom. In his works towards computational wisdom, René V. Mayorga defines wisdom as, "Wisdom: the ability to discern inner qualities and relationships and the exercise of good judgment/ knowledge."[46] Mayorga also relates the concept of wisdom to the concept of intelligence. "Intelligence" would be the ability to choose a proper action by analysis of the situation and thus, attain a local goal; while "wisdom" not only includes detailed analysis of the underlying conditions, but also proper synthesis to act in a way that leads to "the attainment of global objectives".

Wisdom is commonly seen as the acme of human existence that is based on knowledge and judgmental capabilities. Though there are generic interpretations of what could be part of wisdom in different domains, there is no specific, widely accepted definition. It is universally agreed that a certain type of knowledge is needed to develop wisdom[47] but the definite type is hard to portray. Wisdom is neither pure rationality, nor pure emotion based; it creates a certain kind of "intuition". Solutions elicited by wisdom, approach a problem by using a creative interconnection of knowledge and experience. Wisdom is acquired based on experience and knowledge.

The metaphorical analysis of the DIKW hierarchy provides a number of interesting insights. With the deluge of data, the quantity of information generated increases beyond a manageable, manipulable size, resulting in loss of its relative structural relationships and its usefulness as knowledge. By adding structure to data to make information and structuring information according to a certain perspective, one can avoid generation of tacit knowledge and create knowledge which is explicit and unequivocal. The 'knowledge pyramid' conceptualises distillation of large amounts of data to a manageable quantity of information, which is then aggregated to create more distilled, actionable and widely applicable knowledge.

Conclusion

In the context of cyber espionage and surveillance, the mission preparedness and befitting response depends on 'early warning' of potential malevolent events and the "motivation and resources" of an adversary. For the process to be meaningful and result oriented, it is imperative to have situation specific and contextual knowledge, discerning disposition and homogenised actions. The information and intelligence garnered through the infrastructure of surveillance and communication systems that support effective decision-making is a culmination of training efforts, experience and technical sophistication. These qualities, either acquired through training or accumulated with experience, coupled with intuitive ingenuity and intuitional perceptions, make surveillance in cyber space a widely used and useful construct.

The constant evolution of cyber threats is a cold hard reality which will continue to cause cataclysmic upheavals in the cyber landscape. Its scope, magnitude and implications are limited only by the ingenuity and intent of the perpetrators and the technological advancement. The most traditional information security programmes are repeatedly circumvented with impunity. Nations around the world are in a race to develop, consolidate and refine cyber warfare capabilities. To mitigate the associated risks, organisations need to evolve their current surveillance capabilities and augment these with positional and temporal accuracies by using technological innovations with persistent reconnaissance to produce timely and actionable intelligence.

Notes

1 P.K.Gautam, "One Hundred Years of Kautilya's Arthasastra", *IDSA Monograph Series*, No. 20, July 2013, p.1.

2 R.P. Kangle, *The Kautilya Arthasastra, Part 3: A Study* (Delhi: Motilal Banarsidass, 2010), p.258.

3 National Security Decision Directive 298, *The National Operations Security Program : Compendium of OPSEC Terms* (Greenbelt, MD: IOSS, 1991).

4 Michael Warner, *The Rise and Fall of Intelligence: An International Security History*

(Georgetown: Georgetown University Press, 2014), p.2.

5 US Military Intelligence Handbook, *Strategic Information, Procedure and Developments*, (Washington, USA: International Business Publications, 2011), p.249.

6 J.K. Petersen,*Handbook of Surveillance Technologies, Third Edition* (New York: CRC Press, 2012), p.571.

7 Ibid., p.569.

8 Will Gragido, and John Pirc, *Cybercrime and Espionage: An Analysis of Subversive Multi-Vector Threats* (Burlington : Elsevier, 2011), p.111.

9 Thomas Boghardt, *The Zimmermann Telegram: Intelligence, Diplomacy, and America's Entry Into World War I* (Maryland: Naval Institute Press, 2012), p.31.

10 Miloslav Dusek, Norbert Lutkenhaus and Martin Hendrych, *Quantum Cryptology Progress in Optics, Volume 49* (Amsterdam : Elsevier, 2006), p. 385.

11 Ibid.

12 The US Federal Bureau of Investigation, *Oversight of the Federal Bureau of Investigation, James B. Comey, Director, Federal Bureau of Investigation, Statement Before the Senate Judiciary Committee*, Washington, D.C, December 9, 2015, https://www.fbi.gov/news/testimony/oversight-of-the-federal-bureau-of-investigation-8 Accessed on January 20, 2016.

13 Krebsonsecurity, "How Many Zero-Days Hit You Today? ", http://krebsonsecurity.com/2013/12/how-many-zero-days-hit-you-today/. Accessed May 1, 2016.

14 "VeriSigniDefenseThreat Intelligence Services Overview", https:// www. verisign. com /static / 031415.pdf. Accessed May 1, 2016.

15 "Why Did We Create the Zero-Day Initiative?", http://www.zerodayinitiative.com/about/ . Accessed May 1, 2016.

16 Google Security Rewards - 2015 Year in Review, "Google Security Blog", https://security.googleblog.com/ 2016/01/google-security-rewards-2015-year-in.html. Accessed May 1, 2016.

17 2015 Highlights: Less Low-Hanging Fruit, "Facebook Bug Bounty", https://www.facebook.com/BugBounty/. Accessed May 1, 2016.

18 " Microsoft-Pay-Out-First-100000-Bug-Bounty", available on http://nakedsecurity.sophos.com/2013/10/09. Accessed May 1, 2016.

19 Stefan Frei, "The Known Unknowns : Empirical Analysis of Publicly Unknown Security Vulnerabilities", NSS Labs, p.14.

20 "Vulnerability in Server Service Could Allow Remote Code Execution", http://support.microsoft.com /kb/958644 MS08-067. Accessed May 1, 2016.

21 Talitha Nabbali, and Mark Perry. "Going for the Throat: Carnivore in an Echelon World—Part I," *Computer Law & Security Review*, 19.6, 2003, pp. 456-467.

22 Ted Bridis, "FBI Develops Eavesdropping Tools", Centre for Research on Globalisation (CRG), November 23, 2001, http://globalresearch.ca/articles/BRI111A.html, accessed April 23, 2016.

23 Ibid.

24 107th Congress (2001-2002), "H.R.3162 - Uniting and Strengthening America by Providing Appropriate Tools Required to Intercept and Obstruct Terrorism (USA PATRIOT ACT) Act of 2001", https://www.congress .gov/bill/107th-congress/

house-bill/3162. Accessed April 23, 2016.

25 110th Congress (2007-2008), "H.R.3773 - FISA Amendments Act of 2008", https://www.congress. gov/bill/110th-congress/house-bill/3773?q=%7B%22search%22%3A%5B%22FISA+Amendments +Act%22%5D%7D&resultIndex=1. Accessed April 23, 2016.

26 Nick Davies, "Afghanistan War Logs: Story Behind Biggest Leak in Intelligence History", *The Guardian*, July 25, 2010, http://www.theguardian.com/world/2010/jul/25/wikileaks-war-logs-back-story. Accessed April 23, 2016.

27 Glenn Greenwald, Ewen MacAskill and Laura Poitras , "Edward Snowden: The Whistleblower Behind the NSA Surveillance Revelations", *The Guardian*, June 11, 2013, http://www.theguardian.com/world/2013/jun/09/ edward- snowden -nsa-whistleblower-surveillance. Accessed April 23, 2016.

28 Spencer Ackerman and Dominic Rushe , "NSA Director: Edward Snowden has Caused Irreversible Damage to US", *The Guardian*, June 17, 2013http://www.theguardian.com/world/2013/jun/23/nsa-director-snowden-hong-kong. Accessed April 23, 2016.

29 Suzanne Goldenberg, "Al Gore: NSA's Secret Surveillance Program 'Not Really the American Way' ", *The Guardian*, June 14, 2013, http://www.theguardian.com/world/2013/jun/14/al-gore-nsa-surveillance-unamerican. Accessed April 23, 2016.

30 Steven Musil, "Obama Approves Sweeping Reforms to NSA Phone Surveillance", *CNET*, June 2, 2015, http://www.cnet.com/news/senate-approves-sweeping-reforms-to-nsa-phone-surveillance/. Accessed April 23, 2016.

31 US National Security Agency, "PPD-28 Section 4 Procedures", January 12, 2015, https://fas.org/irp/nsa/nsa -ppd-28.pdf. Accessed April 23, 2016.

32 Reform Government Surveillance, "Global Government Surveillance Reform", https://www.reformgovern mentsurveillance.com/#111614. Accessed April 23, 2016.

33 Ibid.

34 Scott J. Shackelford, *Managing Cyber Attacks in International Law, Business, and Relations: In Search of Cyber Peace* (New York: Cambridge University Press, 2014).

35 Paul Mozur and Jane Perlez, "Gregarious and Direct: China's Web Doorkeeper," *New York Times*, December 2, 2014, http://www.nytimes.com/2014/12/02/world/asia/gregarious-and-direct-chinas-web-doorkeeper. html?_r=0. Accessed July 21, 2015.

36 David Bandurski "Lu Wei: the Internet Must Have Brakes," *China Media Project*, November 11, 2014, at http://cmp.hku.hk/2014/09/11/36011/Lu Wei: the internet must have brakes. Accessed July 21, 2015.

37 Cecilia,"China E-Commerce Market in Q1 2015," *China Internet Watch*, July 16, 2015, at http://www.chinainternetwatch.com/13430/e-commerce-marketq1-2015/. Accessed April 21, 2016.

38 Fireeye Labs, "APT30 and the Mechanics of a Long-Running Cyber Espionage Operation: How a Cyber Threat Group Exploited Governments and Commercial Entities across Southeast Asia and India for over a Decade", https://www2.fireeye.com/rs/fireeye/images/rpt-apt30.pdf. Accessed April 21, 2016.

39 Alex Hern, "Great Cannon of China Turns Internet Users into Weapon of Cyberwar," *The Guardian*, April 13, 2015athttp://www.theguardian.com/technology/2015/apr/13/great-cannon-china- internet-users- weapon-cyberwar. Accessed April 21, 2016.

40 Royal United Services Institute for Defence and Security Studies, Neil Couch and Bill Robins, "Big Data For Defence And Security," Occasional Paper, September 2013.

41 Mark Burgin, *Theory of Information: Fundamentality, Diversity and Unification* (Singapore: World Scientific Publishing Co, 2010), p. 188

42 Rajendra Akerkar and Priti Sajja, *Knowledge-Based Systems* (Massachusetts: Jones & Bartlett Publishers, 2010).

43 Katja Franko Aas,*Sentencing in the Age of Information: From Faust to Macintos* (London: Glasshouse Press, 2005), p. 56.

44 Anett Hoppe et al.,' "Wisdom - The Blurry Top of Human Cognition in the DIKW-Model?" 7th conference of the European Society for Fuzzy Logic and Technology, July 2011

45 R.L. Ackoff, "From Data to Wisdom", *Journal of Applied Systems Analysis*, vol 16, 1989, pp. 3-9.

46 Rene V. Mayorga and Leonid I. Perlovsky, "Integration of Knowledge Intensive Multi-Agent Systems," IEEE International Conference, 2005, http://www.uv.mx/jnegrete/workshop/kimas _2k5 _sapient systemsmonograph.pdf. Accessed September 30, 2015.

47 Hoppe et al., n. 44.

6

Cyber Security and Critical Information Infrastructure Protection

The overarching and pervasive societal dependence on the cyber ecosystem has made efficient *implementation of strategic measures and strengthening of the cyber ecosystem* not only inevitable but also irrevocably imperative. The structural integrity, subsistence and growth of the cyber ecosystem is threatened by an expanding panoply of individuals and groups with malevolent disposition, requisite intent and possessed capabilities. The threat of a cyber attack capable of disrupting critical services, causing catastrophic economic damage and colossal physical destruction is very real and existential. The proliferation of potential threats capable of culminating in sophisticated targeted attacks – unremitting in severity and unprecedented in consequences—has dramatically changed the cyber threat landscape. The challenges of cyber security have been further exacerbated by transformational changes propelled by the meteoric penetration of social media, cloud computing, the Internet of Things (IoT), big data, data analytics and big data applications.

The cyber ecosystem resources constitute a vital component of the national security policy. A nation's Critical Infrastructures (CIs) include physical and cyber assets, systems and functions in the public and private domains, vital to its national security, economic and political stability, citizenry empowerment and public safety. The CI encompass a number of sectors, including sectors catering to many basic necessities of our daily lives, such as food, water,public health, emergency services, energy, transportation, information technology and telecommunications, banking and finance, and postal services and shipping.[1] Critical infrastructures do not work in isolation as independent entities, rather are intricately interrelated and inextricably interdependent. Any delay, distortion or disruption in the functioning of these CIs can easily lead to political upheaval, economic loss, social volatility or national instability. Most nations have put in place sophisticated,comprehensive and collaborative frameworks and mechanisms to protect their critical infrastructures and to facilitate coordination, cooperation, collaboration and participatory engagements among all the stakeholders. To foster a harmonised framework and to develop an overarching strategic plan to guide national efforts to protect CIs across the whole spectrum of cyber threats, nations have adopted multifaceted approaches. These approaches ranging from plugging or reducing vulnerabilities, mitigating the effects of cyber attacks, effectively containing the damage to the individual infrastructure post cyber attack, preventing spillover effects to other infrastructures, taking appropriate actions against cyber criminals, and evolving defensive strategies against cyber terrorism have succeeded in resolving many cyber challenges faced by critical infrastructures. However, due to the complexity, context-dependent nature and situation-specific elicitation of cyber weapons, a universally effective and generalised model for the protection of all critical infrastructures is difficult to articulate.

Critical Information Infrastructures (CIIs)

The understanding of what amounts to critical infrastructure is subject to multiple interpretations and context specific connotations. The definition of "critical infrastructure" has been evolutionary, reflecting the felt need of a society for its efficient functioning. The term has also been used in the context of the adequacy of the nation's public works such as schools, health facilities, electric power production, fire safety, waste disposal, and communications services. In the year 1983, the US Congressional Budget Office (CBO) defined "infrastructure" as facilities with "the common characteristics of capital intensiveness and high public investment at all levels of government. They are, moreover, directly critical to activity in the nation's economy."[2] The US National Infrastructure Protection Plan (NIPP) defines "infrastructure" as, "The framework of interdependent networks and systems comprising identifiable industries, institutions (including people and procedures) and distribution capabilities that provide a reliable flow of products and services essential to the defence and economic security of the United States, the smooth functioning of government at all levels, and society as a whole."[3]

Then came the information revolution and changed the way information is viewed, reviewed, leveraged, used, misused and abused. From being an intangible entity largely under the patronage of academia, information has become a catalyst for sustaining the growth momentum and development thrust of various sectors in the social, financial, technological, scientific and military fields. Concomitant with the emergence of the systems using all-pervading and ubiquitous information technology, is the emergence of new vulnerabilities and threats. The scope and opportunities for exploitation of these vulnerabilities—by a number of nation-states, malevolent actors, mischievous pranksters and 'cyber espionage', etc., with different motives and tactics—have exponentially expanded over the last decade or so. In the US, taking cognisance of the growing threats to national security, President Bush issued the "Executive Order 13231" on October 16, 2001, on "Critical Infrastructure Protection in the Information Age" emphasising, "The information technology revolution has changed the way business is transacted, government operates, and national defense is conducted. Those three functions now depend on an interdependent network of critical information infrastructures. It is the policy of the United States to protect against disruption of the operation of information systems for critical infrastructure and thereby help to protect the people, economy, essential human and government services, and national security of the United States, and to ensure that any disruptions that occur are infrequent, of minimal duration, and manageable, and cause the least damage possible."[4]

According to the US Department of Homeland Security, Critical Information Infrastructure (CII) is

> Any physical or virtual information system that controls, processes,transmits, receives or stores electronic information in any form, including data, voice or video that is:
>
> - Vital to the functioning of critical infrastructure;
> - So vital to the United States that the incapacity or destruction of such systems would have a debilitating impact on national security, national economic security, or national public health or safety; or
> - Owned or operated by, or on behalf of, a state, local, tribal, or territorial government entity.[5]

In the Indian context, great strides made in information technology—amalgamated with robust and prudent national efforts and vision—have positioned CIs on the cusp of even greater transformational progress. The convergence of communication technologies and shared information systems has increased the dependency of critical sectors on their CIIs. These interdependent, interconnected and complex CIIs, functioning from geographically diverse locations, are inherently vulnerable to various attack vectors ranging from a single targeted attack to coordinated cyber attacks by cyber criminals to widespread debilitating cyber attacks orchestrated at the behest of a nation-state.

Critical information infrastructure is dependent upon, and/ or made up of, various sub-parts/services across the whole gamut of information technology such as e-mail services, web services, client services, SCADA services, Wi-Fi services, VPN services, network services, VOIP services, DMZ services, etc.[6] An array of state-sponsored or self-motivated malicious hackers/attackers with malevolent intent, motivation or purpose are incessantly threatening the CIIs by exploitation of vulnerabilities and weaknesses associated with these services. Ever-evolving technologies, coupled with craftiness and resourcefulness and a disposition dominated by capricious greed, has given rise to a new breed of malicious actors without any moral or ethical compulsions. The prodigious and potent cyber weapons can be used to execute cyber attacks with devastating consequences. In spite of the potential getting lost in the lexical labyrinth, it is worth mentioning some of them, such as attacks using malwares, APTs (Advanced Persistent Threats), DOS/ DDoS attacks, client side attacks, web application attacks, network attacks, brute force attacks, social engineering attacks, war diving attacks, MITM (Man-in-the-middle), interception attacks,routing attacks, supply chain contamination attacks, DNS attacks, targeted attacks by evading/bypassing perimeter protection devices, etc.[7]

Section 70 as amended by the Indian Information Technology (Amendment) Act , 2008, specifies: "Critical Information Infrastructure means the computer resource, the incapacitation or destruction of which, shall have a debilitating impact on national security, economy,public health or safety".[8] Though the rationale of the definition is well thought out and analysed, it leaves us grappling with a question of gargantuan proportion: how to identify CIIs? The potentiality of information infrastructure characterised as critical, makes it important for the economic prosperity of the people and sovereignty and integrity of the nation. In effect, in a real life paradox, the degree of importance is directly proportional to the degree of post-attack consequences. The differentiation between critical and less important infrastructures and the degree of their influence and effect on a wide range of societal and national security issues rests on the fringes of subjective interpretations. It needs to be deliberated on, and decided, with the requisite diligence, investigation and attention. An amalgam of integrated networks consisting of nodes and links characterises the 'network society'. The criticality associated with a node—in influencing and altering the functioning of other nodes —once compromised, can cause serious disruption of governmental functions or societal interactions. Additionally, its existence as an integral part of an ensemble of nodes and its malfunctioning can trigger cumulative malfunction amplifying to a cataclysmic level in the overall functioning of the nation. The inherent dynamism of cyber space makes the task of securing CIIs a challenging one. The central government has granted itself the authority to "prescribe the information security practices and procedures for such protected system[s]."[9]The existence of cyber space vulnerabilities opens it up for exploitation by hostile elements, including state sponsored actors, ideological and political extremists, data harvesters and financial scammers, disgruntled insiders, organised criminal groups, lone-wolf criminals and even by cyber-dilettantes.

Cyber Threats to Critical Information Infrastructure

The Internet, with its overarching presence and ubiquitous usage, provides the underpinning and support for the information infrastructure of a nation riding the cyber juggernaut of modern times. The Internet owes its genesis to the felt need among the scientists to share research information without a second thought about the possibility of its abuse or misuse by unscrupulous actors. The transmutation of the Internet, from being an esoteric entity within the confines of certain laboratories to a gargantuan, all-pervasive network of networks encompassing the whole of the globe, catalysed the growth of information systems. Today, the Internet connects millions of computers facilitating and sustaining the functioning of a nation's essential services and infrastructures. The computer networks have blurred the boundaries between the digital and physical realms and are increasingly being used to control physical objects such as power transmission, transportation, operations on factory floors, air traffic controlling, handling of hazardous material, etc.

The emergence of new risks and vulnerabilities during, or consequent to, the development and utilisation of new technologies makes it logical to further our understanding by systematically studying interrelated factors and actors. Beginning with technical issues and then threading our way through an entangled thicket of systems, actors, threats, vulnerabilities, consequences and, finally, culminating our journey after addressing the issues of counter-measures/mitigation might bring some much-needed elucidation. Vulnerabilities in the context of cyber space can be defined as the intersection of a system susceptibility or flaw, access to the flaw and the capability to exploit the flaw.[10] It can also be defined as "a flaw or weakness in a system's design, implementation, or operation and management that could be exploited to violate the system's security policy".[11] In addition vulnerabilities can also exist as loopholes or back doors that can be exploited by an attacker to take control of the system either to access and steal the information, impair the system's functioning or render it incapable of undertaking legitimate tasks. Numerous vulnerabilities, either deliberately introduced or a result of oversight and carelessness, exist at different levels. The critical components of any infrastructure and their interdependencies rely on many congruent systems and services for optimal performances to produce the intended results consistency.

For tackling the strategic challenge of securing cyber space and protection of CIIs, coordinated, collaborative and collective efforts from each and every stakeholder, with a holistic and integrated approach, are required. In order to reduce, or with utopian optimism, to have a secure, robust and resilient cyber space, all stakeholders have to ensure that national vulnerability to cyber attacks is minimised.

Threats and vulnerabilities to CIIs in cyber space emanate from multifarious factors. A spectrum of malicious actors, lurking in the dark alley of cyber space, can, and does, exploit the vulnerabilities associated with critical information infrastructures. The primary threat - of closely coordinated and meticulously planned cyber attacks against the CII—weakens the CII's functional effectiveness, jeopardises its existential or physical security and imperils the ability of the CII to carry out the assigned missions. Though the technical sophistication required to carry out attacks against a protected CII is high, this does not offer an excuse to get ensconced in a cocoon of complacency. In the past,the organised attackers have exploited even minor vulnerabilities as a prelude to future activities of greater destructiveness and disruption. The cyber security community is still trying to understand the motivation, intent and/or capability acquisition processes of several observed attacks. Bolstered by easy access to attack tools and methodologies, the technical capability and sophistication required for carrying out cyber attacks has been acquired by a multitude of criminals. The threat quotient due to cyber attacks on CIIs is consistent, though in varying degrees, irrespective of their social or political affiliations, economic imperatives or security underpinnings. In peace-time, adversaries conduct espionage on governments, companies and individuals with an aim to map information systems, identify key targets or infect CIIs with trap doors or other means of access for exploitation at a later stage. During tumultuous times, these exploits may be leveraged to carry out cyber strikes. In a period of heightened tensions or during war conditions, adversaries may seek to undermine each other's political will by carrying out cyber attacks against each other's critical infrastructures.

Strategic Approach for Critical Information Infrastructure Protection

The strategy to secure CIIs against cyber attacks can be articulated by setting four national priorities. The first priority focusses on improving our ability to respond to cyber incidents and reduce the potential damage from such events. The others aim at reducing the number of cyber threats and overall vulnerability to cyber attacks. These are:

- ***Expeditious, Collaborative and Effectual Response System***
  Rapid identification and prompt remediation can often mitigate the damage caused by malicious cyber space activity. For the effectiveness of these activities, there has to be a cooperation agreement at various levels between governments and industries to perform analyses, issue warnings and coordinate response efforts. Because no cyber security plan can be impervious to a concerted and intelligent attack, information systems must be

able to operate while under attack and must have the resilience to restore full operations quickly.

- ***Vulnerability Identification, Mitigation, and Remediation***
  By exploiting vulnerabilities in cyber systems, an organised attack may endanger the security of CIIs. These vulnerabilities are not confined to the information assets and functionality of CIs. The external supporting structures, such as the networks and Internet also have weak points. Vulnerabilities stem from the weaknesses in technology and their improper implementation. It needs to be ensured that cyber attacks against critical infrastructures are prevented at all levels. In the case of cyber attacks, the damage is contained and expeditious mitigation or resolution efforts are undertaken to minimise the recovery time.
- ***Cyber Space Security with Definite Attribution and Explicit Non-Repudiation*** Many
  Cyber vulnerabilities exist because of a lack of cyber security awareness on the part of computer users, systems administrators and technology developers. Such awareness-based vulnerabilities present serious risks to critical infrastructures. Lack of trained personnel and the absence of widely accepted, multi-level certification programmes for cyber security professionals complicate the task of addressing cyber vulnerabilities.
- ***National and International Cyber Space Security Cooperation***
  India's cyber space links it to the rest of the world. A network of networks spans the planet, allowing malicious actors on one continent to act on systems thousands of miles away. Cross-border cyber attacks are launched with impunity as definite attribution of the source of the malicious activity is difficult. A nation must be capable of safeguarding and defending its critical systems and networks. The capability to do so becomes much more credible if a system of international cooperation — which facilitates information sharing, reduction of vulnerability identification time and effective prosecution of malicious actors —is put in place.

The scope for exploitation of cyber space to carry out activities detrimental to the national interest of India has grown exponentially. Hence, it is essential to build capabilities and capacities and to lay down a framework which ensures secure, "cyber robust"and "defensible" information infrastructure. This framework has been provided by formulating polices, and various agencies/ organisations have been entrusted with the responsibility for their implementation.

Assessment and Integration of Threat,Vulnerability, and Risk[12]

In order to evolve a viable and workable methodology, the first step would be to assess and integrate threats, vulnerabilities and risks and based on the results obtained, use these for apportioning the resources in proportion to the assessed risk severity. The assessment will involve the following steps:

- ***Assets Identification and Criticality Determination***[13]

  Assets can be broadly defined as human beings, non-human objects or entities, whether tangible or intangible, that the nation depends on for its security, economic and social activity, the public health and welfare of its citizens. People, activities and operations, information, installations, institutions, equipment and materials fall within the broad definition of assets. Criticality of an asset is a measure of the consequential loss or damage associated with the degradation of that particular asset. The criticality calibration of an asset is done based on its impact on the functioning, survivability or usefulness of its immediate owner/handler/operator and on overall mission viability, consequent to its loss or degradation. In addition, while evaluating criticality, the immediate impact is an important determinant, so too, are the time, efforts and resources required to regain or replace the lost capability. A small consequence over a long period of time may prove as debilitating as a large immediate disruption contained and reconstituted quickly and cost-effectively.

- ***Threat Identification, Characterisation and Assessment***[14]

  Threats can be defined as circumstances or events with the potential to cause loss or damage to an asset detrimental to the owner's interests. The process of characterisation of threats requires information from intelligence and law enforcement agencies, domain specialists, news reports, analysis, investigations of past incidents and own vulnerability assessment. Threat assessment can be deterministic, speculative or assumptive based on the garnered information, which may be comprehensive, scant, incomplete or vague. Once potential threats have been identified and characterised, a threat assessment estimates the "likelihood of adversary activity against a given asset or group of assets". The propensity and gravity of the threats vary with the asset criticality, motivation of the attackers and the owners' vulnerabilities, therefore 'threat assessment' has to be a dynamic and evolving process, made effective by analysing spatially and temporally explicit data.

- ***Risk Reduction and Mitigation***

  Risk reduction and mitigation can be realised in a number of ways: by reduction of threats, by reduction of vulnerabilities and reduction of the impact or consequences. The efficacy of a potential counter-measure can be assessed based on its capability to reduce risks associated with an asset. A series of counter-measures may be required for risk reduction of a particular asset. The sum total of the potential of all counter-measures will provide a measure of effectual overall risk reduction. The cost of each counter-measure is also an important determinant in the overall risk reduction process: the incurred financial costs with equipment, installation and training, the long-term operational costs, including maintenance and repair, the opportunity costs due to committing of precious resources to a non-productive process, etc. After an assessment of a set of counter-measures, stakeholders would have to consensually define their priorities to choose the best suited risk reduction strategy. After judicious selection, other measures such as apportioning of responsibilities, mechanisms of implementation and periodic assessment of effectiveness need to be established.

Identification of Critical Information Infrastructure (CII)[15]

All the sectors, irrespective of government or private ownership, need to undertake a comprehensive identification, prioritisation and categorisation programme of their respective internal critical infrastructures and key resources. Commensurate with the functionality and criticality, degree of interdependencies and complementarities with other key resources of a particular CII, the assessment and remediation strategies need to be formulated, validated and maintained. This constitutive process, with its inherent dynamism and technology dependence needs periodic reviews to address evolving challenges, circumstances and evidence. CII identification is a part of the national risk assessment which will constitute a holistic view of all the risks to national security.

- ***Functionality***[16]

  The functionality determination of a CII is an inherently dynamic process imbibing the economic, social, political and security perspectives driven by a set of functions, procedures and/or capabilities associated with it or with its constituent parts. The degree of functional uniqueness or functional interdependence of a particular CII is a major determinant in its overall rating.
- ***Degree of Criticality***[17]

  The scale of criticality is determined by the empirical appraisal of the degree to which the CII influences the overall security assessment. The empirical appraisal needs to be multi-dimensional, including availability, access, utilisation, stability and consummation for determination of its criticality quotient.
- ***Degree of Interdependence***[18]

  The degree and mutuality of interdependence is a measure of functional linkages, synergic associations and temporal reliance among various CIIs. A truncated or limited functionality may result in the failure of one or more systems and compromise the functionality of other CIIs in a cascading manner.

- ***Political, Economic, Military and Social Underpinnings of National Strategy***[19]
  The CIIs, as the lynchpins of a nation's political stability, social harmony, economic prosperity and security, demand deeper and higher securitisation and protection.
- ***Temporal Relevance***
  The temporal relevance of a CII in its identification and categorisation is important. The degree of criticality of a CII may or may not vary with time.

Most critical infrastructure systems interact through tangible and intangible linkages and relationships. These linkages can occur through direct connectivity, policies and procedures, or geospatial proximity.[20] These interactions often create complex relationships, dependencies and interdependencies that cross infrastructure boundaries. A through understanding and well-reasoned comprehension of interplay of interdependence between infrastructure systems equip us with the requisite ability to protect our critical infrastructure systems. While undertaking important research on 'critical infrastructure interdependency modelling' the inherent underlying dynamics and interactions among critical infrastructures need to be understood from prior knowledge, past experiences and through scenario-building for future vulnerabilities and risks. During chaotic times, the effective response and coordinated remedial measures at the national, regional and personal levels – involving governments, designated agencies, international organisations and the private sectors—will bolster the rescue, recovery and restoration efforts and will accelerate the rebuilding process. CIIs should be viewed holistically with due consideration to all vertical and horizontal interdependencies with other CIIs or resources.[21] Vertical interdependency is a measure of the symbiotic relationship between organisational layers within an organisation and that between organisations and subsidiaries, if any. Horizontal interdependency encompasses both the in-bound and out-bound interdependencies. In-bound interdependencies are dependencies in terms of roles and services expected from an organisation by other organisations, while out-bound dependency is a measure of service expectation by one particular organisation from others.[22]

The onus of protecting its own infrastructures against all cyber threats lies with each department, industry, banking establishment, public utility provider, law enforcing agency, etc. This also includes the responsibility to ensure willing cooperation and diligent coordination with other agencies where appropriate. Infrastructure by its inherent nature is pervasive, highly networked, without perceptible visibility and acts as the arterial framework, entwining most of the national assets. The infrastructure system of systems is exposed to a number of threats that can affect its functioning and compromise its ability to be productive in terms of quality and quantity of services and introduced eficiency in meeting demands, delays in time and cost overruns. The threats emanating from natural or human-made risks or from intrinsic technical failures need to be tackled by infrastructure operators by averting or mitigating these threats, minimising potential damage, prompt remedial actions and rapid recovery. With cyber threats looming large over the horizon, infrastructure operators need to integrate all aspects of infrastructure protection, and innovate and adopt new security measures specific to the cyber risks.

A Framework for Risk Analysis and Management for CIIs

The migration from a less efficient and labour-intensive manual process to an efficient and effective automated process is an irrevocable necessity for infrastructures as these have grown complex and interconnected and are subjected to increasing demands for productivity, reliability and flexibility. As infrastructure become more and more automated and new systems are added, the associated complexities and functionalities also increase. The multiplicity of lateral and vertical interconnections expands the threat surface. The dependence on networking technologies introduces new threats to the functionality and reliability of CIIs. The efficiency of a "Framework for Risk Analysis and Management for CIIs"[23] can be gauged by the thoroughness and quality of risk assessment which produces interpretable and actionable results. The framework should be able to identify the potential targets, the directly or indirectly affected stakeholders and the impact on the asset's tangible functionality. The process involves:

Fig 6.1: Framework for Risk Analysis and Management for CIIs

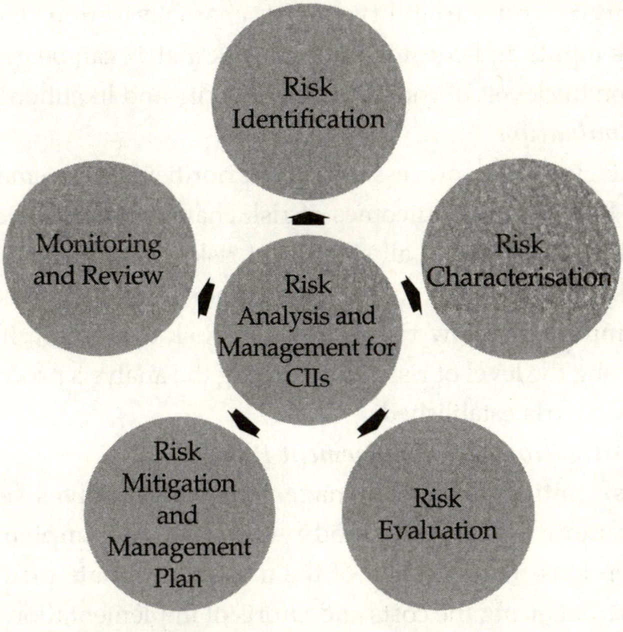

- ***Risk Identification***[24]

  The risk identification process involves identification of sources of risk and their impacts on areas of critical importance. The sources of risk which can negatively influence the functional environment also need to be factored in. Comprehensive identification of risks is critical because an unidentified risk can potentially cause serious and adverse events due to the lack of a corresponding mitigative mechanism. Risk identification should also include examination of the knock-on and cascading effects of particular consequences.

- ***Risk Characterisation***
  Risk characterisation involves consequences and the likelihood of risks occurring and other attributes. The confidence in risk characterisation and its sensitivity to preconditions and assumptions should be factored in the analysis and communicated to all stakeholders. Factors such as divergence of opinion among experts, uncertainty, availability, quality, quantity and ongoing relevance of information, or limitations on modelling, add subjectivity and variability to risk characterisation. Based on various inputs and considerations, a risk matrix can be generated based on the levels of consequential severity and likelihood levels.
- ***Risk Evaluation***
  The risk evaluation process assists in prioritising risk remediation efforts based on the outcomes of risk characterisation. Decisions should take account of all significant risk exposures and should be judicious enough so that disproportionate resources are not committed to low risk exposures. Risk evaluation involves comparing the level of risk found during the analysis process with the risk criteria established.
- ***Risk Mitigation and Management Plan***[25]
  The risk mitigation and management plan involves selecting one or more options for modifying risks and implementing those options. The selection of the most appropriate plan option involves balancing the costs and efforts of implementation against the benefits derived. For mitigating/ managing risks, a number of treatment options applied either individually or in combination can be used. A particular risk treatment option can manifest in unintended outcomes within the organisation or for interdependent stakeholders. Therefore, when selecting risk treatment options, these must be communicated to the other stakeholders and the

organisation must be responsive to their requests and factor in their concerns

- *Monitoring and Review*

  The organisation's monitoring and review processes should encompass all aspects of the risk management process for the purpose of ensuring that controls are effective and efficient in both design and operation. [26] The time, cost and result effectiveness of a risk treatment plan is a measure of its performance and a vital element in subsequent impact assessment or adaptation measures.

National Critical Information Infrastructure Protection Centre (NCIIPC)

As part of a national effort to enhance the understanding of the impact of cyber attacks on CIIs and to strengthen cyber security and the resilience of CIIs, the establishment of the National Critical Information Infrastructure Protection Centre (NCIIPC) of the National Technical Research Organisation (NTRO)is a significant milestone. NCIIPC is responsible for the mitigation, securitisation and protection of identified CIIs against cyber threats. By gathering, processing, reporting, analysing and sharing key information garnered through a qualitative analysis, capturing and linking all facets of the cyber threat landscape, the vulnerability analysis of CIIs and the consequential study of actual cyber attacks, NCIIPC will be able to fulfill its assigned role effectively. The organisation's purpose as reflected in its mission statement sums up the core concept and the overarching strategy and states: "To take all necessary measures to facilitate protection of Critical Information Infrastructure from unauthorised access,modification, use, disclosure, disruption, incapacitation or destruction through coherent coordination, synergy and raising information security awareness among all stakeholders".[27]

Under the provisions of Section 70A(1) of the Information Technology (Amendment), Act 2008, the Government of India has designated NCIIPC as the nodal agency for taking all measures, including associated R&D for the protection of CIIs in India.[28] In addition, under section 70 of the IT Act, the identification of a CII for declaration as critical information infrastructure shall be jointly done by NCIIPC and CII stakeholders.[29] NCIIPC has identified 17 sub-sectors designated as CIIs and is already implementing measures across a broad spectrum of potential cyber threats for seven sub-sectors. The list of CIIs is likely to expand as many sub-sectors have legitimate and strong reasons for being included as a sub-section for protection from any form of cyber sabotage, espionage and attack; and to be extended all measures across the entire spectrum of protection as specified by NCIIPC.

NCIIPC provides a list of 40 critical controls[30]that have been identified through a consensually agreed set of criteria between the government and industry security professionals and derived from empirical-analytic research. These are the minimum number of controls recommended by NCIIPC to be followed in each and every CII. These controls will be updated periodically by NCIIPC to stay in tune with emerging protocols and technologies. The agency has also been entrusted with the responsibility to prevent classified or critical information from being compromised and timely dissemination of relevant and valid information to the authorised elements in each identified CII[31]. NCIIPC has envisioned the following guiding principles to achieve its mission:[32]

- Develop a mechanism to facilitate identification of CII, protection of CII through risk management and ensure compliance of NCIIPC policies, guidelines, advisories/ alerts etc. by CIIs.
- Lead and coordinate national programmes and policies on critical information infrastructure.
- Establish national and international linkages / initiatives for the protection of CIIs, including R&D.
- Promote indigenous R&D relating to protection of CIIs, including modelling and simulation of complex CIIs, development of CIIs protection tools and threat scenarios.
- Develop a mechanism to facilitate sharing of information

on information security breaches, incidents, cyber attacks, espionage, etc. among CII stakeholders as well as with NCIIPC.

- Develop the capability for a real time warning system and facilitate sharing of information on emerging threats, cyber attacks, vulnerabilities, etc. with CIIs.
- Establish sectoral CERTs to deal with critical sector specific issues.

NCIIPC has proposed establishment of an Information Security Department (ISD) in every organisation within a critical sector, which should be headed by a Chief Information Security Officer (CISO).[33] The ISD, in addition to undertaking the above mentioned tasks will be an interface between the organisation and NCIIPC for spearheading, coordinating, and directing departmental efforts to ensure functionality even under extreme conditions. The ISD specific to a particular sector, in its role to plan, develop and lead viable strategies, resource allocation and effective implementation will undertake the following tasks:

- ***Planning***[34]
    - Based on the organisation's strategic objectives, drawing up of an annual security roadmap outlining key security goals and incorporating these into an effective and sustainable security framework.
    - Defining and delineating the scope of the information security programme.
    - Understanding the legal and regulatory issues impacting the implementation strategy and their compatibility with existing legal frameworks.
    - Management and forecasting of budgetary and logistic requirements for planning, maintenance and management of information security.
    - Defining the risk management framework and establishing the context for the risk management process by setting up the criteria against which the risks will be assessed

- ***Development***[35]
  - Identifying, developing, implementing, and maintaining information security policies, standards, guidelines, processes, procedures, and best practices to protect information assets, assuring the organisation's objectives accomplishment[36]
  - Design and development of information assets' classification based on value, sensitivity and degree of assurance required.
  - Development of organisation specific information security policies, procedures, processes derived from inputs, feedbacks,magnitude and degree of interdependence with various stakeholders.
- ***Management***[37]
  - Dissemination of the information security policies, procedures and guidelines to all concerned and apportioning the responsibility in accordance with their place in the hierarchical order.
  - Conducting risk assessments and risk audits for conscious, systematic attempts to evaluate risk management procedures.
  - Managing incidents through the process of mitigation, preparedness, response and recovery.
  - Post-incident reporting for qualitative and quantitative response analysis and lesson learned.
  - Creating an information security-conscious environment by way of security awareness training and education.
  - Making information security processes an integral part of the organisation's policy and embedding these in the organisation's business processes.
  - Periodic evaluation and review of actions for making mid-course corrections whenever necessary.
  - Conducting mock drills for evaluating the degree of preparedness , gauging the veracity of their responses and effective implementation of all security policies and guidelines.

    - Periodic and appropriate installation of security patches, routine verification of patches, updates and hotfixes, including periodic scanning to detect known vulnerabilities.
- ***Oversight***[38]
    - Evaluating the effectiveness of ongoing security operational processes, containing exploitable vulnerabilities and establishing compliance monitoring processes.
    - Evaluating compliance with legal provisions, regulatory requirements and organisational guidelines for information security.
    - Ensuring information security audit for the existence and adequacy of all physical, logical, networks, application security. After the post audit risk assessment and efficacy evaluation of remediation measures, evaluating the degree of overall risk reduction achieved.

Information Security Policy Management in Protection of CIIs

Information security policy management refers to the practices and methods used to create, maintain and enforce security policies sufficiently crystallised to be enacted and communicated to all concerned. These must convey, clarify and reinforce the organisation's position on high-level security principles. The policies, standards, guidelines, processes, and procedures created in accordance with information security imperatives, functionality protection, applicable laws and regulations and government guidelines must be able to protect the information and information systems from unauthorised access, disclosure, disruption, modification, recording or destruction.[39] The policy also needs to clearly spell out specific actions to remediate deficiencies that contribute to *security violations* and restore functionality. The policy must embody the CIA (*Confidentiality, Integrity and Availability)* triumvirate in its enunciation.

Security policy management encompasses all the strategic, operational, human and managerial issues, which after due considerations, deliberations, extrapolations and evaluations have been documented and disseminated to the intended recipients at different levels of the organisational hierarchical structure. An organisation may have different security policies covering different categories of information for different groups, with different perspectives, approaches and requirements. An organisation may have layered policies, with high-level policies addressing issues at the enterprise level and lower-level policies addressing specific responsibilities and information protection methods. [40]The specific, contextual and situational provisions of these policies must be disseminated unambiguously to all the employees, stakeholders, external and internal partners, contractors and business associates with clear instructions on adherence, abidance and compliance, including planned corrective actions in case of violations.

Awareness Training and Skill Building and Upgrading

Building knowledge, skill and awareness is a crucial and indispensable determinant of an organisation's performance, progress and productivity. The intense entwining of information technology in every facet of the organisation's operations, consequent vulnerabilities and high potential exploitability have made these far more important and overarching than in the past. It is not the technology but the instructional implementation of the technology that determines its effects on learning.[41] Formulation, implementation and enforcement of training strategies, policies and plans will create an organisational atmosphere in which information security policies and instructions translate into self-motivating goals for informed and knowledge-driven employees, who consciously and purposely try to achieve these. The development and implementation of realistic and result oriented training strategies will reinforce best practices, promote willing compliance and nurture information security conscious behaviour from all stakeholders. The training strategies, plans and programmes must be periodically reviewed for relevance to current organisational requirements and changes emerging from identification of new vulnerabilities, adoption of new capabilities and role enhancement or functional augmentation.

Conclusion

The critical infrastructures that expedite and influence the way the government functions, business is conducted, civic amenities extended and financial transactions facilitated are either partially or fully owned by the government or by private entities. For protecting these, the responsibility for setting goals and striving to achieve them, rests primarily with the government. However, the effectiveness and sincerity of all the measures and steps required to ensure the implementation of security policies to reduce the vulnerability of privately owned assets depends upon the private sector's financial incentives, knowledge and commercial imperatives. For many, the cost of reducing vulnerabilities outweighs the benefit of reduced cyber risk.

Privately owned companies have been slow to recognise the adverse effects of disasters in the form of terrorist attacks, global economic meltdown, power grid failures or natural disasters such as earthquakes, floods, tsunamis, fire, etc. These failures or disasters can cascade into unanticipated catastrophes. Similarly, the realisation that cyber vulnerability exploitation can result in functional degradation, financial loss and credibility erosion is yet to dawn on private companies. In addition, risks to critical infrastructure industries are becoming more and more interdependent as the economic, technological, and social processes of globalisation intensify. For private companies, the ubiquitous "cyber security externalities" need to be considered and corrected to achieve the objective of a robust and resilient cyber space. A synergic combination of private organisational strategies and government policies will ensure protection of CIIs.

Organisations are most likely to account for vulnerabilities that are linked to their own core activities. There is just not enough incentive to bolster defences against vulnerabilities which may have an indirect or intangible effect on their core activities or affect only other interdependent entities. For such organisations, with a limited understanding of interdependencies and security externalities, determining the source of a cyber attack and quantifying the consequential loss caused by the attack will be difficult and complicated. The uncertainties are compounded by the fact that potential attackers can engage in "adaptive predation," in which they purposefully adapt their strategies to take advantage of weaknesses in prevention efforts.[42]

Beyond infrastructure vulnerability assessments, the structural, organisational, and financial strategies of organisations need to be revamped to support the national effort. The viability determination of strategies to protect CIIs depends upon their political and economic sustainability. Sustainability may be enhanced by a deliberate policy of seeking win-win options that promise public and private benefits beyond vulnerability reduction.

Notes

1. Keith Rhodes et al., *Technology Assessment : Cybersecurity for Critical Infrastructure Protection*, United States General Accounting Office, GAO-04-321 (Washington D.C.: United States Printing Office, 2004), p. 3.
2. David L. Lewis et al., *Public Works Infrastructure: Policy Considerations for the 1980s*, US Congressional Budget Office (Washington D.C.: United States Printing Office, 1983), p. 1.
3. US Department of Homeland Security, "US National Infrastructure Protection Plan", http://www.dhs.gov /xlibrary/ assets/NIPP_Plan_noApps.pdf. Accessed July 20, 2015.
4. US Department of Homeland Security, "Executive Order 13231 of October 16, 2001Critical Infrastructure Protection in the Information Age", http://www.dhs.gov/xlibrary/assets/executive-order-13231-dated-2001-10-16-initial.pdf. Accessed July 20, 2015.
5. Department of Homeland Security Cybersecurity Authority, "Sec. 242 Title II of the Homeland Security Act of 2002",https://www.whitehouse.gov/sites/default/files/omb/legislative/letters/dhs-cybersecurity-authority.pdf. Accessed July 20, 2015.
6. National Critical Information Infrastructure Protection Centre (NCIIPC), National Technical Research Organisation (NTRO), GOI, *Guidelines for Protection of National Critical Information Infrastructure*, Version 1.0 (June 2013), p. 3.
7. Ibid.
8. Harish Chander, *Cyber Laws and IT Protection* (New Delhi : PHI Learning Pvt. Ltd, 2012), p.198.
9. Ibid.
10. A. Kiyuna, L. Conyers, *Cyberwarfare Sourcebook* (North Carolina: Lulu.com,2015)), p. 42.
11. R. Shirey, *Internet Security Glossary : RFC 2828* (North Arlington : The Internet Society, 2000), p. 189.

12. John Moteff , *Risk Management and Critical Infrastructure Protection: Assessing, Integrating, and Managing Threats, Vulnerabilities and Consequences*, CRS Report for Congress, p. 1, February 4, 2005, https://www.fas.org/sgp/crs/homesec/ RL32561.pdf. Accessed July 20, 2015.
13. Ibid., p.4.
14. Ibid., p.6.
15. n. 6, p. 5.
16. Ibid.
17. Ibid.
18. Ibid.
19. Ibid.
20. P. Pederson, et. al., *Critical Infrastructure Interdependency Modeling: A Survey of US and International Research* (Idaho National Laboratory, 2006),
21. n. 6, p. 8.
22. Ibid., p. 9.
23. Eric Luiijf Pieter Hartel, *Critical Information Infrastructures Security 8th International Workshop, CRITIS 2013, Amsterdam, The Netherlands,*(London : Springer, 2013), p. 84.
24. Ibid., p. 90.
25. Ibid., p. 94.
26. Bureau of Indian Standards, *Risk Management — Principles and Guidelines IS/ISO 31000 : 2009* (New Delhi : BIS, 2011), p. 20.,
27. n. 6.
28. Ibid., p. 1.
29. Ibid., p. 90.
30. Ibid., p. i.
31. Ibid., p. 9.
32. Ibid., p. 6.
33. Ibid., p. 9.
34. Ibid., p. 10.
35. Ibid.
36. http://www.cio.ca.gov/ois/government/documents/pdf/iso_roles_respon_guide.pdf
37. Ibid.
38. Ibid., p.11.
39. In Lee, *From Government to E-Governance: Public Administration in the Digital Age*, (Pennsylvania: IGI Global, 2013), p.192.
40. Elaine Barker, *Framework for Designing Cryptographic Key Management Systems* (Collingdale, PA: Diane Publishing Co, 2010), p. 20.
41. B Collis Betty, "Anticipating the Impact of Multimedia in Education: Lessons from Literature," *International Journal of Computers in Adult Education and Training*, 2.2, 1991, p. 146.
42. Philip E. Auerswald, et al., *Seeds of Disaster, Roots of Response: How Private Action Can Reduce Public Vulnerability* (Cambridge: Cambridge University Press, 2006), p. 7.

7

Cyber Defence: Prevention and Mitigation Against Cyber Attacks

The evolving character and influence of cyber space has succeeded in altering the scope of cyber threats of multifarious dimensions and manifestations, differentiated in terms of the kind of destruction, disruption or loss caused as well as the required level of defence.[1] Defending against cyber attacks demands cooperative approaches, collective efforts and pooling of resources, guided by policy guidelines derived from widely shared experience and empirical analyses and not from a disjointed variety of ad hoc sources. The integration of military, economic and political instruments at each level within the national security framework only can ensure that cyber defence matters remain central to national security determinations in the future.[2]For guarding national security and protecting national interests against cyber attacks, cyber defence strategies and defensive capabilities are being developed, refined and consolidated by almost all nations. However, the existing cyber security measures always appear to be in the 'catch up' mode to the challenges and ubiquitous reliance on cyber space. The burgeoning growth of networked systems, devices and platforms is a testimonial to the deep inroads made by cyber space into an increasing number of enterprises, crucial for a nation's security and economic growth, and the well-being of its citizens. Capability argumentation and consolidation across the whole spectrum of cyber defence strategies is an inalienable imperative rather than a conceptual presumption. To bolster defence against cyber attacks, updation and consolidation of existing capabilities and dynamic development of new capabilities through empirical observations, technology innovations and enumeration of threat vectors and actors is a mandatory prerequisite. The evolution of cyber warfare strategies, like strategies in other domains of warfare, has in its roots, the cardinal imperative of protecting the security of cyber space, defending cyber assets and cyber infrastructure, thwarting or hindering the enemy's advance in cyber space and disrupting the enemy's cyber space to greatly undermine its will and debilitate its cyber capabilities.

Deliberate and well-orchestrated military efforts to thwart an aggressor's attempt directed towards disruption or destruction of military information infrastructure and capabilities, critical information infrastructure and civilian and government information technology-based economies are termed as preventive measures in the realm of cyber warfare. The ability to effectively wage preventive cyber warfare is essential to defend against a myriad manifestations of offensive information warfare. It is, therefore, imperative to develop, consolidate and practise such capabilities, either independently or as an adjunct to other means. The fruition of these strategies takes years and is resource intensive: however, the investments made in terms of expertise, capital and resources are worthwhile in the long run and the advantages accrued will justify the efforts.

Securing cyber space is a national security imperative and an overarching concern for the protection and progression of national interests, economic development and societal growth. The employment of a number of long and short-term strategies, synergised with a coherent and pragmatic policy framework and involving all the stakeholders, will augment and aggrandise efforts towards this objective. This vision can be realised by articulating the following strategic priorities.

Recognition of Cyber Space as an Operational Domain[3]

The resources that make up cyber space differ in composition, functionality and architecture in comparison to resources that make up other domains. These resources are created, nurtured and matured by humans encapsulating innate traits of intelligence, diligence and perseverance. Most of these are privately owned and dominated by civilian usage. Nonetheless, treating cyber space as an operational domain is critical for allaying a nation's security concerns. This makes it imperative to organise, train and equip for cyber space on the same lines as in other domains of human activities: air, land, maritime and space. Enhanced and specific training and orientation, greater situational awareness, creation of secure and resilient network environments and information assurance are some of the measures that can be utilised for cyber space risk management. The increased level of vertical and lateral collaborations, smart and synergistic partnerships, strengthened self-defences and a shared understanding of cyber security threats will fructify in strengthening cyber defences. The development of integrated capabilities through shared competencies and information-sharing among security agencies, academia, industry and military will ensure rapid delivery and optimal deployment of innovative capabilities.

From the warfare perspective, mission accomplishment in the face of degraded cyber space conditions for extended periods will be a great challenge. During exercises and training, integration of the complete spectrum of the cyber space scenario into a wide variety of contingencies will prepare the armed forces to respond quickly and effectively.[4] A cornerstone of this activity will be the inclusion of simulated rogue cyber actors in war games and exercises followed by critical deliberations, viable and vital recommendations and formulation of workable operating procedures. Operating under cyber attacks and threats requires capabilities as well as resilience for mission assurance and preservation of critical operating capabilities. These efforts need to be bolstered by investing time and capital in the development of resilient networks and systems. During contingencies emanating from network failure or a disrupted cyber environment, the armed forces must have redundant capacity and spare resources to remain operationally effective. At the same time, the capability to isolate and neutralise the impact in the shortest possible time will bolster cyber defence capability.

Protection of Networks and Systems

Today, the stability and functional integrity of cyber space is any mission's operational success. Implementation of cyber hygiene best practices, deterrence and mitigation of insider threats, apportioning of accountability, continual monitoring and information management capabilities – all these will bolster the cyber defence mechanism against a number of cyber threat actors and vectors. An active cyber defence capability, reinforced by a concept of operations which have proved has successful in the past, shapes the adaptive and dynamic defence in cyber space. Advance cyber attacks seldom comprise a single discrete event. For a cyber attack to be successful, an aggressor takes several steps: each step a logical extension of the previous step and in preparation for the next step. Although an adversary's overtures can be thwarted at any point, engaging with an attacker at the early stage requires expertise and experience.

The exploitation of most of the vulnerabilities and execution of malicious acts can be arrested through good cyber hygiene. The notion of 'cyber hygiene' is rooted in the notion of the individual's responsibility and accountability. The observance of cyber hygiene by users and administrators alike strengthens a nation's cyber security bulwark. In the cyber domain, like in any other system, people are the first line of defence. Mitigation of the insider threat and prevention of accidental or deliberate disclosures of sensitive and classified information will strengthen cyber security and reduce vulnerabilities. All efforts must be concerted to foster a strong culture of information assurance within the workforce. This will help in shaping the behaviours and attitudes of individuals through accountability, encouragement and support. In addition, through the imposition of higher costs for malicious activities, a deterrence posture will be firmly established. This cultural shift will be enabled by new policies, new methods of personnel training, and innovative workforce communications.[5]

Public-Private Partnership for Evolution of Comprehensive Cyber Security Strategy

A nation's cyber security challenges are growing in complexity and severity. Efforts to tackle these challenges require collaborative partnerships between the public and private sectors. However, each sector is saddled with its own peculiar and intractable problems. The private sector is driven by a profit motive and is inherently keyed to look for new business opportunities, whereas the public sector is often more geared towards stability, order and the established way of doing things.[6] This acts as a limiting factor for the establishment of a framework dynamically flexible and extensible and fails to establish the well delineated nature and scope of such relationships. Legal, strategic and pragmatic obstacles often impede effective public-private sector cooperation, which are compounded by regulatory and liability risks.[7] Different private and government organisations have competing roles and interests.[8] Due to the multifaceted challenges of cyber security, the traditional modalities of interaction between the government and private sector—between the regulators and the regulated—do not always tackle the cyber security challenges.

The challenges to cyber security and cyber crime have grown steadily. Indeed, the proverbial trickle has literally turned into a flood of Biblical proportions threatening to inundate and overwhelm cyber security participants, measures, apparatuses and procedures. The technology is often complicated and constantly evolving, the vulnerabilities are innumerable and elusive, and the laws are muddled and fragmented. The diverse range of resources, priorities and perspectives on these issues, at times, are not complementary but competitive. At the strategic level, there is a need to align the shared objective of developing effective strategic solutions to cyber security challenges. The focus must be on convergence of collective resources of both the public and private sectors to make the cyber ecosystem secure, resilient and compliant with the strategic vision.

The ownership and control of many of the critical systems that need to be protected are with a diverse range of agencies. The private sector often has more resources for recruiting top technical and information security talent and is not restricted to operate within the constitutional and statutory gamut that restrictively governs the government's cyber activities. The companies are often reluctant to involve government agencies for fear of collateral consequences. In this characteristically 'Orwellian paradox' most of the critical systems are owned and operated by private companies while the government is expected to ensure the security of these systems.

While the private sector has crucial insight, expertise, and resources to successfully combat cyber threats, the government is uniquely positioned to investigate, arrest, and prosecute cyber criminals; to collect foreign intelligence on cyber threats; and potentially, to provide a certain statutory protection to companies that share information with the government[9].The government is also well placed to have access to threat information—collected from both domestic and foreign sources—before its disclosure in the public domain and can disseminate information across the sector. In this way, the government can provide actionable intelligence on an evolving threat for effective mitigation actions.

Since both the public and private sectors are endowed with expertise, resources and disposition to address the cyber threats, collaboration is the key to feasible and effective cyber security solutions. Despite the collective desire to harmonise the efforts of the government and private sector in cyber security, the way ahead is marred by parochial hurdles. These hurdles have discouraged many companies from extending whole-hearted cooperation even in the face of pervasive and persistent cyber threats.

Leveraging the Nation's Cyber Workforce and Rapid Technological Innovation[10]

To defend its security interests in cyber space, a nation needs to muster the expertise, talent and ingenuity of its people and garner contributions from various stakeholders. A collective pool of talented individuals drawn from the scientific and academic fields, corporate honchos and military personnel will foster a culture of rapid innovation,enhanced capacity building processes and effective cyber space operations. The investments made in people, technology and R&D will accrue capabilities and resources vital to national security. The demand for cyber personnel with the requisite expertise and proficiency is commensurate with the severity and pervasiveness of cyber threats.

A secure cyber ecosystem, maintained and sustained by a prepared and trained cyber security workforce—supported by far-sighted policies—is vital to our nation's security and prosperity. However, there are inconsistencies in the defining and understanding of the cyber security work and requirements, which, in turn, hinders the nation's ability to establish a baseline of capabilities, identify skills gaps and an adequate pipeline of future talent. The unique aspects of cyber security work make it imperative for the cyber security workforce to keep up with emerging risks, threats, vulnerabilities and associated technologies that may require more rapid skill and knowledge acquisition than other functional areas. The importance of establishing a common lexicon and taxonomy is vital for cyber security work to tackle the challenges of the associated severity of cyber threats. The expertise development in this area serves as an overreaching framework facilitating consolidation of an agile, highly-qualified cyber security workforce.[11]

For building the nation's enduring capability to prevent and defend against the ever-increasing menace of cyber threats, it is vital to describe its cyber security work and workforce down to the minutest detail, along with the greatest possible consistency. Armed with this understanding, organisations can analyse the dynamicity and diversity of the task at hand commensurate with the growth, structure and quality of the workforce. This, in turn, will provide a predictive framework for a nuanced approach in anticipating the requirements, needs and priorities related to critical strategic and operational issues.

Active Cyber Defence

Active Cyber Defence (ACD) describes a range of proactive measures to engage, contain and thwart an adversary before and during a cyber attack. ACD can bolster efforts to prevent, detect and respond to sophisticated cyber attacks.[12]A large number of stakeholders are undertaking and weaving ACD activities into their 'concepts of operations'. The evolving nature of cyber threats has made ACD an increasingly important area of cyber security in both the private and public sectors. The contemporary cyber threat landscape is no longer at great risk from cyber dilettantes, teenage hackers or petty criminals, although such actors do pose a threat albeit at a lower level. Instead, sophisticated criminals and state-sponsored malicious actors pose the greatest danger for businesses and governments. The term 'Advanced Persistent Threat' or APT, is often used to describe state-sponsored cyber spies who deliberately target specific organisations, use sophisticated means to penetrate those organisations and evade detection within those organisations for weeks, months or even years in order to gather information.

Passive cyber defences are simply too ineffectual to address APT, which is widely recognised as "first and foremost a new attack doctrine built to circumvent the existing perimeter and endpoint defences".[13]Passive defences constitute measures that are generally retrospective in nature and lack proactive approaches. In cyber space, passive defence measures such as basic cyber hygiene practices, patching vulnerabilities, limiting access to systems, etc. can limit or contain low-level cyber attacks. Passive defences, though intricately incorporated and inextricably woven into any cyber defence programme, fail in mitigating security risks arising from sophisticated attacks. The typical advanced attack vectors can stealthily sneak into cyber systems, conceal themselves within the network, stay undetected or remain unnoticed for a substantial period of time. Once inside a victim system, the attack vectors have plenty of time to undertake reconnaissance, adopt, modify and lie in wait for an opportune time to reach their ultimate objective such as stealing intellectual property or financial assets.

In cyber space, the defenders have to function in an asymmetric environment in which the enemy is always at the gates, ready to exploit even an ephemeral weakness thereby stretching the defender's resources to their limits. For every bulwark raised by the defenders, a plethora of attack vectors and methodologies is invented, refined and employed. The battle is asymmetric, in the sense that the terms of engagement are dictated entirely by the adversary that is not governed by any rules or constrained by any moralistic notions. Though the defence has its own inherent advantage, an aggressor can shape the cyber battlefield and secure strategic advantage.

Cyber Attack Reconstruction and Synthesis[14]

The understanding of the kill chain progression from the adversary's perspective provides valuable insight into the analysis of intrusions. A malware detected in isolation will typically provide a limited set of attributes, but further analysis spread over all phases of the cyber kill chain will unearth its many other attributes and manifestations. By detecting an intrusion in one phase and carrying out a backtrack investigation in the preceding phases, the defenders would be able to identify and analyse attacks that had already been executed but were not detected.[15] The information gathered will help in preventing or disrupting future attacks earlier in the kill chain.

The importance of analysis of an attack from its inception till its detection cannot be overemphasised. It is equally important to analyse the effects of successfully thwarted cyber attacks by reconstructing scenarios in which these attacks escaped detection and made their way to the intended end-state. By conjuring up a worst case scenario, the defenders will have an understanding of techniques that the attacker planned to employ in the subsequent phases. For example, in a hypothetical situation, an adversary uses a spear phishing e-mail which contains an embedded zero-day exploit and the anti-virus software at the gateway fails to detect the intrusion. However, the delivery mechanism associated with e-mail provides an emerging pattern associated with a known APT campaign. The intrusion is then blocked at the delivery phase. The malicious code is debugged, the zero-day exploit identified and shared. The adversary, unaware of these developments, does not change the delivery mechanism and the defenders will be able to successfully detect and catch the intrusion. This analysis facilitates the development of a resilient mitigation mechanism, proactive defensive posturing and prioritising defensive processes.

Cyber Attack Detection and Forensics

Sophisticated attacks can circumvent passive defences. The ACD techniques can be used to neutralise these threats. The defenders can use honeypots and look for specific traits in the structural and behavioural pattern of an attack,attributable to a specific aggressor. Once a cyber intrusion is detected,the attack vector is thoroughly analysed to gather the following information:

- **Type of Attack:** Is it an act of cyber espionage, cyber crime, terrorism or hacktivism?
- **The Extent of Damage Prior to Detection of Attack:** Quantification of damage in terms of information stolen, importance of stolen information, destruction or alteration of data within the organisation or monetary loss.
- **The Perpetrators of Attacks:** Who is the progenitor and orchestrator of the attack? A cyber dilettante, an inveterate cyber criminal, a criminal organisation or a nation-state?

The search for answers to such questions, formally and scrupulously, will provide valuable inputs to base decisions on how to respond. An organisation can gather this information by using resources at its disposal or by reaching out to others. The honey-pots and honey-nets are digital network baits used for deception and to attract intruders. A honey-pot to an attacker appears to contain exploitable vulnerabilities in a legitimate machine or network. By design, it is made to appear vulnerable to attack. As long as the hacker is lured into believing the authenticity and legitimacy of the honey-pot, system administrators can analyse the attack mechanism to collect data on the identity, intent, access and methods used by the intruder.

Cyber Intelligence

The exercise for identification of dominant factors that shape the cyber defence strategy and strengthen its bulwark, will not be difficult if the understanding is rooted in conventional principles of warfare and furthered through the existing military doctrine. By learning about the intent, motivation, capabilities, resources, patterns of operation and methods of vulnerability exploitations, one can garner actionable information and disseminate it within its temporal relevance to the right people, including forewarning of identified threats and forecast of potential threats. The intelligence gathering may become more structured if we analyse it through a framework of established concepts or paradigms unequivocally consistent throughout conventional warfare: the strategic, operational, and tactical levels.

At the strategic level, cyber intelligence activities are directed towards the determination of objectives and intents of the highest organisational entity (a group or organisation) and their willingness to commit available resources towards achievement of those objectives. In this context, the risk characterisation starts with a multifaceted, far-reaching and all-encompassing analysis of the assets, capabilities, and core competencies that are coveted, feared or reviled by others, including the implications, cumulative effects and repercussions due to compromise, loss, impairment, disruption or destruction of these.[16] This also includes all-round security measures and a defensive bulwark for their protection.[17] After a through risk assessment, an organisation needs to carry out threadbare analysis of the cyber threat landscape to identify the enemy's intent, design and possible *modus operandi*. Intelligence gathering is the lynchpin of the strategic-level decision-making process. While red flagging gathered intelligence is of strategic importance, the military leadership should focus on empirically derived interpretations and objective perceptions of intelligence.

At the operational level, adversaries plan their campaigns based upon inferences drawn from their own intelligence to achieve strategic goals. They build the capabilities (botnets, malware, delivery methodology [phishing], etc.) needed to support the tactical operations and stealthily manoeuvre in cyber space to position capability at vulnerable points for their tactical missions. The planning of operations and campaigns to defend against cyber operations at this level is largely in the realm of active cyber defence. The allocation of operational information technology systems, identification of the type of attack and the potential perpetrators and pooling of resources and capabilities to neutralise such attacks are some of the steps directed towards strengthening cyber defences at the operational level. The actionable intelligence gleaned from various sources, its veracity and credibility provides information about the objectives and capabilities of malicious actors and immensely helps in maintaining an overall deterrence and defence posture, which is credible, flexible, resilient, adaptable and capable of thwarting their actions. The tactical level of the cyber domain is where malicious actors and network defenders are pitted against each other, constantly manoeuvring to try and outwit, outfight and outgun their opponents. At this level, cyber weapons are directed towards a specific target, unleashing their payloads at opportune times. This is the area of intense attention and analysis, and acts as a pivot around which most of the cyber defence is focussed. The acquired capabilities at this level, just as the two preceding it, are strengthened when built on credible intelligence.

Cyber Conflict Termination

The conflict termination process works on the presumption of an ongoing conflict, which at least one participant wants to end. The willing participant brings the other party on the table for conflict resolution by way of coercion, subjugation or annihilation. However, classic conflict termination definition does not fit in the mould of the cyber environment. A cease fire in cyber space is supposed to be a declaration of complete cessation of hostile activities. However, verification of such claims rests entirely on subjective perceptions, thereby precluding objective verification due to technical limitations. In some cases, ongoing offensive operations undertaken by third parties may be mistakenly attributed to conflicting parties. In a kinetic military environment, a variety of technical means (e.g., photo reconnaissance aircraft and satellites, ocean-scale sonar arrays) is capable of monitoring movements of military personnel and equipment and provide information that is generally regarded as reliable. However, because of the ephemeral footprint of cyber forces and the subtle signatures of the activities, it is difficult to establish cyber conflict termination criteria and a set of quantifiable benchmarks that functions as a basis for implementing conflict termination provisions. Each party will naturally have concerns about its adversary's commitment to adhere to the terms of a cyber ceasefire, especially in the aftermath of a conflict.

Applicability of International Laws and Cyber Defence

In spite of the severity, complexity and violence associated with war, it is still not untouched by inherent human traits like empathy and compassion. The general consensus among states to adhere to the provisions of the Geneva Convention by signing on the dotted line is indicative of the general acceptance of the rights of persons *hors de combat* and those who do not take a direct part in hostilities, of their lives and their moral and physical integrity. Article 36 of the 1977 Protocol I, additional to the Geneva Convention, makes it obligatory on each state that any new weapon it deploys or considers deploying, complies with the rules of International Humanitarian Law (IHL). However, new weapons and means and methods of warfare could marginalise laws and treaties, as their intended use, effect and outcome after deployment might not have been comprehended well over the entire spectrum.

The evolution of cyber warfare has the potential of rendering the provisions of the Geneva Convention ineffective. Computers and networks are so intricately linked that, if attacked, infiltrated or blocked by an adversary, as a strategic or tactical move to gain advantage, they may put the lives of civilians at great risk by depriving them of basic essentials like medical care, food and potable water. Critical infrastructures such as power plants, dams, railways-network and aircraft control systems may also be vulnerable during cyber attacks because of their reliance on computers and networks.

In the cyber environment, one of the major challenges is the applicability of various provisions of international laws governing cyber operations, whether in offence or defence. The International Court of Justice has pronounced the applicability of international laws to "any use of force regardless of weapons employed" in an armed conflict. In the same breath, one can interpret the laws as pronounced by the Permanent Court of International Justice, that acts not forbidden in international law are generally permitted. The lack of definitive guidance on the subject of cyber operations in an armed conflict does not relieve the states of their obligation to ensure the safety and moral and physical integrity of civilians.

A number of states are in the process of revisiting their policies regarding potential military responses to threats in the cyber domain. As a punitive or retaliatory action against an attack in the cyber domain, these states may resort to the use of conventional weapons or cyber counter-attacks to destroy, deny, disrupt or degrade an adversary's capability to use cyber space as a domain of warfare. At the same time, concerted national, regional and international efforts are underway to assess the risks associated with military use of cyber offence, how to insulate non-combatants and innocents from cyber offence as well as the applicability of various international laws in this context. The United Nations, European Union, and North Atlantic Treaty Organisation have initiated formal processes for finding multilateral approaches to securing the cyber domain.

United Nations

The United Nations General Assembly has put forward a number of resolutions related to cyber security with the objective of drawing attention to cyber challenges. The General Assembly adopted two resolutions in 2003 and 2004 respectively dealing with the creation of a "Global Culture of Cyber Security and the Protection of Critical Infrastructures". Resolution A/57/239 of 2003 calls for more awareness and responsibility by capable states to "act in a timely and cooperative manner to prevent, detect and respond to security incidents".[18] Resolution A/58/199 of 2004 invites all relevant international organisations and member states "that have developed strategies to deal with cyber security and the protection of critical information infrastructures to share their best practices and measures that could assist other member states in their efforts to facilitate the achievement of cyber security".[19]

In 2010, the General Assembly approved Resolution (A/RES/65/41) constituting a new Groups of Governmental Experts (GGE) to study the existing and potential threats in the cyber domain and to lay down a framework for possible cooperative measures to address them. The logical extension of this will be "to develop some specifics on what the implementation of the recommendations might look like and—equally importantly—designate a forum for discussion of transparency and confidence building measures in cyber space".[20]

On September 12, 2011, the permanent representatives China, the Russian Federation, Tajikistan, and Uzbekistan submitted a proposal for discussions on an International Code of Conduct for Information Security in the framework of the United Nations. This draft model basically concerns the maintenance of the information and network security. The proposed code will mandate the member-states to pledge "not to use information and communications technologies, including networks, to carry out hostile activities or acts of aggression, and pose threats to international peace and security or to proliferate information weapons and related technologies".[21]

International Telecommunication Union

The ITU (International Telecommunication Union) is the specialised United Nations agency for information and communication technologies and allocation of the global radio spectrum and satellite orbits. The ITU is in the process of expanding its realm to encompass the issues related to cyber security. On May 17, 2007, as a framework for international cooperation to promote cyber security and enhance confidence and security in the information society, the ITU launched the Global Cyber Security Agenda (GCA). The GCA seeks to encourage collaboration amongst all relevant partners in building confidence and security in the use of Information and Communication Technologies (ICTs). The agenda is built on five pillars: legal measures, technical procedures, organisational structures, capacity-building, and international cooperation.[22] The agenda seeks to form partnerships with different stakeholders and enable states to implement concrete measures for cyber security.

Convention on Cyber Crime

The 2004 Budapest Convention on Cyber Crime is the first international treaty seeking to address issues related to cyber crime by strengthening and harmonising national laws, making investigative techniques more effective, and enhancing cooperation among nations. It provides a framework for states to conceptualise, draft and ratify national legislation on cyber crime and for international cooperation. In one of the conferences, the member states of Europe highlighted the human rights aspects of cyber security, trying to draw parallels between Internet freedom and fundamental rights. This was vehemently opposed by some of the members and a general consensus could not be reached. However, it has been consciously agreed by the members to endorse cyber attacks as illegal, regardless of their motivation. Presently, only 37 states have joined the treaty and of these, only Japan and the United States have ratified it.

Framework for "International Law Applicable to Cyber Warfare"

In order to provide a framework for "International Law Applicable to Cyber Warfare", a project was undertaken by a group of experts at the initiative of the NATO Cooperative Cyber Defence Centre of Excellence based in Tallinn, Estonia. The group was mandated to study international laws and prepare a draft on the applicability of these laws to govern 'cyber warfare' encompassing both *jus in bello* (the law of armed conflict or international humanitarian law) and *jus ad bellum* (the set of rules to be consulted before engaging in war). It commenced in 2009 and the fruition of the project culminated in the production of a manual on the law governing cyber warfare, known as the "Tallinn Manual". The assemblage of the group in Estonia was a matter of great significance as Estonia had been the victim of much publicised cyber-attacks in 2007, which has energised the on-going legal debate on the nature of cyber warfare, especially between states.

The preparation of the Tallinn Manual is an exercise in *lex lata,* i.e. an exercise in the laws which are in existence and not an attempt to create a whole set of new laws. The experts based their deliberations on several established treaties and regulations, including the 1949 Geneva Convention and 1907 Hague Regulations. Some of the provisions in the Tallinn Manual have been framed anew as no corresponding analogous provisions could be found in existing treaties or customary international laws. This is a deliberate attempt to fit cyber warfare within the framework already established under the gamut of international laws.

- **Sovereignty, Jurisdiction and Control:** The Tallinn Manual begins with the statement: "A State may exercise control over cyber infrastructure and activities within its sovereign territory." This is indicative of acceptance of the fact that the cyber infrastructure of state may be a part of a more global network, but will remain under a state's sovereignty.[23] However, the intentions of a state exercising its sovereign rights over cyber infrastructure for securing illegitimate objectives become contentious and mala fide. At times, exercising sovereign rights and protection of human rights create a poignant situation pitting the rights of states against the rights of individuals. Denying access to the Internet, as has been happening in the Syrian conflict for the last two years, can be quoted as one of the examples. A state may exercise its jurisdiction:

- Over persons engaged in cyber activities in its territory.
- Over cyber infrastructure located in its territory.
- Extra-territorially, in accordance with international law.

The exercise of territorial jurisdiction as envisaged under the provisions of the Tallinn Manual includes 'subjective' and 'objective' jurisdictions. The state exercises subjective jurisdiction when the cyber operation has been initiated within a state's territory, irrespective of where the effects occur. When the effects of cyber operations initiated outside a state's territory are felt within it, it falls under the preview of objective jurisdiction. The process of establishment of well-defined jurisdiction within cyber space may prove a daunting and ambiguous task because of the distribution of cloud or grid systems over many nations' territory. The complex and international nature of network infrastructures distributed among many states is not in consonance with the traditional notions of territorial sovereignty. This may precipitate in a situation wherein multiple states may enjoy jurisdiction over a particular cyber incident. However, a state is within its right to exercise sovereignty even if it does not hold exclusive jurisdiction over the organisations or infrastructures used to perpetrate an act of cyber operation.

State Responsibility

As per Rule 6 of the Tallinn Manual: "A State shall bear international legal responsibility for a cyber operation attributable to it."[24] In cyber space, the perpetrators can be nation-states or non-state actors. The act will be considered a breach of international obligations by a state, even if the perpetrator (person or entity) is not an organ of the state but has been empowered by the law of that state.

In the realm of cyber warfare, the question of determination of state responsibility is a piquant one. Let us examine a hypothetical situation, where a group in State A assimilates computers located in State B into its botnet and uses the botnet to overload computer systems in State C based on instructions received from State D. The attributability of the conduct squarely rests with State D. State A and State B can be exonerated from the responsibility of conduct based on the fact that the group was merely located on the territory of State A and the bots were located on the territory of State B. In Nicaragua, although the US had financed and organised the rebels fighting the Nicaraguan government, it did not exercise "effective control" over the rebels, who were the true perpetrators. To sum up, the mere fact that a cyber operation has been launched or otherwise originates from a governmental cyber infrastructure is not sufficient evidence for attributing the operation to that state.[25] Furthermore, the fact that a cyber operation has been routed via the cyber infrastructure located in a state is not sufficient evidence for attributing the operation to that state.[26]

The Use of Force

The International Court of Justice and the United Nations Charter, state that the prohibition of the use of force and the right of self-defence apply to "any use of force, regardless of the weapons employed". In the realm of cyber operations, the operations carried out from an innocuous looking computer can be deemed as 'use of force', though it is radically different from our general perception of traditional weapons or platforms. In an attempt to elucidate further, the Tallinn Manual suggests that 'use of force' in cyber space needs to be determined based on its effects rather than the physical form of the weapons or platforms. Therefore, a cyber operation constitutes a use of force when its scale and effects are comparable to non-cyber operations rising to the level of a use of force[27].

The approach focusses on both the level of harm inflicted as well as certain qualitative elements of a particular cyber operation. The identification of cyber operations that are analogous in scale and effect to other non-kinetic or kinetic actions, described as 'use of force' by international laws, is to be done based on qualitative evaluation of certain parameters. The parameters determining the causal effects are as follows:

- **Severity:** A cyber operation which results in damage, destruction, injury or death is likely to be considered a use of force. Severity obliviously tops the list of factors in the analysis. Operations resulting in mere inconvenience or irritation will not be included in this category.
- **Immediacy:** An act in cyber space is likely to be categorised as 'use of force' if the outcome of the operation produces immediate quantifiable and palpable results.
- **Directness:** Cyber operations in which there is a distinct link between cause and effects may be characterised as use of force.
- **Invasiveness:** The degree of intrusion achievable with cyber operations into the targets of interests of the state will determine its declaration as 'use of force.'
- **Measurability of Effects:** A state will characterise actions as use of force when the consequences are apparent. Though in cyber space, the identification and quantification of consequences may prove to be subjective, the state will assess and evaluate the situation in specific terms when determining whether the level of cyber attack tantamounts to 'use of force'.
- **Military Character:** A cyber operation undertaken as a mean to invade or intrude into another state with the objective of threatening its territorial integrity, undermining its sovereignty or severely damaging its economy is akin to an operation with a military overhang. This act will be categorised as 'use of force.' As many as 15 nations have developed offensive cyber capabilities and may use these as instruments of power projection.
- **State Involvement:** Most states have, overtly or covertly, recognised the potential of undertaking cyber operations to secure their national interests. Cyber space is populated with

state as well as non-state actors, with objectives having overtures of sovereignty, patriotism, territorial integrity, national interest or of terrorism, fraudulent or crime. When the state or an entity empowered by the state undertakes cyber operations against another state, it tantamounts to 'use of force'.

Self-Defence

A state that is the target of a cyber operation that rises to the level of an armed attack may exercise its inherent right of self-defence. Whether a cyber operation constitutes an armed attack depends on its scale and effects. In cyber warfare, the adversary may adopt one of following approaches: the effects-based approach, the target-based approach or the instrument-based approach. In this context, the effects-based approach is very dynamic owing to its subjective interpretation due to lack of foreseeability. Essentially, the main criterion for categorising an attack as armed is that the act needs to be grave. It is not clear as to which point death, injury, damage, destruction, or suffering caused by a cyber operation qualify as an armed attack.

An attempt to transpose pre-existing rules and principles to the domain of cyber space is not without pitfalls as it raises a number of important questions. Some of these questions can be resolved by judicious interpretation of pre-existing treaties, whereas some require a unanimous and consensus policy decision by the international community and states. Till date, while the effects of cyber warfare have not resulted in dramatic humanitarian consequences, the growing dependence on computers, networks and computer-controlled systems for our sustainability and subsistence has made the cyber entity an indispensable and inalienable one. State-sponsored cyber attacks are not a distant possibility and these attacks have the requisite potential to generate a humanitarian crisis of unparalleled proportions.

Concerted national, regional and international efforts are underway to generate a consensus among member states to assess the risks associated with the military use of cyber offence, how to insulate non-combatants and innocents from the acts of offence in the cyber domain as well as from cyber crime. Although till date, no formal agreement has been signed by the nation-states, every stakeholder in cyber space is conscious of the dangers associated with its misuse. This collective consciousness may, in the near future, precipitate into adoption of certain guidelines by consensus among the states.

Conclusion

By establishing a framework for an analysis of defensive cyber warfare strategies and laying down agendas for policy-makers and military planners, cyber defence capabilities will be bolstered, making cyber defence an integral part of broad-based collective defence. The biggest cyber defence challenge *is* not one of confronting a set of known rogue groups and malicious individuals; it is, instead, a challenge of identifying, in the first place, who is a potential threat to the nation's security. The future of cyber warfare will be much more than the continuum of present events and will evolve, mutate, transform or morph into something more dangerous and destructive capable of catapulting the world into so-called 'cyber Armageddon'. We have reached a point of inflection, where new, malicious cyber attack capabilities are being created at a much higher rate than the capabilities for cyber defence. The government, military and industry triumvirate needs to capitalise on their strengths and to pool in their respective resources for capacity and expertise aggrandisement for building an all-encompassing framework for defending cyber space which is doctrinally pragmatic, strategically all-inclusive, operationally meaningful and tactically viable. Universally, recourse to war has been viewed as a rational alternative for the preservation or furtherance of the state's interests and its justification or condemnation and characterisation as just or unjust is measured by perceived outcomes and the value placed on those outcomes. The inherent fluidity in the global and regional geopolitical space, the scourge of global terrorism and the human disposition for greed, power and violence, will always threaten national sovereignty and interests in all spheres of social, political, economic and military activity. This has made it imperative to take every measure to strengthen and bolster the defences in all areas and domains, including cyber space.

Notes

1. Sai Felicia Krishna-Hensel, *Order and Disorder in the International System* (Surrey: Ashgate, 2010), p.13.
2. Laura K Donohue, "High Technology, Consumer Privacy, and US National Security", *Georgetown Law Faculty Publications,* Paper 1457, 2015, http://scholarship.law.georgetown.edu/facpub/1457. Accessed June 15, 2015.
3. Douglas Lovelace, *The Obama Administration's Second Term National Security Strategy* (New York : Oxford University Press, 2015), p. 263.
4. United States. Department of Defence, *Department of Defense Strategy for Operating in Cyberspace* (Pennsylvania: Diane Publishing Co, 2012), p.5.
5. Ibid., p.7.
6. Preston L. Schiller, Eric Bruun and Jeffrey R. Kenworthy, *An Introduction to Sustainable Transportation: Policy, Planning and Implementation* (Washington DC: Earthscan, 2011), p. 240.
7. Judith H. Germano, *Cybersecurity Partnerships: A New Era of Public-Private Collaboration* (New York: Centre of Law and Security, New York University School of Law, 2014) , p.1.
8. Ibid.
9. Ibid., p. 4.
10 n. 3, p.10.
11. National Initiative For Cybersecurity Education, "National Cyber Security Workforce Framework", http://csrc.nist.gov/nice/. Accessed April 23, 2016.
12. Irving Lachow, *Active Cyber Defense: A Framework for Policymakers* (Washington, DC: Centre for a New American Society, 2013), p.4.
13. Ami Kaufman, "Anatomy of an Attack", https://blogs.rsa.com/anatomy-of-an-attack/. Accessed April 23, 2016.
14. Lt Gen Charles Croom (Retd), USAF, "The Cyber Kill Chain: A Foundation for a New Cyber Security Strategy", *High Frontier*, August 2010, p.53.
15. Ibid.
16. Joseph M. Mazzafro, *Operational Levels of Cyber Intelligence* (Arlington, VA:Intelligence and National Security Alliance Cyber Intelligence Task Force, 2013), p.12.
17. Ibid.
18. United Nations, *Creation of a Global Culture of Cybersecurity,* UN document A/RES/57/239, January 31, 2003, p. 2.
19. United Nations, *Creation of a Global Culture of Cybersecurity and the Protection of Critical Information Infrastructures,* General Assembly, UN document A/RES/58/199, 30 January 2004, p. 2.

20. B. Baseley-Walker,"Transparency and Confidence-Building Measures in Cyberspace: Towards Norms of Behavior", *Disarmament Forum*, no. 4, 2011, p. 37.
21. United Nations General Assembly, letter dated September 12, 2011 from Permanent Representatives of China, the Russian Federation, Tajikistan and Uzbekistan to the United Nations, addressed to the Secretary-General, UN document A/66/359, 14 September 2011, p. 4.
22. The International Telecommunication Union, "Global Cybersecurity Agenda (GCA)", www.itu.int/osg/csd/cybersecurity/gca/new-gca-brochure.pdf. Accessed February 1, 2016.
23. Michael N. Schmitt, *Tallinn Manual on the International Law Applicable to Cyber Warfare* (Cambridge: Cambridge University Press, 2013), p.15.
24. Ibid., p. 29.
25. Ibid.
26. Ibid., p. 36.
27. Ibid., p. 45.

8

War Over Internet Governance: Oxymoronic or Opportunistic?

The Internet, as we know it today, is often hailed as a *beacon of knowledge*, a harbinger of freedom through empowerment, a strong proponent of freedom of expression and a place for exchanging ideas without the fear of prosecution or punitive action. The birth of the Internet shook the very foundation of sovereignty as propagated by the dominant 'Westphalian conceptions'. The Internet was wild, unhindered and unencumbered by anyone or anything, transcending physical boundaries with impunity and hubris. The virtual space used by the Internet and operatives became so well recognised that it was even christened with an appropriate name: "cyber space". Independence was the structural yarn used for weaving the fabric of the Internet as we know it today. The agnostic nature of the used standards and protocols do not differentiate between creed, culture or countries. An attempt to block the Internet traffic is treated as a technology hitch and the traffic is rerouted through seemingly infinite networks. "The Net interprets censorship as damage and routes around it."[1] There is a widely held view that it "is not a physical place—it defies measurement in any physical dimension or time-space continuum. It is a short-hand term that refers to the environment created by the confluence of cooperative networks of computers, information systems, and telecommunication infrastructures, commonly referred to as the World Wide Web."[2]

The precursor to the Internet were the collective efforts in the backdrop of strategic imperatives of the US to design a system capable of withstanding missile attacks. The Cuban missile crisis of 1962 was arguably a catalytic factor that fuelled the dramatic development of the Internet. During the 'the Cuban crisis', the lack of exchange of information, cogently and coherently, among several of the powers involved, exacerbated the situation and brought the world to the brink of a global nuclear war. Taking cognisance of its impact on the situation, under direct orders from President Kennedy, the National Security Council (NSC) constituted an interdepartmental committee to examine the communications networks and institute changes. In 1963, in order to provide better communication support to critical government functionaries during emergencies, President Kennedy established the National Communications System (NCS). The NCS was mandated to link, improve and extend communication to components of various federal agencies, focussing on interconnectivity and survivability. In this backdrop, in August 1962, computer scientist JCR Licklider at the Massachusetts Institute of Technology (MIT) conceptualised the Intergalactic Computer Network,[3] envisioning a global network of computers through which everyone could quickly access data and programmes from geographically dispersed sites. Later that year, Licklider moved over to the Defence Advanced Research Projects Agency (DARPA) to head the development project. In 1964, Paul Baran of the RAND Corporation, proposed the architecture of a new kind of network of computers, a packet-switched network, capable of surviving an enemy attack due to its inherent resilience[4]. In 1967, driven by Licklider's vision and Baran's architecture, ARPA embarked on a research project to build a network. The first four nodes of the ARPAnet became operational in early 1970. By 1981, the ARPAnet had grown to about 200 nodes and a basic suite of protocols (TCP/IP, FTP, Telnet, SMTP) was developed. During this time, the Europeans' endeavours in the field of networking culminated in the development of the ISO (International Standards Organisation) , a seven-layer model of protocol architecture. By 1990, the emerging Internet had grown to over 150,000 computers and was expanding exponentially.

The Birth of the World Wide Web

In the year 1989, Tim Berners-Lee, a computer scientist specialising in networking, was working at the "Conseil Européen pour la Recherche Nucléaire" or European Council for Nuclear Research (CERN) in Switzerland. Using the initial vision of Licklider and Nelson as the springboard, he proposed a paper on the information management system for, "the problems of loss of information about complex evolving systems.... and derives a solution based on a distributed hypertext system."[5] Though termed as *"vague but exciting"* by his boss, Berners-Lee was permitted to continue on the project. By 1990, Berners-Lee could define the Web's basic building blocks, the URL, http and html and wrote the first browser and server software. Working on the 'NeXT' computer at CERN, he named the first web server as "Info. cern.ch" and world's first web page was addressed as "http://info. cern.ch/hypertext/WWW/ Project.html", containing information and details of the World Wide Web project. As CERN was primarily using particle accelerators and detectors to boost beams of particles to high energies and was at the helm of high-energy-physics, in 1991, an early version of the world wide web system was released to the high-energy-physics community that included a simple browser, server software and a library of essential functions for designing custom software. In 1993, CERN put the Web in the public domain, ensuring that it would remain an open standard and released the source code of Berners-Lee's hypertext project, "World Wide Web" the same day. The move, while heralding the expansive and unhindered growth of the Internet, saw the World Wide Web accounting for most of the Internet traffic.

On October 24, 1995, the Federal Networking Council (FNC), in consultation with members of the Internet and intellectual property rights communities, came up with the definition of the term "Internet".[6] As per definition, the "Internet" refers to the global information system that:

- Is logically linked together by a globally unique address space based on the Internet Protocol (IP) or its subsequent extensions/ follow-ons.

- Is able to support communications using the Transmission Control Protocol/Internet Protocol (TCP/IP) suite or its subsequent extensions/ follow-ons and/or other IP-compatible protocols.
- Provides, uses or makes accessible, either publicly or privately, high level services layered on the communications and related infrastructure described herein.

The Geopolitics of Internet Control and Policies

The Internet, conceived in the era of limited computing and time-sharing, has not only survived but thrived, and grown by leaps and bounds. The new technology, standards of networks and computational methodologies have been seamlessly adopted and assimilated by the Internet. An enterprise, conceived developed and nurtured by a small group of dedicated researchers, from a humble beginning has grown to become an all pervasive entity, intricately woven into the fabric of the social and political life of all *inhabitants of this planet*. A sterling example of commercial success, the Internet dictates the way the business is negotiated, facilitated and conducted. If we take into account the indelible impact of the Internet on today's society, the issues related to its management and governance become paramount over the insular and parochial interests of individuals, societies and nations.

The Internet has become the significant harbinger of the information society, but too often it seems that it is merely reflecting albeit in distorted form, scourges that have plagued mankind for many centuries: crime, espionage, warfare, terrorism, stalking, reputation tarnishing, etc. Human vices manifest in all kinds of available environments and cyber space provides an easily accessible platform for exploration,targeting and exploitation of human frailties. Threats emanating in cyber space are potent, pandemic, inimical and perilous. Today, nations use Computer Network Operations (CNO) to defend sovereignty and to project power, and cyber conflicts may soon become the rule rather than the exception.[7] Cyber attacks have now been recognised as capable of creating a significant threat to national security, foreign policy or financial stability, and in the post-Stuxnet era, the "cyber war" is no larger an oxymoronic construct but a stark reality.

In some quarters, there is a popular perception that systematic cyber espionage activities by China against the US and other countries are comparable to those of the Communist plan of world domination in the bygone era, albeit from a different source, following a different methodology. Some believe this is reminiscent of the Cold War era of the 1960s, when the erstwhile Soviet Union became the nemesis of the US, forcing the US to direct most of its political, economic, military efforts to curb and contain the Communist sphere of influence. This metaphoric comparison foreshadows a bleak future for the Internet and may contribute to its militarisation. Some nations are trying to shape the Internet policy landscape to suit their real and imagined security concerns. Some of the conflicts among nations over the Internet show a similarity with conflicts during the Cold War era. The conflict between "the champions of Internet freedom" and "advocates of regulatory jurisprudence" has turned cyber space into a battlefield, with a clear delineation between the two.

The genesis of the Cold War lies not in the fact that the Soviet Union had comparable military might or knew better ways of governance over its people. It was, rather, the widely held apprehension that the Soviet system could leverage post World War II political upheavals to tip the balance of power in its favour. The post-war popularity of Communist ideology and the emergence of nationalistic movements with a Communist inclination in the former colonies of Europe, were increasingly perceived as threats and fanned the fear that emerging nations and part of Europe would toe the Soviet line, either politically or economically. The Cold War rivalry was further exacerbated by technological advances in weaponry, especially with the development of nuclear weapons. In an effort to gain strategic advantages, a nuclear armed race was triggered between the US and Russia, culminating in the development, production and stockpiling of arms capable of apocalyptic destruction of the world. Mutually

Assured Destruction (MAD) prevented a direct military conflict between the two;nevertheless, the fierce rivalry sometimes resulted in violent conflicts in other areas. The Cold War was ultimately won, not because of superior military capabilities,but by the conscientious and collective desire of the world community at large to adopt the liberal capitalistic democracy model which would produce wealth for its citizens, provide them with political freedom, and enhance their well-being.

Are we witnessing an ideological division in the Internet sphere? Is this division similar in its ideological orientation towards the capitalism vs. socialism and democracy vs. Communism divisions? There is an ideological difference between two distinct issues: the institutional form of Internet governance vs. the substantive aspects of the communications policy.[8] The authoritarian states are in favour of a prominent role for sovereigns in policy formulation, while stakeholders in academia, the technical community and civil society and some states advocate open and participatory institutional mechanisms for Internet governance. There are states with authoritarian political systems wanting to reassert sovereign power over the Internet in their efforts to maintain a tenuous political equilibrium and to keep the political aspirations of their citizens at bay, and insular to global trends. The societies in the developed world and in many parts of the developing world are increasingly clamouring for Internet freedom without censorship, surveillance and monopolistic controls, while supporting freedom of expression, privacy and innovation. However, unlike the Cold War, this competition has not translated into a power struggle between two great power states, trying to attract or coerce other nations into their spheres of influence. During the Cold War, siding with one superpower entailed severing of most of the ties—diplomatic, economic and social—with the other side. Physical boundaries were constructed to restrict immigration, trade and travel between East and West. However, this kind of restriction, severe isolation and minimal interaction is not possible today.

Internet Governance

Since the time the Internet made its foray into the public domain and opened to commerce, the term "**Internet governance**" has come into the lexicon. The term, at first, referred to the policy issues for its portability, operability, sustenance and reliability, and later encompassed the issues related to management of domain names and IP addresses. As the Internet became ubiquitous, the definition also broadened considerably. In 2005, the UN-sponsored World Summit on the Information Society (WSIS) defined Internet governance as "the development and application by governments, the private sector and civil society, in their respective roles, of shared principles, norms, rules, decision-making procedures, and programs that shape the evolution and use of the Internet."[9] An equitable distribution of Internet resources, unfettered and multilingual access to all and a stable and secure functioning of the Internet constitute the core of Internet governance.

Technologies which the Internet rides on, and resides in, historically, came into being during the initial development, consolidation and refinement phases. With the emergence of new challenges such as freedom of expression, Internet infrastructural security and stability, policy role of Internet companies, efficacy of Internet protocols, Internet control systems such as the Domain Name System (DNS) and the relationship between intellectual property rights enforcement and the Internet architecture, the issue of Internet governance has become more complex and variegated. Preservation of national security, prevention of societal disharmony, protection of economic interests and containment of internal dissident elements are some of the concerns, adding further complexities to the already tumultuous realm of Internet governance.

At the heart of Internet governance is the designing and administration of the technologies necessary to keep the Internet operational, followed by a formal and substantive mechanism governing the use of these technologies. This technical scaffolding involves critical Internet resources, technical standards for integrity and interoperability, interfaces for man-machine interaction such as search engines, information access and exchange points, etc. Some of the challenges need to be addressed pragmatically and ethically before a consensus and conceptual framework for Internet governance many be built.[10]

Agnostic Arrangement of Technical Architecture

The technical foundation used to build the Internet may appear pragmatic and agnostic in nature, free from the shackles of political and cultural imperatives. However, as Jasanoff puts it, technology "both embeds and is embedded in social practices, identities, norms, conventions, discourses, instruments, and institutions— in short, in all the building blocks of what we term the social." [11] Technology, *per se* is an inanimate entity used as a tool to set in motion, and to sustain, the momentum generated by the Internet. Internet governance decisions are often based as much as upon technological imperatives as on how to regulate and control the usage of these. For example, technology dictates that the domain name and corresponding Internet address need to be globally unique, but allocation and control calls for institutional coordination and control. The issue has become central to the global struggle for Internet governance since the early Nineties.

Use of Internet Governance Technologies for Content Control and Information Censorship

The enactment of policies governing the use of Internet technologies for content control and censorship has become a norm, albeit a draconian one, among many nations. In the garb of intellectual property rights protection, law enforcement functions or for strangulation of voices calling for political reforms, Internet governance technologies are being increasingly leveraged for curtailing the free flow of information and for content control. Traditionally, institutionalised centres of power have resorted to censorship of information and after sieving the information through the mesh of their perceived values and interests, made it accessible to the masses. The Internet has deprived these centres of the power of being selective or in denial mode about information and its flow,deemed detrimental to their core interests. The Internet governance infrastructure is routinely used to block, filter or censor access to information, to disseminate misinformation or to create a system of mass surveillance.

Privately Owned and Controlled Internet Governance Technologies

Historically, most of Internet governance functions were executed out of the domain of governments,via private ordering, technical design and new institutional forms. Internet governance policies were enacted in specific contexts of technological and social change. Sovereign governments, in an effort to regulate activities within or through their boundaries, as constitutionally and legally mandated or otherwise, oversee many Internet governance functions such as enactment of laws against cyber crime, cyber terrorism, espionage, computer fraud or social disharmony.

Internet as an Instrument in Global Conflict

The use of the Internet as a coercive and exploitative instrument tool—by manipulating its implicit character via technology, policy formulation and restrictive regulation, for political, commercial and security reasons—has given rise to global tensions. In a blatant digression from its promised goal of upholding democratic values and freedom of expression,Internet governance control is being used for content censorship, mainstream media control, mass surveillance of citizens and shaping of public opinion for the furtherance of nefarious designs. Central to Internet governance are conflicts over issues of ethicality, morality, cultural and political rights,intellectual property rights protection and national security.[12] Ernest efforts for conflict resolution over these issues require technical innovation, governments' intent and private participation. Articulation and implementation of policies and procedures for Internet control/regulation have directly exacerbated in building up global tensions.

Parochial Geopolitical Outlook in Internet Globalisation

The stability and security of the Internet is in the common interest of all nations. Nations have to deal with enduring global problems such as terrorism, environmental degradation, climate change and contagious diseases, which require cumulative, collective and congruent efforts. While losing sight of greater goals, the petty squabbling for a larger share of the pie over Internet governance is denying the global aggrandisement of Internet governance.

Globally, a loose consensus, comprising certain shared fundamental economic, political and social beliefs, is developing to unshackle the Internet from the historic and hegemonic control of US companies supposedly protecting US interests. Central to this debate is disagreement among many Internet governance stakeholders, over who controls the "Critical Internet Resources (CIR)." Though not physical, these virtual resources are finite and indispensable for use, access and operation of the Internet. Without the virtual resources such as Internet addresses, domain names, and Autonomous System Numbers (ASNs), even with the swankiest computer and high speed fibre optic network, the Internet will be as elusive as the proverbial unicorn.

An Internet Protocol (IP) address is a numerical value assigned to each device (e.g., computer, printer) willing to be a part of a network that uses the IP for communication.Every device accessing the Internet requires a unique binary number called an IP address. The domain name provides a humanly recognisable and easily memorable form, dispensing with the requirement of making sense of an esoteric string of binary numbers. Domain names such as www.google.com are used to locate websites. A domain name, when typed into a browser address bar, is translated by the Internet's Domain Name System (DNS) into unique binary numbers for locating the web site. An ASN is a binary number assigned to a network operator that connects to the global Internet. These network operators are usually described as autonomous systems. ASNs are valuable because receiving a globally unique ASN is a prerequisite for an

Internet service provider's network to become part of the global Internet.

The structural framework over which the Internet governance infrastructure is stitched together came into being as part of viable and workable technological solutions. No legal or commercial considerations were factored in during the development phase. The growth and transnational reach of the Internet has seen significant changes in objectives, roles and administrations of institutions responsible for coordinating CIRs. Understanding the functioning of these groups involves circumnavigating through the acronym thicket of global institutions, including Internet Assigned Numbers Authority(IANA),Internet Corporation for Assigned Names and Numbers (ICANN), Regional Internet Registries (RIRs), root zone server operators, domain name registrars,registries, and various other entities. The nuances of Internet governance can be captured by familiarisation with institutional structures that centrally oversee critical Internet resources,control root zone files, operate DNS servers, manage the registrar system for assigning domain names and distribute Internet numbers via RIRs.

IANA and ICANN

In early Internet history, management of names and numbers began with a single person. Christened as the "God of Internet", Jon Postel, a computer scientist from the University of South California (UCLA), who was involved in the early work of the ARPAnet, along with his colleagues, performed the role of a central coordinating functionary for the assignment of names and numbers. At IANA, Postel and colleagues, under contract with the US Department of Commerce, were responsible for:

- The coordination of the assignment of technical Internet Protocol parameters.
- The administration of certain responsibilities associated with the Internet DNS root zone management.
- The allocation of Internet numbering resources.

- Other services related to the management of the Address and Routing Parameter Area (ARPA) and INT Top-Level Domains (TLDs).[13]

Though the work was crucial, it was bereft of any major controversy. During that period, the network was primarily an American phenomenon and was yet to realise its full potential of having a global presence and close to 4 billion users. IANA eventually became a function under ICANN. Formed in 1998 under a contract with the US government, ICANN is a private, non-profit entity with an official mandate to provide technical coordination of core Internet resources, most notably domain names. Though incorporated in the state of California, it wields considerable authority, directly or indirectly, over all users of the Internet. To rein in unbridled growth of the Internet without order and regulation, ICANN is mandated to create, enact and promulgate enforceable regulations. However, depending on one's frame of reference, the creation and functioning of ICANN can be described as a panacea or branded as the root cause of the ailments.

Transition of communications over the Internet is different from our understanding of the classical communication process, which requires establishment of a dedicated channel over which transition of information takes place as one unbroken entity. Over the Internet, messages are broken into manageable packets and are exchanged over many independent networks following different paths, from source to destination. The lack of a central communication channel or information pathway makes the process of policy promulgation and enforcement across all the information traffic over the Internet extremely difficult. ICANN realises this through its control of the Internet's DNS. Internet addressing, as realised in the DNS, is centralised and provides the control point from which to regulate users. Denial of access to domain names is the equivalent to declaring someone a pariah from the Internet community. The DNS also defines jurisdictions on the Internet. The logical organisation of the DNS allows authority to be mapped onto distinct zones. Collectively, these features render ICANN capable of governance.

Root Zone Management

Root zone refers to the highest level of the DNS structure. It contains the names and the numeric IP addresses for all the top level domain names such as the generic top-level domain (gTLDs) (.com, .net, .org, .jobs), and all the country code top level domains (ccTLDs), for example, (.us, .uk.ph), including the entire list of all the root servers.[14]"Root Zone Management" involves the processes by which changes are made to the root zone file and Root WHOIS (a query and seek protocol for querying databases of registered users of the Internet resource). Root zone management involves three roles performed by three different entities mandated to do so under the provisions of legal agreements.

- IANA is responsible for managing the content of the root zone based on the policies adopted by ICANN. It transmits requested changes in TLD data to the root zone maintainer (Verisign) and the administrator (NTIA).
- The NTIA as administrator approves any changes, additions or deletions from the root zone file.
- Verisign, under a cooperative agreement with NTIA, performs the role of root zone maintainer. After approval from NTIA, Verisign implement changes in the root zone file. While IANA is supposed to determine the content of the root zone file, VeriSign actually edits the root zone data, cryptographically signs it and distributes the resulting content to the root server operators.

Operation of Root Name Servers

The root zone files are contained in a group of servers for distribution of this information to the world. This system of root name servers is controlled by 12 organisations with 13 distinct root server implementations. Each of the root name servers contains the most current root zone database. These root servers are the gateway to the DNS, so operating these servers is a critical task involving great responsibilities in both logical and physical management. Many of these server implementations are operated by American institutions such as governmental agencies, including, the NASA and the Department of Defence, American universities, including the University of Maryland and corporations, including VeriSign and Cogent.

Controlling Internet Number Distribution

Internet access is possible only with a legitimate IP address, which usually is provided through an Internet Service Provider (ISP). ISPs generally are allocated with a block of IP addresses for sub-division. In addition, to be a network operator further requires an ASN. The organisations that control the allocation and assignment of these numbers serve an essential Internet governance function. IANA has retained its historic role as the organisation centrally responsible for allocating IP addresses and ASNs, albeit now formally under the auspices of ICANN. IANA, in turn, delegates reserves of addresses and assignment authority to five Regional Internet Registries (RIRs), central and influential institutions in the Internet governance landscape. For example, APNIC (Asia Pacific Network Information Centre) has been delegated with the responsibility of the Asia-Pacific region. These RIRs, in turn, allocate address space to Local Internet Registries (LIRs) or selected National Internet Registries (NIRs) for further allocation or assignment to ISPs and end user institutions. For example, the Indian Registry for Internet Names and Numbers (IRINN) provides allocation and registration services of IP addresses and ASNs in India.

Critical Internet Resources' Management

The availability and accessibility of Critical Internet Resource (CIR), coupled with the historical legacy and future aspirations, has triggered a high profile, prolonged and hostile debate over centralised control, consensually agreed regulations and enactment of legally binding rules. A number of formally enacted agencies as well as a multitude of loosely governed organisations are providing platforms for debating

Internet governance issues, championing the cause of specific groups of stakeholders.Topping them all is the lack of consensus over the acceptance of a global model for Internet governance. There are proponents and opponents of the 'multistakeholder' and 'multilateral' models who are at loggerheads with each other due to various reasons. There is still another school of thought propounding the idea of identifying the Internet as one of the 'Global Commons' at par with the high seas, the atmosphere, Antarctica and outer space, outside of the political reach of any one nation-state. Many advocate the 'multistakeholder model' in which all stakeholders, whether from the private sector, government, academia, civil society or non-governmental organisations, participate in the policy development process. The multilateral model provides a level playing field for participants in which all participants (mostly nation-states) have an equal say in policy decisions.

Multistakeholder vs Multilateral Model of Internet Governance

Both the terms 'multistakeholderism' and 'multilateralism', have evolved contextually in reference to the Internet governance ecosystem over the last decade. The debate on multilateral versus multistakeholder has largely centred on what should be the roles and responsibilities of different stakeholders in various Internet governance mechanisms. This also raises further questions such as:

- What entities fall under the category of relevant and legitimate stakeholders?
- Have nation-states exclusively been mandated to make policies even when the issues have larger demographic ramifications?
- Can the Internet, which does not operate within geographically defined precincts, be governed by rules applicable to sovereign nation-states?
- Are the stakes of different stakeholders quantifiable to decide on the quantum of their participation in the Internet governance mechanisms?

The multistakeholder approach advocates inclusivity – a recognition of the fact that an open participation process and a bottom-up policy approach produce consensus driven outputs more or less loosely binding on individual members. In contrast, the multilateral approach is characterised by participation which is limited to member states and a top-down policy process that advocates voting for resolution, and produces outputs that are more binding on its members.[15] The critics of the multistakeholder approach see it as favouring US-based big IT companies such as Facebook, Google, Yahoo, etc. thereby reaffirming the dominant position of the US in the Internet arena. A multilateral approach, on the other hand, is seen as reinforcing the dominant position of member states at the expense of curbing the participation of legitimate stakeholders.

Emergence of Working Group on Internet Governance

The US has a dominant say on how the issues of Internet governance are to be addressed. The US dominance stems partly from traditional advantages accrued during the development phase of the Internet and partly from the location of critical infrastructure such as root name servers in the US and in countries closely allied with the US. At various international fora, many nations have clamoured for years to get rid of US dominance and have sought a more assertive role for themselves on issues related to Internet governance. However, the US is thwarting such moves as it sees this as an organised effort by other nations to wrest control of one centralised resource of the Internet that was both "unilateral and centred in the US".[16]

At the World Summit on the Information Society (WSIS), the endorsement by the UN General Assembly of the "Tunis Agenda for the Information Society' of 2005 saw the creation of the "Internet Governance Forum" (IGF) as a platform for the multistakeholder policy dialogue. The IGF aims to provide a unique multistakeholder platform for discussions on public policy issues related to key elements of Internet governance in order to foster the sustainability, robustness, security, stability and development of the Internet.[17] In its official statement at the NETmundial in Brazil, India endorsed that "international law and in particular the Charter of the United Nations, is applicable and is essential in maintaining security and stability and promoting an open, secure, peaceful and accessible ICT environment. All governments should have an equal role and responsibility for ensuring the stability, security, and continuity of the Internet."

The inequitable distribution of power in managing the Internet resources and greater influence wielded by a few countries has been an issue of discord for India and other developing countries since the Tunis phase of the WSIS. However, replacing the multistakeholder and dispersed model of Internet governance entirely with a centralised model may not translate into empowering the users. The government led control may be used to limit, restrict or deny content on the Internet. This will result in strengthening of the 'content control mechanism' at least in countries with oppressive, autocratic and oligarchic governments.

NETmundial

Edward Snowden's revelations comprised a defining moment in more ways than one. These have amply demonstrated that Internet technologies, though transformative and emancipatory, have actual, foreseeable and potential risks to cause global disharmony. The general disposition among those who feel alienated and angry, after Snowden's revelations can be gauged by the tone and tenor of the discussions at the NETmundial on the "International Telecommunication Union (ITU) Plenipotentiary in November 2014" in São Paulo, Brazil, on April 23 and 24, 2014. On the implementation of a different model of Internet governance, the Brazilian government and representatives of the European Commission articulated that Internet governance should be:

- Open, multilateral and democratic governance , carried out with transparency by stimulating collective creativity and the participation of society, governments and the private sector;

- A real multistakeholder governance model based on the full involvement of all relevant actors and organisations[18].

During the NETmundial, a roadmap for a different model of Internet governance was proposed, incorporating the following:

- Combating all violations of human rights in cyber space.
- Consolidation of a decentralised multilateral Internet governance, interoperable and truly established in a consensual way with all users of public space: the governments, the entrepreneurs of the private sector and the civil society organisations.
- Guarantee of defence of net neutrality, against the restrictions arising from the economic interests of some monopolies in the business of telecommunications.
- Construction of mechanisms to prevent the illegal practices of the surveillance and espionage of the military and private industries in cyber space.
- Restoration of the confidence, credibility and tranquillity in cyber space, by the creative and collective work maintained by representative actors of governments, entrepreneurs of the private sector and civil society organisations.[19]

India and Internet Governance

India is at pole position to swing the outcome of any debate on Internet governance. India's assertive role in this respect is highlighted by the opening statement made by the Indian representative at the NETmundial: "With over 400 million Internet users, soon going to cross half a billion in the coming years, over one billion mobile telephone subscribers, and a thriving and robust Internet ecosystem, India is well poised and willing to play an important and constructive role in evolving the global Internet governance ecosystem and, in the process, make it more credible."[20] India's position on Internet governance can be gauged by its official position at various international platforms for debating the issue. Acceptance of India's viewpoint and its assimilation in policy formulation in the future may be speculative at this point of time, but there is global acceptance that the existing Internet governance ecosystem needs reforms, irrespective of these being multistakeholder or multilateral in nature. On the issue of Internet governance, both the terms 'multistakeholderism' and 'multilateralism' have been used in many platforms by the Indian government.

- In 2011, India proposed the establishment of the United Nations Committee for Internet Related Policies (CIRP) as the new institutional mechanism. The CIRP was to take inputs from IGF and was to comprise 50 member states, based on equitable geographic representation. The CIRP was envisaged to have multistakeholder representation.[21]
- At the Budapest Cyber Space Conference in October 2012, India endorsed the status quo position of the ICANN-led Internet governance. According to the then Minister of State for Telecom, Sachin Pilot, who led the Indian delegation to Budapest, India would pursue enhanced cooperation with ICANN through wider dialogue.[22]
- At the NETmundial, India in its official submission, while acknowledging the importance of an open, stable and secure Internet—as crucial to global connectivity, innovation and economic development—recommended a transformational shift from the Internet of today to the "Equinet" of tomorrow. While proposing the structure of Internet governance as multilateral, transparent, democratic and representative, with the participation of governments, the private sector, civil society and international organisations, in their respective roles, India acknowledged these as the foundational principles of Internet governance. Though the Indian representatives did not support the consensus view on the NETmundial outcome document, the country's active participation was a measure of willingness to bridge the "trust deficit". The Indian government has articulated its position on Internet governance at the NETmundial in the following official statement:
  - For global credibility and universal acceptability, the Internet governance ecosystem needs to be "representative,

democratic, transparent and accountable, involving governments and other stakeholders as per the Tunis Agenda"[4].

- Second, "given its profound importance, there is also a need for the various facets of the [*sic*] Internet governance, including the core Internet infrastructure, to be anchored in [an] appropriate international legal framework"[5].

These two statements echo the Indian government's resolve to tackle "strategic and policy challenges" to bring in more credibility and transparency into the global Internet governance ecosystem. It has unequivocally raised the following concerns:

- Lack of a truly representative and democratic nature of the existing systems of Internet governance, including the management of critical Internet resources, leading to a trust deficit in the system.
- Need for the Internet governance ecosystem to be sensitive to the cultures and national interests of all nations, not just of a select set of stakeholders.
- Apparent inability of the current structures of Internet governance to respond to some of the core and strategic concerns of the member states.
- Need to broad base and internationalise the institutions that are invested with authority to management [*sic*] and regulate the Internet.[23]

- On June 22, 2015, in Argentina, at the opening conference of the ICANN, Information Technology Minister Ravi Shankar Prasad unveiled an "Indian vision for the Internet"and said that "India recognises that all stakeholders are the key and multistakeholderism is perhaps the only way to keep the system integrated, growing and expanding."[24]

The endorsement of multistakeholderism at the highest political level allows India to engage substantively with Internet governance concerns at multiple fora.[25] Mr. Prasad, in his statement, supported multistakeholderism in general, without spelling out the nuances from the Indian perspective on the multistakeholder model. The Indian government's endorsement of multistakeholderism is crucially timed as the demand for transition of the IANA function from the US government to the global multistakeholder community has gained considerable momentum. The IT minister's remarks are an assertion of the Indian government's role in offering constructive inputs that enhance ICANN's accountability to users and will ensure that Indian Internet users and businesses have an equitable say in the ownership of new and lucrative top-level domain names (like .kids, .books, .pharmacy). The Indian government's endorsement of multistakeholderism facilitates the bottom-up approach on key Internet concerns such as net neutrality, freedom of speech and expression on the web.[26] It is a step in the right direction to create democratic space for debating Internet policies to "sustain a future of equity, innovation, collaboration and inclusion", as Ravi Shankar Prasad eloquently put it to an applauding audience in Argentina.

Conclusion

Internet governance is a highly complex and ever evolving form of governance which requires cognitive and technical scaffolding and ICT resource management to fulfil the aspirational goals of civil societies, uphold civil liberties and address national security imperatives. From being executed under the supervision of one person, today its enormous complexity has rendered even a multitude of agencies grappling to find viable and workable ways to make the Internet governance ecosystem globally acceptable to all users. The policy-making has also evolved from predominantly US institutions to new global entities. India is at the cusp of the digital revolution and at pole position to swing the outcome of any debate on Internet governance. Though the US has declared that it (US) would eventually transfer key Internet domain name functions to a global multistakeholder community, one has to watch with bated breath for this to really happen. In an official release, Dr. Stephen D. Crocker, chairman of ICANN's Board said, "Even though ICANN will continue to perform these vital technical functions, the US has long envisioned the day when stewardship over them would be transitioned to the global community. In other words, we have all long known the destination. Now it is up to our global stakeholder community to determine the best route to get us there." [27] India needs to leverage this opportunity for furtherance of its envisaged objectives for Internet governance by formulating a coherent policy and creating a team of technocrats, diplomats and members from academia for spearheading its efforts.

Notes

1 "John Gilmore's Maxim", http://techpresident.com/networked-public-sphere. Accessed January 25, 2015.

2 Thomas c. Wingfield, "The Law of Information Conflict: National Security Law in Cyberspace", August 21, 2000.

3 "Internet Hall of Fame Pioneer J.C.R. Licklider", http://www.internethalloffame.org/inductees/jcr-licklider. Accessed January 25, 2016.

4 "Paul Baran and the Origins of the Internet", http://www.rand.org/about/history/baran.html. Accessed January 25, 2016.

5 "The Birth of the Web", http://home.web.cern.ch/topics/birth-web. Accessed January 25, 2016.

6 "Definition of Internet", https://www.nitrd.gov/fnc/Internet_res.aspx. Accessed January 25, 2016.

7 https://ccdcoe.org/sites/default/files/multimedia/pdf/CS_organisation_HUNGARY_2015-10-12.pdf

8 Milton Mueller, "Are we in a Digital Cold War?" Paper presented on May 17, 2013, at the GigaNet workshop on The Global Governance of the Internet: Intergovernmentalism, Multistakeholderism and Networks, Graduate Institute, Geneva, Switzerland.

9 Château de Bossey, "Report of the Working Group on Internet Governance", June 2005, p.4.

10 Laura Denardis, *The Global War for Internet Governance* (Yale University Press, 2014), p. 7.

11 Sheila Jasanoff, *States of Knowledge: The Co-Production of Science and the Social Order* (Routledge, 2004), p. 3.

12 Ibid.

13 "C.2.9 of Contract between US Department of Commerce (DoC) and Internet Assigned Numbers Authority (IANA) dated Jul 02, 2012", http://www.ntia.doc.gov/files/ntia/publications/sf_26_pg_1-2-final_award_and_ sacs.pdf. Accessed January 30, 2016.

14 "Root Zone", http://icannwiki.com/index.php/Root_Zone. Accessed January 25, 2016.

15 Rekha Jain, *Model for Internet Governance and Implications for India* (Ahmedabad: Indian Institute of Management, W.P. No. 2015-03-23, March 2015), p. 31.

16 M. L. Mueller, *Networks and States: The Global Politics of Internet Governance* (Cambridge: MIT Press, 2010), p. 75.

17 "World Summit of the Information Society WSIS Action Lines Executive Summaries (Achievements, Challenges and Recommendations) WSIS+10 High-Level Event Geneva 2014",www.itu.int/wsis/review/ inc/docs/phase6/v/r /wsis10-5-3.pdf. Accessed January 25, 2016.

18 "Roadmaps for a Multilateral Decentralized Internet Governance ",http://content.netmundial.br/ contribution / roadmaps-for-a -multilateral-decentralized-internet-governance/217". Accessed January 25, 2016.

19 Ibid.

20 "Statement by Mr Vinay Kwatra, Indian representative at the Global Multistakeholder Meeting on the Future of Internet Governance in Sao Paulo (April 23-24, 2014)",http://mea.gov.in/Speeches-Statements.htm? dtl/23246/Statement by Mr Vinay Kwatra Indian representative in Sao Paulo April 23, 24 2014. Accessed January 25, 2016.

21 Ibid., p. 24.

22 Shalini Singh, "On Internet Rules, India now More Willing to say ICANN," *The Hindu*, October 13, 2012, http://www.thehindu.com/news/national/on-internet-rules-india-now-more-willing-to-say-icann/article3994985.ece. Accessed March 23, 2016.

23 Ibid.

24 Arun Chinmayi and Sarvjeet Singh, "Yes to Multi-Stakeholderism," *The Hindu*,July 20, 2015, http://www.thehindu.com/opinion/op-ed/on-multistakeholder-governance-of-the-internet/article7440857.ece. Accessed June 23, 2016.

25 Arun Mohan Sukumar , "India's New 'Multistakeholder' Line Could Be a Gamechanger in Global Cyberpolitics," *The Wire*, June 22, 2015. Accessed June 23, 2016.

26 Ibid.

27 "Administrator of Domain Name System Launches Global Multistakeholder Accountability Process", https://www.icann.org/resources/press-material/release-2014-03-14-en. Accessed January 28, 2016.

9

Offensive Potential of Cyber Attacks

The fundamental underpinning of the present-day conflicts is information and the outcome of any conflict is largely decided by the ability to generate, distribute and manipulate information with appropriate temporal and spatial relevance. Exchange of information facilitated through information technology, computers, networks and telecommunications is considered as the ontological keystone of war in any domain. The dynamism, sustainability, survivability and mission accomplishment of a functioning war-fighting entity is directly linked with reliable, secure, resilient and survivable information infrastructure. Many erudite discourses and lucid expositions have been made and a great deal of attention has been paid to the problem of how to defend information technology systems and networks against debilitating cyber attacks in both military and non-military contexts. However, the possibility of a sovereign state, leveraging and engaging its cyber assets and capabilities for perpetrating cyber attacks for the protection and furtherance of its national interest is rarely discussed in public. From a cyber warfare perspective, the dangers of cyber attack are so imminent across a multitude of national interests that the issue deserves a wide-ranging, robust and open debate to exploit all the tenets of the military, intelligence craft and international law, without prejudice or reservation.

The overarching dependence of many societal functions on information technology and the cyber infrastructure has made the growing challenges of defending cyber space against a multitude of threats emanating from various sources,a top national security priority. The national security and national interests of a sovereign nation are intricately linked and inextricably dependent upon its ability to maintain a strong cyber security posture, with proportionate emphasis on defensive strength and offensive capabilities. In other warfare domains, both defensive and offensive components add up and synergistically combine to provide comprehensive national security. The principle conventional military doctrinal exposition primarily focusses on the offence-defence balance that determines the relative efficacy of offensive and defensive security strategies. In the realm of cyber security, the primary focus of attention remains deeply skewed towards defence. As states become increasingly involved in cyber space for military purposes, the cyber domain has emerged as a critical component of the overall security paradigm.

Passive defensive measures in the cyber warfare context facilitate attainment of a strong defensive posture capable of thwarting a cyber attack. Nevertheless, these measures offer only enhanced deterrents, not fool-proof defence. An adversary pays no penalty for failed attacks and an attack needs to succeed only once out of numerous attempts to shatter the credibility of the passive defensive posturing. This defensive posture often weighs down heavily on overall preparedness and results in an asymmetric disadvantage. This bring to the fore the question of exploring other approaches which might bolster the defensive posture. One approach advocates elimination or degradation of an adversary's ability to successfully prosecute an attack. In that case, the severity of a malevolent cyber attack perpetrated by an adversary would be much diminished,because of taking a lot of wind out of the sails of the attack as a consequence of lost or degraded capabilities. An equally effective possibility would be to make the costs of undertaking a cyber attack so prohibitive and overwhelmingly deleterious that they far exceed the expected gains from the attack. Cyber attacks will be inhibited or deterred because of the threat of punitive reprisal and if a deterrent threat is created before the cyber attack is even contemplated,[1] the motivation, severity, magnitude and frequency of cyber attacks will be much more diminished even when undertaken by a determined and capable adversary. In general, there are many options for imposing costs on an adversary, including economic penalties such as sanctions, diplomatic penalties like snapping of diplomatic relations and even kinetic military action. In-kind military action—a counter-cyber-attack—is also a possibility.[2] The initiation of these possible actions can be construed as part of the 'active defence strategy'. But some of the actions undertaken in the realm of active defence are often captured under the rubric of offensive acts.[3] The limitations of passive defence necessitate consideration of evaluating attack options for defensive purposes. An acquired attack capability bolsters an active cyber defence posture with the possibility to use this for other non-defensive purposes. Attack capabilities also give teeth to the nation's credible deterrence posture.

Strategic and Political Dimensions of Cyber Attacks

Cyber attacks are increasingly being used as instruments and agents of conflict enunciation, resolution and reconciliation, both as independent entities and in conjunction with broader military operations. The effects and implications of such attacks on variegated targets may be large or small, ephemeral or permanent; cyber attacks have shut down networks, cut off access to essential information and services, damaged industrial infrastructure and disrupted banking services. Even if the needle of suspicion points to state-sponsorship of cyber attacks, the relative anonymity under which actors operate in cyber space makes definite attribution a distant possibility. This highlights the importance of a measured and nuanced professional debate on this unequivocally important issue and interweaving the tenets of offensive cyber attacks into the concept of operations.

- **Empirically Supported and Efficaciously Applicable National Policy on Cyber Attacks:** The nation should have a declaratory policy on the use of cyber space for offensive cyber operations. A befitting analogy that highlights the veracity of public discourse on the 'potential of cyber attacks' was the debate during the initial enunciation of India's nuclear doctrine. Initially, a shroud of secrecy was drawn over all nuclear policy issues, preventing an animated public debate about them. However, some of the seminal works undertaken by prominent thinkers mobilised public opinion and their subsequent incisive work outside the precinct of government organisations had a real impact in the formulation of nuclear doctrine. The potential relevance of cyber attacks across the whole spectrum of national interests in both war and non-war situations makes it imperative to constitute a study committee, mandated to closely examine various aspects of cyber attacks, factoring in perspectives from members from diverse backgrounds. The amalgam of expertise of domain practitioners with acquired domain-specific competence through experience will fructify in the emergence of a national policy on 'cyber attacks', capable of addressing, and responding to, issues from a national security perspective. The study committee may provide guidelines for the setting up of an organisational framework for planning, managing and evaluating offensive cyber capabilities. Based on the dynamic and qualitative assessment of acquired capabilities and evaluation of their 'deterrence quotient' against present, potential and perceived threats, the committee may decide the quantum and extent of the offensive cyber operations after identifying situations warranting such use.

A comprehensive policy framework in this area will enable various stakeholders to weigh the accrued advantages vis-à-vis the risk potentiality of cyber attacks in their concepts of operations and will *establish functioning guidelines*, operational precincts and appropriate yardsticks. An overarching policy framework will guide the armed forces, intelligence agencies and others in a domain which still is not adequately governed by national and international laws. The existing laws are ambiguous in expression and lend themselves to idiosyncratic interpretations, leading to fragmented understanding of the impacts and ramifications of cyber attacks across the whole range of national issues.

- **National Decision-Making Apparatus with Strategic Priorities for Offensive Cyber Operations:** The establishment of an informed, clear and inclusive decision-making structure capable of deciding on the quantum, timing and risks associated with the perpetration of a cyber attack will accelerate the decision-making process due to the enhanced overall effectiveness and contextual relevance of *actionable decisions.* The decision-makers should include, or, at least, ensure consultations with, all stakeholders who might directly or indirectly be involved and affected by the use of a cyber weapon. The decision to undertake a cyber attack should be made after weighing the various military, diplomatic and economic compulsions. For example, if the stakes are high enough to justify the associated risk, the use of a preemptive cyber attack will amount to a *well-thought out and timely* action.

  As such, in the military realm, preventive measures taken to mitigate hostile actions against own resources, personnel, facilities and critical information are the standing rules of engagement. However, if a cyber attack, conclusively, presumptively or speculatively, appears to be emanating from a known adversary, a response action may lead to escalation, especially if the incident occurs during times of strained relations and the effects of retaliatory cyber attacks post execution far exceed the effects anticipated during the planning phase. For such reasons, the decision to launch a cyber attack should be taken after weighing the various equities (military, diplomatic, economic) by the appropriate competent authorities.
- **Support to the Enactment of International Laws/Treaties with Enforceable Mechanisms:** The understanding of key issues on cyber attacks among most of the nations has yet to reach a level that can address a broad range of related issues. The far-reaching manifestations and consequences of cyber attacks will only grow in severity and invasiveness, with the potential to cause financial

crisis, social upheaval and political instability. Enacting laws with enforceable mechanisms and creating international standards or rules for abidance by all states may rein in the malevolent use of cyber attacks. The efforts in this direction will evoke a common understanding for policy formulation and quantification of the degree of international outrage consequent to a cyber attack. This will foster better coordination and information sharing and will avoid misunderstandings. At the very least, it will help in developing mechanisms for coordinating cyber attacks to avoid collateral and unintended consequences. It is equally important to engage with ambiguous and perfidious allies as well as with existential and conceivable adversaries on these issues. Though such consultations could prove be inconclusive, contentious or politically fraught,these would at least help in mutual understanding of the stakes involved and the expectations from their perspectives.

- **Acquisition, Maintenance and Consolidation of Effective Cyber Attack Capabilities:**[4] The nation must have credible, potent and flexible cyber attack technologies at its disposal with the requisite intent to wage a cyber war. The methodologies should be consistent with the potentiality of the situation with the necessary command and control. The type, quantum and period of cyber attacks should be based on intelligence garnered through various sources with assured mission success and minimum collateral damage. Such capabilities, while providing operational advantages also act as a credible deterrent against cyber adversaries.
- **Extent, Causes and Consequences of Cyber Attacks:** The cyber attacks, in the realm of cyber warfare have been relegated to footnotes rather than being incorporated and assimilated into the main narrative, thereby denying a template to base a conceptual framework. It is difficult to categorise some activities as constituting a cyber attack and their subsequent quantification of damage or harm in definite terms of economic loss, losses of

strategic assets, disruption of critical information infrastructures or the suffering of civilians. The losses as a result of cyber attacks can reasonably be construed as a threat to national security. Some of the consequences after a cyber attack may constitute a "use of force" and an "armed attack"and can invoke a state's right to use force in self-defence.

- **Severity, Extent, and Duration of Planned Cyber Attack to be in Conformity with Moral and Ethical Standards:**[5] The laws of armed conflict governing cyber attacks, both *jus in bello* (the law of armed conflict) and *jus ad bellum* (the set of rules to be consulted before engaging in war), should have moral and ethical underpinnings even when cyber weapons are used covertly. The computers and networks that make up cyber space are so intricately linked and inextricably interconnected that, if attacked, infiltrated or blocked, as part of strategic or tactical moves, may have far-reaching spillover effects on the people, establishments and institutions that are likely to enjoy immunity in a conventional war. The basic rule of the law of armed conflict that "during war between similarly matched armies, civilians and other noncombatants enjoy immunity from direct or intentional harm"[6] needs to be followed in the case of cyber attacks also. Even during war, adherence to established ethical benchmarks in the context of cyber attacks, though difficult, will provide the moral compass for guiding actions righteously.
- **Creating a Pool of Trained Personnel with the Requisite Skills:** Understanding of strategic, conceptual and operational complexities associated with cyber conflict requires specialised expertise in operations, intelligence and technology. Similarly, policy understanding and formulation related to cyber attacks requires integration of domain experts from the defence, industry, academic, diplomatic, intelligence and corporate communities. For planning and execution of cyber attacks to achieve the intended results, an involved workforce rigorously trained, with a high premium placed on professionalism, is a mandatory prerequisite.

These needs are in consonance with the history of how cyber attacks have evolved: from being innocuous endeavours to pernicious enterprises. The personal computers and later the World Wide Web are at the forefront of the information technology revolution ubiquitously impacting the way sectors of society, including the military, interact, engage and operate. The notion of attacking an adversary's networks and computers as an instrument of warfare is burgeoning and growing, with the senior military leadership embracing the potential of such possibilities seriously. Against this backdrop, the full realisation of the challenges, opportunities and consequences of cyber attacks need to be understood by the entire spectrum of personnel involved. Because cyber conflicts are interdisciplinary in nature, a comprehensive and integrated human capital development programme focussed on establishing cross-linkages between different entities, promoting cross-fertilisation of ideas and furthering cross-disciplinary interactions, will be able to meet the variegated challenges of cyber attacks.

Technical and Operational Considerations in Cyber Attacks

The complexity, implications and nuances of cyber attacks cannot be captured within a simple formal definition. Activities in cyber space do not have a comparable template vis-a-vis principles that govern armed conflict under the conventional laws of war. Analysis of the potential consequences of a cyber attack has yet to emerge in definitive form from speculative accounts. The US National Research Council defines cyber attacks as "deliberate actions to alter, disrupt, deceive, degrade, or destroy computer systems or networks or the information and/or programs resident in, or transiting, these systems or networks."[7]

The Shanghai Cooperation Organisation (SCO), a security cooperation group which includes India as an observer, has adopted a much more expansive means-based approach to cyber attacks. The organisation has "express[ed] concern about the threats posed by possible use of [new information and communication] technologies and means for the purposes [*sic*] incompatible with ensuring international security and stability in both civil and military spheres."[8] It defines an "information war" as "mass psychologic[al] brainwashing to destabilise the society and state, as well as to force the state to take decisions in the interest of an opposing party."

The approach towards the use of cyber weapons in an offensive role needs to be goal-based rather than means-based. The emphasis needs to be on the results and their significance. In cases, where methods become a priority over results, the unbounded ramifications may be calamitous. A goal-based approach requires capabilities across the spectrum of present, potential and perceived threats, and not on a limited number of threats. Depending upon the intent, opportunities and envisaged results, the corresponding capability suitable for achieving the objective with minimum collateral damage may be used. Any of the means—hacking, logical bombing, malware infection, forceful intrusion and advance persistent attack—can be leveraged for perpetuating cyber attacks to undermine, disrupt or destroy the adversary's cyber assets or use them as a conduit to attack dependent physical assets. The means and weapons for carrying out cyber attacks have the following distinct characteristics:

- **Incidental and Collateral Effects of Cyber Attacks are Indiscriminatory and Unpredictable:**[9] A cyber attack targeting a particular computer system or network, in addition to causing system specific degradation, causes indirect or follow-on effects on interdependent systems and devices and on the people who depend on these for numerous societal functions and sustenance needs. Cyber attacks in effect neither satisfy the 'principle of proportionality' nor are in conformity with the 'principle of discrimination'. The cascading and spillover effects, consequent to a cyber attack, will be unpredictable and unquantifiable and may be well above the planned and intended objective.
- **Post Cyber Attack, Effects Quantification is Uncertain due to Complex Determinative Mechanisms:** The outcomes post cyber attacks are often highly uncertain as cascading effects rapidly cut across societal sectors, critical infrastructures and vital institutes,

causing disruption across a wide array of domains. The incidental and collateral damage may far exceed the intended effects. A holistic assessment of a cyber attack across the whole spectrum of infrastructure and operations will be challenging due to the risk of uncertain and unforeseeable consequences. In some cases, the results will be tangible and immediate; in others, they will be more subtle, with long gestation period before their manifestations.

- **Cyber Attack Planning is Often Associated with Obliquity and Complexity:** An offensive cyber attack carried out against a chosen military, economic or societal target, in addition to interrupting, destroying, or limiting the capabilities of the primary target, may also try to elicit and exploit effects on interdependent secondary targets. It makes the pre-attack prediction and evaluation of outcomes an extremely arduous and subjective task. The temporal scales of a cyber attack may stretch from a few seconds to years and the spatial ranges may be anywhere from the immediate neighbourhood to distant places.
- **Identification, Acquisition Maintenance and Consolidation of Cyber Attack Capabilities:** In the military domain, identification and acquisition of effective capabilities to dissuade, deter or defeat potential adversaries and existential enemies is a fundamental and crucial necessity for offence and defence. On assimilation of the newly acquired capability into the 'Concept of Operations' (CONOPS), this needs to be seamlessly dovetailed with existing capabilities to bring in a significant enhancement in the overall operational efficiency and capability. For preserving its operational viability, potentiality and potency, comprehensive and constantly evolving maintenance support is also a prerequisite. For acquisition of cyber attack capabilities, a thorough analysis of potential targets, their strengths and vulnerabilities, weapon-to-target ratio, possible retaliatory response, collateral and spillover effects, and the time and duration of attack will fructify in making congruent qualitative

and quantitative projections. The technical sophistication required to develop a potent and credible cyber attack capability is present and is only limited by resources and motivation. A cyber weapon, once developed and added to the repository of other cyber weapons ready for deployment needs to be constantly evaluated, updated and improved to ensure its effectiveness and potency, if employed.

- **The Problem of Attributability and Accountability Associated with Cyber Attacks:** The perpetrators of a cyber attack can conceal their true identity behind the 'technological fog' and 'digital thicket'.Besides, the follow-up process to assign attributability and establish accountability to an organisation, group or individual is marred by unfathomable complexities specific to cyber space. Cyber attacks are often called bloodless, non-violent attacks, in stark contrast to kinetic attacks which are invariably accompanied with high visibility explosions, violence and body counts. However, cyber weapons have an undeniable capacity to achieve kinetic effects,when used by a determined adversary with the requisite technical sophistication and unwavering intent. By exploiting vulnerabilities in the information systems and processes, cyber attacks can cause direct, incidental or collateral physical damage, injury or death.

Comparison of Key Characteristics of Cyber Attack and Kinetic Attack[10]

The use of a weapon of any kind is for the attainment of a strategic, tactical or operational objective over an adversary by disrupting, damaging, destroying or disabling some of his capability. The effects elicited by the action of a weapon system on an adversary can be direct or indirect, with perceptible gains in terms of asserting dominance, forcing behavioural changes or diminishing belligerent posturing. Weapons are largely perceived as military solutions to belligerent, contentious and complex problems. In the case of kinetic weapons, the immediate targets bear the brunt of the devastation, while other physical entities as follow-up consequences, experience indirect effects such as temporary or permanent disruption, disablement, dislocation or destruction. Cyber attacks are easy to conduct with plausible deniability and are reasonably suited for being instruments of conflict enunciation and resolution. A significant cyber attack can be concealed with relative ease, compared to a kinetic attack. The exponential proliferation of Information and Communications Technology (ICT) devices has expanded the list of possible targets. An assessment of the multivariate characteristics of a cyber attack versus a kinetic attack provides a comparative understanding.

- **Quantum and Significance of Attack:** Kinetic attacks largely rely of achieving physical destruction, decimation, death and injury with high visibility and conspicuousness. 'Shock and awe' is considered as one of the main objectives of a successful kinetic attack. The indirect effects resulting from a cyber attack are not significantly factored in the overall objective. Cyber attacks try to elicit maximum efficacy by relying on indirect effects as follow-up consequences of an attack on an information system or network.
- **Consequences of Attack:** The recovery and reconstruction process post a kinetic attack may be time-consuming and resource-intensive and, in some cases, even irreversible. Cyber attacks have limited effects on physical entities and are often targeted against peripherally located assets as core assets are generally well secured and protected with firewalls, encryption/authentication algorithms and need-based access. The restoration, consequent to a cyber attack, is relatively less time consuming and the effects may be reversed depending upon the consequential manifestations of damage.
- **Associated R&D and Acquisition Costs:** The R&D and acquisition costs and costs of operation of a kinetic weapon system are high relative to the cyber weapons. Besides, the cyber weapons can be designed, tested and used within the close confines of a work station without elaborate infrastructure spread over a large area,

teeming with skilled and unskilled labour and resources. The low entry cost of acquisition of cyber weapons acts as a catalyst for states and terrorist groups, inimical to the sovereignty and integrity of the country, to acquire these with relative ease.

- **Technical Knowhow and Systems Required:** The technical knowhow to develop effective cyber weapons is readily available and the new crop of developers entering the arena for monetary gains and notoriety make it possible to stockpile cyber weapons with ease, away from the prying eyes of international observers.

Offence/Defence Balance in Cyber Space

In strategic thinking and planning, the 'Offence-Defence Balance' (ODB) is a major determinant of the relative efficacy of offensive and defensive security posturing. The tipping of balance of one of the two, the theory suggests, affects the patterns of international relations and foreign policy. The offence-defence theory contends that international conflict and war are more likely when offence has the advantage, while peace and cooperation are more probable when defence has the advantage.[11]When it is believed by one side that its offensive capabilities *far exceed* the other side's *defensive capabilities*, it will be tempted to perpetrate preemptive attacks. On the other hand, when defence is easier than offence, states are more likely to mutually cooperate, embark on confidence-building measures and even take initiatives toward slackening of the pace of arms race.

Heuristically, the viability of the 'offence-defence balance' focusses on identifying important causal variables that are contemporaneous and modifiable. Military prowess alone, however, does not usually suffice as a variable, capable of securing lasting peace.[12]For practical purposes, the major issue with the ODB theory is how to measure this balance. While assessing the ODB in cyber space, one is compelled to accommodate the peculiarities and idiosyncrasies of cyber space. The existence of cyber space in the real and virtual realms populated by the real and amorphous mass of faceless individuals, makes it a peculiar battlefield. Secondly, and equally peculiar, is the centrality of the Internet for both military and non-military actors. While there are differences between civilian and military networks, they mostly use the same hardware and software. In cyber space, the main objective of an offensive action is not to seize and control a geographical entity but to compromise/deplete the effectiveness of a system or network.

The seemingly exponentially growing spate of cyber attacks and resulting multidimensional losses have led to a movement among strategists towards creating a deterrent factor embodied in the use of "counter-offensive strategies".[13] These mechanisms encompass a range of activities that go beyond active cyber defence. Several analysts have succinctly compared the deterrent offered by offensive technologies to the nuclear deterrent. In the early stages of the nuclear era, an attacker with a monopolistic hold on nuclear technology could annihilate an opponent without fear of reprisal. It is worth reiterating that India's nuclear doctrine is based on the notion of 'massive retaliation' to a first strike designed to inflict 'unacceptable damage'. During the period of the Cold War, when the Soviet Union developed its own nuclear capabilities in response to America's burgeoning nuclear arsenal, the dynamics of the world order changed. Attacks could now be made remotely and destruction on a scale unparalleled in human history would surely occur soon after the initiation of the attack. The defensive mechanisms, which evolved against a nuclear attack, were either untested or speculative. The realisation of this new reality motivated the formulation of the MAD strategy. The threat of mutual obliteration emerged as a strong deterrent, reining in the war-mongering stance of both superpowers.

There are a few striking commonalities between cyber warfare and nuclear warfare. Like nuclear warfare, cyber warfare is of an asymmetric nature, with no conventional battlefield and no fool-proof mechanism for protection of targets. To make deterrent threats credible and credible threats with strong deterrent effect, in both cases, the defenders need to respond within a very limited period of time. In the case of cyber warfare, if a response is not initiated almost immediately, the traces of the attack will be lost and the attacker will disappear in an apparently fathomless labyrinth of cyber space, and remain untraceable. For an effective deterrence posture, it must be communicated to the adversaries in no uncertain terms that the costs of the attack would be prohibitively high and reprisals would be swift and severe.

Possible Objectives of Cyber Attacks[14]

Whether a cyber attack is conducted as part of an offensive strategy or an active defence measure, attainment of some objectives in sync with the overall strategy, the possessed capabilities and the envisaged degree of severity, are central to their orchestration. In the larger context of warfare, some types of warfare are characterised by the 'employed means', which, in most cases, happens to be a weapon. For example, in the case of nuclear warfare, the 'employed means' would be a nuclear weapon. Other types of warfare focus on the 'objective' in the form of a target-based approach for neutralisation. In the means-based approach, the result is an outcome of a specific weapon's capability, lethality, and survivability. In the objective-based approach, the objective accomplishment by any means at disposal is the priority. In the context of cyber warfare, an objective-based approach *captures its nuances* and complexities more fittingly than the means-based approach.[15] The orchestration of cyber attacks is invariably linked to the attainment of objectives in furtherance or pursuance of some military, political or economic goals.

- **Manipulation Through Information Exploitation:**[16] In the present scenario, our society can be termed as an ubiquitously interconnected information society in which the creation, distribution and manipulation of information have become the most significant drivers for most societal activities. In an information society, the social, political and economic underpinnings are primarily exchange of information facilitated through information technology, computers, networks and telecommunications. The inclusive growth, continuity and dynamism of the information society are directly linked with a reliable, secure, resilient and survivable information infrastructure. In effect, securing information has become a major challenge for national security. Cyber attacks directed against critical information systems for stealing, altering, modifying or deleting crucial information will undermine the adversary's capability to respond to threats across a broad spectrum of military, economic and political contingencies.

- **Cyber Attacks in Conjunction with Kinetic Attacks:**[17] Cyber-attacks may be carried out in conjunction with, or as an adjunct to, a conventional kinetic armed attack intended to maximise the cumulative war-waging efforts for neutralisation of the adversary's defensive and command and control systems.[18] A potent cyber attack can create widespread pandemonium and confusion in the rank and file of the enemy, disrupting command, demoralising forces and taking the wind out of the sails of the war efforts. The state of disarray is exacerbated manifold when cyber attacks are used in conjunction with a kinetic attack.
- **Destroying Data on a Network or a System Connected to the Network:**[19] A cyber attack might be conducted to delete and permanently erase data files or to wipe clean all memory storage devices that it can find. Moreover, destruction of a network will have an adverse cascading effect on other interdependent systems connected to it. For example, power generation facilities controlled and operated by a network will come to a grinding halt if the controlling network is disabled.
- **Donning the Guise of a Bona Fide User for Propagating Spurious Information:**[20] A cyber attacker might masquerade as a senior official or agency head and issue bogus orders or pass faked intelligence information. This virtual impersonation of someone who calls the shots and is on the high rung of the hierarchical ladder, will facilitate a cyber attacker to take over the control of a trusted machine. By obtaining the authentication and encryption keys, the malicious activities will be interpreted as legitimate to other machines/persons.

- **Clandestine Data Manipulation in Data Repository.**[21] The military relies on detailed planning, resource management and allocation of tasks to achieve its objectives. The central repository for such information in the form of data is used in the entire course of the operation. For example, the logistical support to the armed forces, such as deployment of weapons, replenishment of ammunition, repairing of weapon systems and delivery platforms or the management of complex technological systems, is driven by data manipulation that apportions responsibilities, manages spares and produces coherent and appropriate sequences of tasks. A corrupted database may compromise the intended effectiveness or efficiency of the mission.
- **Degradation and Denial of Service on a Network:**[22] A cyber attacker might try to degrade the quality of services available to network users by overwhelming communications channels with a huge influx of bogus traffic. A cyber attacker with the intent to degrade the quality of service may overwhelm the communications channels with a huge influx of bogus traffic. A denial-of-service attack on a network controlling factory floor operations and other interconnected activities might shut it down. By taking control of a telecommunications exchange, a cyber attacker may acquire the ability to wreak havoc with the functioning of an organisation with anomalous calls and wrong or random cross-connections. A denial-of-service attack on a communication system might force an adversary to resert to the use of a less secure method which could fall easy prey to cyber exploitation.
- **Wresting Control of a Network to Modify Interconnects, Services or Privileges:**[23] An attacker might wrest control of an Internet service provider in an adversary nation and, depending upon its strategic objectives, deny or curtail services and privileges to the extent as deemed essential for mission success. By intentionally and clandestinely limiting the bandwidth to key users, the transmission of large files (e.g., images or video)

would be made agonisingly slow to rob them off their real-time relevance. Delays in transmission might cause time lags between decision-making and communication of decisions to the forces for tactical action, thereby missing important deadlines.

Attacks on Cyber Physical Systems

The inextricable conjoining and interdependent interplay between the cyber domain and physical resources has accelerated the convergence and integration of computer systems with the physical realm over a wide spectrum of industrial and military endeavours. The economic and societal potential of such systems is vastly greater than what has been realised and major investments are being made worldwide to develop the technology.[24] The Cyber Physical Systems (CPS)technologies are ubiquitously used in devices, systems and sectors including critical infrastructure control systems, defence systems, avionics, automotive systems, medical devices, automotive systems, industrial processes and research laboratories. The use of CPS is only limited by the innovation of the technology and by the demand, willingness and acceptance on the part of users or consumers. It is not difficult to envision a future in which the cyber systems will be used with such prolificacy that they will permeate, and proliferate into, all the societal, industrial and military domains. Unfortunately, unbridled proliferation of CPS will also act as a catalyst for an unrelenting creation of,and inexorable search for, new vulnerabilities. While, the possibility of widespread mayhem and apocalyptic destruction through cyber attacks targeted at CPS, which have been vividly and convincingly conjured up by so many screen writers and novelists, currently appears far-fetched, the possibility of physical damage,superficial or grievous injury and intentional death through the exploitation of vulnerabilities in information systems, either inherent or introduced, is no longer an imaginary threat. In the past, a number of cyber attacks have caused physical damage to physical entities, disrupted physical systems and sabotaged physical processes.

Kinetic cyber attacks, on the one hand, are a menacing and growing threat to national and international security. On the other, they offer an opportunity to be exploited by the interweaving of their transformative potential with the doctrinal framework of offensive cyber operations. Cyber attacks do not fit neatly into the conventional paradigm of warfare in terms of violence, death and destruction. Nonetheless, the effects consequent to a cyber attack on a CPS can be comparable to an actual kinetic attack causing intentional, incidental or collateral damage to physical resources and claiming human lives as casualties. In 2010, Iran faced the full wrath of a kinetic cyber weapon when the 'Stuxnet' worm ravaged its Natanz nuclear facility. Though not as spectacular as the Stuxnet, the example of numerous other cyber attacks, with varying success, has unwittingly compelled many states to throw their hats into the ring, ushering in a new and more insidious phase of an already diabolical cyber arms race. In October 2011, the discovery of the 'DuQu', which shared a similar code as that of the Stuxnet but differed in functionality, jolted the security agencies across the world. It was designed to clandestinely acquire information about the industrial control systems for planning and executing potential future attacks.[25] In June 2012, it was reported that the Iranian oil industry had been a victim of a sinister malware, 'Flame', which, while masquerading as an innocuous and routine Microsoft software update, penetrated the computers of senior Iranian officials and allegedly stole a treasure trove of sensitive data in preparation of a cyber attack.[26]

Cyber physical attacks aimed at severing the interactions between cyber and physical components within a CPS have been used many times. Conversely, it is also possible to cause disruption, incapacitation or destruction of cyber assets by carrying out attacks on physical assets and infrastructures. Computers and network devices connected to one another, using common protocols for exchange of data, are the building blocks of cyber space. These devices themselves are physical objects, with inherent vulnerabilities similar to those associated with other physical assets. In effect, both cyber and kinetic attacks can be used against cyber and physical assets and the choice is largely determined by the possessed capability, the target's vulnerabilities and the ability to absorb a retaliatory blow.

Cyber Attacks as Force Multipliers for Military Operations

Today, military operations have become much more complex, geographically dispersed and often represent lightning temporal and spatial transitions from minor skirmishes to full campaigns. Against this backdrop, defence policy-makers have to tackle challenges which have substantial contextual differences from those of the past. Even if a single, large military engagement may seem a distant possibility, the potential for multiple and disparate operations of varying intensities calls for capacity building that entails bolstering numerous tangible and intangible military resources. There is also a need for putting in place mechanisms and corresponding tools across the diplomatic and military space to respond to challenges arising from rogue states, state sponsored terrorist organisations and radical religious groups. Traditional military systems will have to continuously evolve and redefine their roles for meeting the challenges of the future. Compressed timelines, an amorphous mass of enemies, a high tempo of operations, and a remote and unfamiliar battlefield are leading to the development of highly specialised niche platforms and military systems.

Cyber attacks are endowed with some attributes that are well aligned to this evolving threat landscape. From a life-cycle cost perspective, though cyber weapons have comparable research and development costs, the production and deployment costs of cyber weapons are relatively low. A cyber attack can be applied across a wide gamut of military activities, either as a stand-alone system or integrated into information operations. In addition, missions outside the realm of military prowess may also be successfully accomplished by using cyber exploitation.

- **Cyber Attacks in Support of Defence and Other Information Operations:**[27] Offensive cyber capabilities, as a preemptive weapon, have the potential to neutralise an eminent threat emanating from a belligerent adversary. Some nations, including the US, have declared cyber attacks as acts of war due to the increasing realisation that the measures of functionality and severity consequent to a cyber attack are comparable to those of kinetic attacks. Even so, the problem of traceability, attributability and accountability makes cyber attacks a more lucrative and preferred option in comparison to kinetic attacks.

- **Psychological Operations:**[28]A cyber attack designed to inundate adversary decision-makers with bogus e-mail messages or insinuating telephone calls could disrupt their cohesion and derail their decision-making process. The contents of e-mail messages may include disturbing and incriminating information in order to create distrust, disharmony or dissension among members of the organisation. Fanning the fear psychosis with threats of public exposure of aberrant behavioural traits may force some decision-makers to tweak or modify their decisions. Another way of leveraging Psychological Operations (PSYOPs) is by launching a small and easily manipulated cyber attack with a very high degree of visibility with the intent to undermine the adversary's confidence in its systems and networks.
- **Military Deception and Operations Security:**[29]Cyber attacks can be used against specific adversary sensor systems with an aim to either render it inoperative or to flood it with fabricated information to manipulate the adversary's decision-making capabilities to elicit decisions and actions that can be accurately anticipated or favour own operational plans. Cyber attacks directed against the command and control centres of an adversary may render it incapacitated of taking viable operational decisions. While injecting misinformation regarding capabilities, intentions, force deployments and favourable courses of action of friendly forces may undermine the adversary's war-fighting efforts.
- **Electronic Warfare:** The ubiquitous proliferation of software-defined and hardware-dependent devices such as radio

communication, radars, satellite links has added vulnerabilities that were non-existent just a few short years ago. Cyber attacks against an adversary's software-defined radios may degrade wireless battlefield communications, air defence radars and other systems. In fact, EW capabilities could be leveraged to support cyber attacks. For example, the computer systems connected through wireless links may be rendered useless if these links are jammed using EW capabilities. In effect, jamming may be construed as a denial-of-service cyber attack against such networks.

- **Cyber Attacks Augmenting Traditional Military Operations:**[30] Cyber attacks could also be used to augment a variety of military operations. Targeting Command, Control and Communications (C3) with cyber attacks will diminish the ability of an adversary to manage and dominate the battlefield, achieve the requisite degree of situational awareness and exploit information for operational missions. By using cyber attacks to invoke denial of service, render communication links unusable,impersonate high ranking decision-makers or spoof the identity of a legitimate device, the adversary's planning could be disrupted or altered. With severed tactical links, the forces in the field will be deprived of operational guidance and direction from the higher command authority. Secondly, in air defence operations, monitoring and lateral sharing of information are the core elements of mission accomplishment. The air defence systems are made up of a set of sensors and a set of kill vehicles, collectively called a weapon system. A networked air defence system uses sensors to detect incoming targets and the information is communicated to kill vehicles for the destruction of targets. Disruption of communication links for information sharing in real-time can considerably degrade the performance of the overall system. With the clandestine insertion of spurious signals and the adversary's total incomprehension, the adversary may be led to believe that the distorted air picture is the true picture of an unfolding situation. Thirdly, spurred by technological advancement, the so-called dumb munitions have been transformed into sophisticated smart munitions, with enhanced lethality, precision, stealth and sustainability. The on-board sensors of smart munitions are linked with computers which in real-time guide these munitions through the course of their flight for the most efficient way of engagement and subsequent damage. To guard against such munitions, a cyber attack targeting on-board programmable circuit boards and ground computers for in-flight control of smart munitions may degrade their precision strike capabilities.

Cyber Jurisprudence to Tackle Emerging Issues

Article 51 of Chapter VII of the United Nations Charter acknowledges the inherent right of individual or collective self-defence against an armed attack. [31] It is pertinent to dwell at some length on the issue of an armed attack, especially in the context of cyber space and its consequential effects on national interests. The *Webster's Dictionary* defines weapons as "as an instrument of offensive or defensive combat; something to fight with; anything used, or designed to be used, in destroying, defeating, or injuring an enemy, as a gun, a sword, etc."[32] The weapons achieve their intended goals through the perpetration of particular damage, destruction or injury commensurate with their functionality and lethality. Although the essence of the purpose and functionality of traditional weapons might be captured under the rubric of kinetic warfare, it remains empirically inadequate for capturing the idiosyncratic nature of cyber warfare. A cyber weapon may be used to achieve objectives which may, or may not, be measured against, or compared with, outcomes listed in the definition. The term 'cyber attack' has been used generically to refer to activities ranging from penetration of a network, insertion of malicious codes, implantation of software Trojans, stealing of information, unauthorised downloading of sensitive contents or disrupting the services provided by these networks, with a focus upon the consequential impacts without any inquiry into the legality or the ethicality of these acts. It is the consequence and effect of a cyber attack that determines whether or not the act is in contravention to, or compliance with, the laws of armed conflict. It is both the offensive capability of the malicious code and the intended outcome or effect produced by that code that transforms it into a weapon that would be governed, as with any conventional weapon, by the law of armed conflict.[33]

To encapsulate the belligerent acts committed in cyber space within the definition of "threat or use of force" is not easy. The phrase "threat or use of force," has been used in Article 2(4) of United Nations (UN) Charter which states, "All Members shall refrain in their international relations from the threat or use of force against the territorial integrity or political independence of any state."[34] The logical entailments and empirical evidences require that the international legal norms and the laws of armed conflict,either customary or treaty-based, which apply to the other domains, are applied to activities in the cyber domain. A determination of what is a "threat or use of force" in cyber space needs to be made in the contextual backdrop that led to the occurrence of the event, the purpose of the action in question and its consequences on national interests. In the face of compelling evidence that a particular cyber attack has been perpetrated in conjunction with, or as an adjunct to, a larger military operation and its political and/or military attribution to malevolent intents, a state may invoke its inherent right to self-defence.

The international laws have been articulated to provide a rationale for waging war for legitimate and righteous purposes. The *jus ad bellum* (the set of rules to be consulted before engaging in war) defines the rightful reasons for use of force by states focussing on fulfilling certain criteria that legitimise the war as "just and necessary". In the context of cyber space, the key question is whether a cyber attack constitutes a use of force or an armed attack, invoking the inherent right to self-defence. Governing the belligerent cyber attacks under such rules proves difficult because of the enunciation of these rules in the context of domains without any overlapping linkages with cyber space. For example, the lack of consensus in determining whether or not the 'Stuxnet attack' was an "armed attack" or "use of force" brings to the fore the various issues and problems that emanate from subjective interpretations of various provisions of the UN Charter. The interpretation may differ, as the same event, depending upon the interpreters' perspective and interest, could be termed as an armed attack, an unlawful intervention without the use of force or the use of force not amounting to an armed attack. [35]

Conclusion

Warfare is no longer a sum total of capabilities of putting more personnel, capital and technology on the battlefield, but of better situational awareness, contextual knowledge, discerning disposition and homogenised actions. The technological breakthroughs have profoundly altered and shaped the doctrinal, organisational and strategic contours of warfare. Information technology has revolutionised the way the warfare is conducted. Once made up of solely mechanical and electrical parts, military hardware now comprises complex systems, evolved through a combination of various components and functionalities of sensors, microchips, microprocessors, hardware, software, data storage and connectivity in a myriad ways. These "smart, connected products", bolstered by advancements and improvements in processing power, device miniaturisation and by ubiquitous wireless connectivity have put warfare on the cusp of an epochal shift from the conventional to an information-based virtual age. Embedded sensors, intelligent processors, sophisticated software and seamless connectivity in these products, coupled with data analysis and algorithmically induced decision-making capabilities, are driving unfathomable improvements in product functionality and performance. This wave of cyber-driven transformation is radical, sweeping and innovating, demanding a relook at the established strategic plan and direction for operational enhancements and improved tactical efficiency. Cyber space and cyber systems offer a whole new set of technological solutions to some of the challenges of modern warfare.

The policy and organisational issues which need to be tackled in the wake of acquisition and use of cyber attack capabilities have strong and integrated linkages across the whole spectrum of conflict, from all-out war to small skirmishes to situations below the armed conflict threshold. Outcomes of cyber attacks can vary across an enormous range and they can affect military, intelligence, diplomatic, economic and law enforcement equities.[36]The acquired capabilities to wage offensive operations in cyber space greatly expand the list of options available to policy-makers and practitioners of warfare. A major issue which hinders all aspects of policy formulation for offensive cyber attacks is the collateral nature of effects consequent to a cyber attack which may be unintentional, incident direct or indirect. Although, during cyber attacks, computer systems and networks are primarily targeted, the consequential effects on other systems due to interdependence significantly influences other entities such as people, critical infrastructure, banking, machinery, etc. The consequences of cyber attacks may vary in severity, lethality, intent or geographic distribution and can manifest in complex, dynamic and unpredictable ways, having far-reaching tactical and strategic implications. Nevertheless, the absence of an appropriate publicly stated policy framework for guiding and regulating their use has further exacerbated the complexities involved in the possible use of cyber attacks in support of national interests.

Notes

1 Robert J. Art and Kelly M. Greenhill, *The Use of Force: Military Power and International Politics* (Lanham: Rowman & Littlefield,2009), p.25.

2 William A. Owens, Kenneth W. Dam, and Herbert S. Lin, US National Research Council of the National *Academics, Technology, Policy, Law, and Ethics Regarding US Acquisition and Use of Cyberattack Capabilities* (Washington, D.C.: The National Academies Press, 2009), p. 9.

3 Herbert Lin, "Escalation Dynamics and Conflict Termination in Cyberspace", *Strategic Studies Quarterly*, vol. 6, no. 3, 2012,p.47.

4 Owen, et. al., n. 2, p. 69.

5 Ibid., p. 68.

6 Leslie C. Green, *The Contemporary Law of Armed Conflict* (Manchester: Manchester University Press, 200), p. 124.

7 Herbert S. Lin, "Cybersecurity Symposium: National Leadership, Individual Responsibility: Offensive Cyber Operations and the Use of Force," *Journal of National Security Law & Policy*, vol.4, no. 1, 2010, p.63.

8 Agreement between the Governments of the Member States of the Shanghai Cooperation Organisation on Cooperation in the Field of International Information Security (61st plenary meeting, December 2, 2008).

9 Owens, et. al., n.2, p. 19.

10 Derek S. Reveron, *Cyberspace and National Security: Threats, Opportunities, and Power in a Virtual World* (Georgetown: Georgetown Univeristy Press, 2012), p. 38.

11 Seanm Lynn-Jones, "Offense- Defense Theory and its Critics,"*Security Studies 4*, vol. 4, 1995, p. 660.

12 Andrea Locatelli, "The Offense/Defense Balance in Cyberspace", *ISPI Analysis*, no. 203, October 2013, p. 4.

13 Ibid., p.7.

14 Owens, et. al., n.2, p. 114.

15 Oona A. Hathaway et al., "The Law Of Cyber-Attack", California Law Review, 2012, p.828.

16 Myriam Dunn Cavelty, *Cyber-Security and Threat Politics: US Efforts to Secure the Information Age*, (Oxon, Routledge, 2007), p. 45.

17 Reveron, n. 10, p. 42.

18 Terry D. Gill and Paul A. L. Ducheine, "Anticipatory Self-Defense in the Cyber Context," *International Law Studies*, US Naval War College, vol. 89, 2013, p. 438.

19 Ibid.,p.114.

20 Owens, et. al., n.2, p.115.

21 Ibid., p.117.

22 Ibid., p.118.

23 Ibid.

24 E. A. Lee, "Cyber Physical Systems: Design Challenges" (11th IEEE International Symposium on Object and Component-Oriented Real-Time Distributed Computing (ISORC)), May 2008, pp. 363–369.

25 Symantec Security Response, "W32.Duqu The Precursor to the Next Stuxnet," https://www.symantec.com/ content/en/us/enterprise/media/security_response/whitepapers/w32_duqu_the_precursor_to_the_next_stuxnet.pdf. Accessed November 10, 2015.

26 Ellen Nakashima,Greg Miller and Julie Tate, "US, Israel Developed Flame Computer Virus to Slow Iranian Nuclear Efforts, Officials say ," *The Washington Post* , June 19, 2012, https://www.washingtonpost.com/world/national-security/

us-israel-developed-computer-virus-to-slow-iranian-nuclear-efforts-officials-say/2012/06/19/gJQA6xBPoV_story.html. Accessed November 10, 2015.

27 Owens, et. al., n.2, p. 117.

28 Jason Andress and Steve Winterfeld, *Cyber Warfare: Techniques, Tactics and Tools for Security Practitioners* (Massachusetts: Elsevier, 2011), p. 156.

29 Owens et. al., n.2, p. 178.

30 Ibid., n.2, p.179.

31 The United Nations, "Charter of the United Nations Chapter VII: Action with Respect to Threats to the Peace, Breaches of the Peace, and Acts of Aggression," http://www.un.org/en/documents /charter/ chapter7.shtml. Accessed November 10, 2015.

32 *Webster-Dictionary* online, s.v."weapon". http://www.webster-dictionary.org/definition/Weapon. Accessed November 10, 2015

33 Arimatsu L, "A Treaty for Governing Cyber-Weapons: Potential Benefits and Practical Limitations ," paper presented at the 4th International Conference on Cyber Conflict, Tallinn, Estonia, June 5-8, 2012.

34 The United Nations, "Charter of the United Nations Chapter I: Purposes and Principles,"http://www.un.org/en/documents /charter/ chapter1.shtml. Accessed November 10, 2015.

35 Reveron, n. 10, p. 243.

36 Owens, et. al.,n. 2.

10

Internet of Things: A New Paradigm for Military Operations

Modem warfare has reached a strategic inflection point in the wake of different geopolitical challenges, the global terrorism menace, different economic challenges, violence emanating from religious radicalisation and internal security challenges. Warfare is no longer a sum total of capabilities, of putting more personnel, capital and technology on the battlefield, but of better situational awareness, contextual knowledge, discerning disposition and homogenised actions. The technological breakthroughs have profoundly altered and shaped the doctrinal, organisational and strategic contours of warfare. History is replete with examples in which adoption and assimilation of enabling technologies and corresponding shifts in doctrine, organisation and strategy have endowed the innovator with the capability to avoid attrition and pursue a form of "decisive" warfare.

Based on the outcome of the Persian Gulf War, which witnessed the use of an impressive array of high-technology weapons that allowed the coalition forces to overwhelm the world's fourth largest army in a remarkably short time, many strategists viewed these developments as revolutionary, spurred on by technological breakthroughs rather than as a part of ordinary evolutionary innovations. In the same breath, it is also important to understand that a revolution is not simply a demonstration of new technological capabilities. The revolutionary process is much more than a technology demonstrator, it is an all-encompassing process that requires effective adaptation of such technologies for successful exploitation, corresponding doctrinal and organisational modifications and willingness to digress from the established ways of doing things.

Information technology has revolutionised the way the warfare is conducted. Once made up of solely mechanical and electrical parts, military hardware now comprises complex systems, evolved through a combination of various components and functionalities of sensors, microchips, microprocessors, hardware, software, data storage and connectivity in a myriad ways. These "smart, connected products", bolstered by advancements and improvements in processing power, device miniaturisation and ubiquitous wireless connectivity have put warfare on the cusp of an epochal shift from the conventional to an information-based virtual age. These smart, connected products offer limitless possibilities and opportunities for new functionality, far greater reliability, higher and multifarious product utilisation and capabilities that cut across, and transcend, the traditional domains of warfare. The changing nature of military hardware is also forcing a rethink of strategic doctrines, a reevaluation of concept of operations and a reassessment of the ways of doing things.

Smart, connected military products raise a new set of strategic challenges. The challenges of utilisation of a prodigious amount of new and sensitive data generated, insertion of new technology into legacy systems,redefining warfare outside the traditional military mindset and the role of the military leadership in the backdrop of this new paradigm need to be tackled with due diligence. The phrase "Internet of Things (IoT)" has evolved to collectively identify the growing number of smart, connected products with exponentially expanding opportunities. For exchange of information between people or things, a virtual or physical connectivity is a prerequisite. The connectivity *per se,* is only a conduit and it is the changing nature of the "things", with expanding capabilities and data generation that are ushering in a new era of warfare.

Over the past 50 years, the information revolution radically the reshaped military thinking, concept of operations and strategy. The world is now going to witness another transformation. Before the advent of modern information technology, military hardware was predominantly mechanical, and activities in the conduct of warfare such as planning, resource allocation, exchange of instruction and orders were performed using manual modelling, verbal communication and paper processes. Riding on the IT wave, the adoption of IT enabled services in the realm of warfare saw a dramatic increase in the productivity of these activities, in part due to the enhanced ability to capture and analyse huge amounts of data associated with each activity. With increased connectivity and the rise of the Internet, an IT-driven renaissance has enabled better coordination and integration across individual activities. These developments have made the administration, supervision, operation and coordination of military affairs much more productive, result oriented and temporally relevant.

Now IT has become an indispensable appendage to all military activities. The IT proliferation in military related products is remarkably variegated and prolific. Embedded sensors, intelligent processors, sophisticated software and seamless connectivity in these products, coupled with data analysis and algorithmically induced decision-making capabilities, are driving unfathomable improvements in product functionality and performance. This wave of IT-driven transformation has the potential to be bigger than its predecessors, triggering even more innovation, operational enhancements and tactical utilisation. Smart, connected products offer a whole new set of technological solutions to some of the challenges in modern warfare.

Smart, connected products are made by an amalgam of three core elements: physical components, "smart" components, and connectivity components. Smart components focus on value addition and capability enhancement of the physical components, while connectivity amplifies the capabilities of the smart components. The end result is the evolution of the dynamic process of value addition and improvement. A product's mechanical and electrical parts are termed as physical components while smart components are fabricated by using sensors, microprocessors, data storage, controls, software, embedded operating systems, and enhanced user interface. In many products, software is increasingly used to emulate the functionalities of some hardware components or for enabling a single physical device to undertake multi-tasking at various levels. Connectivity is achieved by using components capable of interfacing/ interacting with the environment, medium or other devices by using ports, antennae, and protocols enabling wired or wireless connections.

Modern Warfare and Internet of Things

The alloying of intelligence and connectivity gives rise to an entirely new set of product functionality and capabilities in four core areas: monitoring, control, optimisation and autonomy. A capability developed in one area is in itself an enabler and energiser and functions as a stepping stone for the next level, ultimately leading to the desired goal. For example, monitoring capabilities are the bedrock of successful command and control operations, optimisation and autonomy.

- **Monitoring:** Smart, connected products facilitate comprehensive monitoring of the pace and magnitude of operations and even subtle changes in the external environment are recorded through sensors and external data sources. By analysing and synthesising the data, the user is alerted to change/ modify circumstances or performance. Monitoring also gives an insight to the product's operating characteristics, history and its utilisation. Intelligence, Surveillance and Reconnaissance (ISR) operations have always been the mainstay of military operations. The ISR operations provide valuable inputs and data which support planning, decision-making and mission accomplishment.

  In some cases, such as in air defence operations, monitoring is the core element of mission accomplishment. The air defence systems are made up of a set of sensors and a set of kill vehicles, collectively called a weapon system. While the sensors are used to detect incoming targets,kill vehicles are assigned to destroy targets. Air defence weapon systems, designed with smart products, will be capable of controlling themselves in a coordinated manner. Based on a pre-evaluated threat threshold, the smart components monitor the evolving air situation and alert operators in advance if the threat reaches a pre-defined threshold. The sensors continuously monitor the assigned area, exchange information laterally with other sensors and allocate weapons to targets based on vicinity and kill probability.

- **Control**: Smart, connected products can be controlled through remote commands or algorithms that are built into the device or reside in the product cloud. Algorithms are rules that direct the product to respond to specified changes in its condition or environment. Control through software embedded in the product allows the customisation of product performance to a degree that previously was not effective or, often even possible. The, same technology also enables users to control and optimise their interaction with the product in many new ways.[1]
- **Optimisation**: The monitoring data garnered from smart, connected products and the capacity to control product functionality allow optimisation of product performance in unthinkable ways—a capability acquisition not possible with earlier technology. Smart products, using algorithmic architecture and data analytics of in-use or historical data, offer improved efficiency and utilisation. In a radar, for instance, a local microcontroller can adjust the polarisation on every revolution during the rains. The radiated power can be adjusted to not only improve the radar's performance but to minimise its impact on the efficiency of he power generating components.

  Real-time monitoring of data on equipment condition and its operational capability enables operators to optimise its utilisation by performing preventive maintenance, and accomplishing repairs remotely, thereby, reducing product downtime and the need for on-site repair teams. Even when the on-site repair requirement is indispensable, advance information about failed components and instructions to accomplish the repairs reduces costs, reduces downtime and improves spare management.

- **Autonomy**: By smart monitoring, adaptive control and functionality optimisation capabilities, the smart, connected products can achieve a previously unattainable level of autonomy. Products equipped with sophisticated components and processes are capable of interacting with their environment, self-diagnosing their own service needs, optimising their output and adapting to the operators' preferences. Autonomy not only reduces the continual presence of operators but improves operational safety in dangerous environments and facilitates operations in remote locations. Autonomous products can also self-synchronise and coordinate with other products and systems, producing results far exceeding the sum total of individual capabilities. The value of these capabilities can grow exponentially as more and more products become connected.

A whole gamut of technologies is driving the IoT evolution. IoT is no longer confined to the traditional range of physical devices. The amalgam of traditional devices, human operators and smart devices in varying temporal and spatial domains, greatly expands the scope of application of IoT. IoT takes the outside physical information as a sensing foundation to realise identification of things, carry out dynamic sensing of environmental information,connect with other devices, and then builds a network by using various wired and wireless network communication technology to achieve information transmission. After sensing, a connection needs to be realised for distributed data sharing by integrating sensing subnets with existing networks. IoT uses high-performance computing technology to achieve intelligent data management and decision-making. Based on the results from the decision-making process, the control of things and the environment is realised.

- **Identification Technology:** For application of IoT, the basic requirement is recognition of things by assigning to each device, a globally unique value for its unambiguous identification. There are many coding rules, such as EPC coding which uses Radio

Frequency Identification (RFID) technology, IPv4 and IPv6 which is based on TCP/IP. For realisation of the full potential of IoT and seamless connectivity, mapping and compatibility issues between different coding methodologies need to be resolved. RFID is a non-contact identification technology for automatic identification of targets and collection of data through its radio frequency signals. The TCP / IP based IPv4 and IPv6 technology is capable of meeting the requirements of a vast number of devices in IoT.

- **Sensing Technology:** Data acquisition in the form of generation, access, transmission, processing and application is an important component of IoT. In IoT, depending upon the type of sensing devices (RFID, infrared devices, TCP/IP based devices, global positioning system devices), the real-time data in various forms are acquired. The data collection process of IoT is mainly through the control of various sensing devices to collect information on the surrounding environment and transfer the data through the corresponding network protocols.
- **Communication and Network Integration Technology:** The transmission of sensing data in IoT mainly relies on network and communication technology The network level of IoT is not limited to the traditional single network structure, but is spread over different types of networks, such as the Internet, 2G/3G mobile communications network and broadcasting and television network. It involves wired,wireless, mobile and other means of access, the unification of heterogeneous network addresses, conversion, packet format, routing options, and other issues.
- **Intelligent Information Processing Technology:** In IoT, the key technology is how to transform physical sensing data into logic data. Intelligent information processing technology integrates the intelligent computation, data mining, optimised algorithm and machine learning, and after processing and analysis of the data, the results are delivered to the intended user.

IoT-centric operations like Network-Centric Warfare (NCW) will enable a shift from attrition-centric warfare to a war-fighting style characterised by expeditious decision-making, versatile networked command and control and self-synchronisation. IoT will accelerate the process of attainment of information superiority,better awareness and understanding of the battle space rather than simply more raw data. With the emergence of new challenges to national security, the changing nature of global terrorism and an ever-growing reliance on network-centric operations, the intelligence agencies have to trawl through vast amount of data to identify subtle and specific signatures to determine the magnitude and timing of conditioned responses. In modern warfare, the key to successful operations is the immediate and appropriate response to fleeting signatures and detour from the time-consuming routine monitoring processes. The consequences of not dealing effectively with these challenges are potentially profound. IoT enabled forces, acting with speed, precision, and reach, achieve the massing of effects versus the massing of forces. The results that follow are the rapid foreclosure of enemy courses of action and the shock of closely coupled events.[2] One of the potential strengths of IoT-centric warfare will be to offset a disadvantage in numbers, technology, or position.

Battlefield Awareness and IoT

According to Carl von Clausewitz, "The great uncertainty of all data in war is a peculiar difficulty, because all action must, to a certain extent, be planned in a mere twilight, which, in addition not infrequently—like the effect of a fog or moonshine—gives to things exaggerated dimensions and unnatural appearance."[3] Situational Awareness (SA) encompasses a wide range of activities on the battlefield to gain information about the enemy's intent, capability and actual position. Throughout military history, seeking of the higher ground for an insightful perception of the battlefield has been the holy grail of warfare. Over recent years, aerial and space reconnaissance assets are being increasingly used to gain SA and thereby penetrate the fog of war. The main determinant of effectiveness in these operations is the speed of delivery of relevant information. IoT can play a vital role in raising SA by collecting, analysing and delivering the synthesised information in real-time for expeditious decision-making for appropriate military action. Defining SA in the realm of IOT requires an understanding of SA from the perspective of the following definition. SA is highly dependent on the following three elements:

- The perception of the elements in the environment within a volume of time and space.
- The comprehension of their meaning and/or comprehension of the current situation.
- The projection of their status in the near future

Perception is the key to all SA because operators perceive the environment differently. Perception, in turn, impacts how each individual perceives and acts upon, information. Comprehension is the ability to take disjointed elements from the perception phase and understand what their meaning and significance are to the greater whole. Projection is the ability to predict future actions, at least in the near term; this is achieved from the knowledge that is obtained from perception and comprehension. IoT enabled devices can enhance the level of perception by adding an objective functionality to complex and abstruse sets of data. The chaotic war-time environmental signatures and stimuli are organised to fit into the human cognitive process for comprehension.

Today, battlefield situational awareness can be enhanced by leveraging real-time and untethered interactions between combatants, decision-makers and machines. Unification of C4ISR systems, sensors, video, voice, data collaboration and secure mobile computing is delivering transformative and emancipator battlefield capabilities. IoT technologies can conjure up an integrated battlefield awareness system for monitoring, planning and reacting to threats as they emerge. An IoT enabled wearable device will transform a war-fighter in the field into a communications node, capable of gathering and transmitting data back to analytics and command centres. The lateral and vertical exchange of information of the battlefield between aerial and space-based sensors, UAVs, monitoring and communication devices, radars and wearable devices will provide real-time assessment of evolving operational requirements that help a military commander use assets effectively in deterring and responding to threats.

Intelligence and Operations

For many intelligence experts, automated analysis technology is the top ISR priority. In the military realm, data comes from a number of sources and platforms. It is varied and increasingly 'unstructured', with large quantities of imagery and video generated every day. It has been commented upon that military operations have "reached an inflection point in data deluge. We are now in danger of data asphyxiation and decision paralysis."[4] The collected data need to be sieved through a mesh of perceived objectives and goals to perform real analysis rather than exhaustive culling of raw data. IoT enabled devices can be used as predictive tools capable of providing coherent and actionable sets of data. IoT devices are capable of performing semantic and pragmatic data analysis to which experts can then apply their experience, intuition and human judgment.

Application of Internet of Things in Military Equipment Logistics

The proliferation of data generated from connected devices and sensors will have an enormous impact on military equipment logistics processes and the way logistics oriented decisions are made. IoT will usher a new era of efficiency, visibility and availability of military equipment in the right hands at the right time. IoT will be a huge enabler of creating efficiencies and unprecedented end-to-end visibility into every logistics activity and transaction. Gen Dennis J. Reimer, chief army of the staff, famously said, "There will not be a revolution in military affairs unless there is a revolution in military logistics." A loose consensus is slowly developing to recognise the

Revolution in Military Logistics (RML) as a necessary pre-condition of the Revolution in Military Affairs (RMA). For the RML, the focus needs to be on:

- **More Accurate and Timely Visibility of Demands:** IoT will further serve this demand by exploiting real-time information connectivity and auto communication by products of their status, health and requirements.
- **Quicker, More Responsive Processes.** Timely, integrated and predictive support even in unforeseeable conditions as the products will accurately provide the information in real time.
- **Increased Support From Afar:** During split-based operations conditions, by sustaining the force from dispersed geographical locations with IoT products, a blow by blow performance evaluation would be possible.
- **Reduced Footprint:** By limiting the extent and magnitude of the logistics support forces from the active theatre, attrition would be reduced.

Every smart equipment in the logistics chain, from intelligent storage to transportation to fitment and finally being declared as operationally suitable, will give off streams of useful real-time data. By leveraging IoT in the logistics process, it will be possible to:

- Collect data coherently across the whole spectrum of military equipment to predict future demand accurately.
- Create efficient shipments and optimisation.
- Prioritise the components availability
- Initiate procurement processes by studying the consumption pattern and inventory held.

IoT and Casualty Mitigation

The care of war casualties, both during their service and as veterans,is the lynchpin of military ideology. Changes in battlefield medical technologies, evacuation of the seriously wounded from the battlefield and assisting those in need of physical and mental succour have profoundly changed the treatment of wounded and injured soldiers. Without proper care of the wounded, the morale of the troops would suffer. IoT is capable of fuelling tremendous growth and improvement in the providence of healthcare services to military personnel by improved monitoring, driving better outcomes, consistency of care and enhancing the domain knowledge of medical experts. IoT can combine human intelligence and diligence with technology advancements to deliver enhanced results. The personalised medical devices and mobile healthcare applications that make up IoT have been increasingly making forays into the defence healthcare programme. IoT can be further exploited to holistically improve all aspects of healthcare by not only managing health, but by disease prevention and fitness promotion. To bolster healthcare for the defence personnel, leveraging the potential of IoT and adoption of IoT driven systems and processes, along with patient participation and subsequent data analysis, will change the way health services are delivered. IoT will continue to evolve fast, leading to impactful and positive changes in the realm of military forces.

The combination of IoT sensors will allow significantly improved measurement and monitoring methods of vital functions (temperature, blood pressure, heart rate, cholesterol levels, blood glucose, etc). Implantable wireless identifiable devices could be used to store health records that could save a patient's life in emergency situations. Edible, biodegradable chips could be introduced into the body and used for guided action. Things are now more and more integrated within the human body. It is expected that body area networks can be formed and that they will communicate with the treating physicians and emergency services.

IoT and Deployment/Mobilisation

Real-time route optimisation of all types of forces, equipped with IoT enabled devices, can be done by studying the steady stream of data generated during movements. The enabling automated capability to support rapid deployment of forces and to furnish accurate and timely data to manage the deployment conundrum has a bearing on the operational efficiency and efficacy. The automated planning, organising, coordinating, and controlling of the deployment activities will provide optimum, cost-effective and need-based solutions to the movement/ deployment of both equipment and personnel, from origin to destination. For example, a system with IoT enabled devices will be able to plan and execute air movements as well as design and analyse force packages by real-time estimation of airlift requirements for a given deployment list, maintenance of pre-planned contingency packages and by automated generation of individual aircraft load plans.

Equipment Maintenance and IOT

The core of military operations are its resources — the combined human and physical assets necessary to perform at peak levels. In today's military Services, keeping major end items military equipment in mission capable condition has been a tremendous challenge in the theatres of operation. The harsh conditions, extended deployments, stretching the limits of their capabilities, have put extensive wear and tear on equipment. The perennial operational readiness requirement of equipment throughout all the branches of the military services is stretching the existing maintenance resources and practices to the limit. There are many diverse and complex factors affecting equipment maintenance, such as the battlefield environment, equipment condition, maintenance resources, technical level of personnel, etc. Therefore, it is of great significance to use advanced Internet of Things technology for advanced equipment maintenance and management.

By using IoT, visualisation techniques and automatic identification technology with a combination of computer platforms, databases, supervision of maintenance personnel and material in important links, nodes and parts of the maintenance process, can be effectively implemented. The safety management system, with intelligent decision-making and automatic monitoring, based on IoT will be capable of combining, optimising and appropriately allocating various resources and processes such as manpower, material, financial resources, information, technology, management level and equipment maintenance objects. For example, modern aviation equipment with high technology integration requires managing and monitoring of each component throughout the entire life-cycle process, from its design, prototype fabrication, mass production, and integration with other components and maintenance.

IoT achieves automatic and intelligent information collection, transmission, processing and connections between objects and objects through a variety of sensing equipment.[5] The management system and process monitoring system based on IoT technology can effectively improve the management efficiency of the equipment maintenance materials. The traceability of management behavior and spares management information can be achieved by means of convenient, fast and accurate acquisition of raw materials.

IoT in Aerospace and Aviation

IoT can help to improve the safety and security of products and services by protecting them from counterfeiting. The aviation maintenance for example, is marred by the problem of Suspected Unapproved Parts (SUPs). An SUP is an aircraft part that is not guaranteed to meet the requirements of an approved aircraft part (e.g. a part that dose not conform to the strict quality requirements). Thus, SUPs pose great risk of undermining the capability of a mission critical aircraft to meet its objective. SUPs can seriously violate the maintenance and security standards, leading to accidents or incidents. This problem can be solved by introducing electronic pedigrees for certain categories of aircraft parts, which document their origin and safety-critical events during their life-cycle (e.g. modifications). By storing these pedigrees within a decentralised database as well as on RFID tags, which are securely attached to aircraft parts, an authentication (verification of digital signatures, comparison of the pedigree on RFID tags and within the database) of these parts can be performed, for example, prior to installing them within an aircraft. Thus, the safety and security of an aircraft is significantly improved. The 'on-condition' wireless monitoring of the aircraft by using intelligent devices with sensing capabilities available within the cabin or outside and connected to the aircraft monitoring systems is another emerging application area that forms the basis for ubiquitous sensor networks. The nodes in such a network will be used for detecting various conditions such as pressure, vibrations, temperature, etc. The data collected gives access to customised usage trends, facilitates maintenance planning, allows condition-based maintenance, reduces maintenance and waste, and will be used as input for evaluating and reducing the energy consumption during aircraft operations.[6]

Challenges of IoT

It has been succinctly commented that "IoT describes a splendiferous future: a dynamic and universal network where billions of identifiable 'things' (e.g. devices, people, applications, services, etc.) communicating with one another anytime and anywhere; things become context-aware, are able to configure themselves and exchange information, and show 'intelligent/cognitive?' behaviour when exposed to a new environment and unforeseen circumstances; intelligent decision-making algorithms will enable appropriate rapid responses, revolutionising the ways business values are generated."[7]

However, the present is not without challenges and tribulations and the current research and developments, though promising, are still too far from realisation of the envisaged vision. The diverse, heterogeneous and time dependent data generated by IoT enabled devices and resources is a major hurdle for the aggrandisation of IoT. The transformation of actionable and reliable knowledge and creation of perceptions from the large amount of data generated by the physical devices and human sensors requires further research and standardisation. IoT requires efficient mechanisms and methods that can handle large amounts of data and respond to the identified phenomenon and events arising from the environment in a timely fashion. Furthermore,security and privacy issues, trust and reliability of the data are also important for IoT-based applications and services, especially those in the military domain. Some of the major challenges are:

- **Inherent Dynamism and Complexity of IoT:** In the military realm, most of the data generated is transient in nature with high spatiotemporal dependencies. While analysis of data for meaningful inferences is possible, the pervasiveness and volatility of the environments require continuous monitoring and updates. This inherent dynamicity becomes a challenging issue when scalability, diversity and network/resource constraints are taken into consideration. The challenge in the future will be further exacerbated in the wake of the mobility and ubiquity of IoT enabled military hardware providing real-time data streaming. The issues of dynamicity and complexity will have a significant impact on many aspects of military operations such as data and resource access services, and maintenance, data analysis, aggregation and mining.[8] Further research, refinement and consolidation for coherent data processing mechanisms are required to address these issues.
- **Scalability of IoT Resources:** Creating domain knowledge models from data garnered from a large number of IoT entities, devices and their related data is critical for data engineering and knowledge harvesting. The data generated during military operations is an expected outcome of different processes, so meaningful interpretation needs to be associated with domain knowledge of resources and entities. Many military specific applications have been developed to maintain their own domain knowledge, but interoperability with cognitive layouts of human operators and algorithmic understanding of other IoT devices is an issue. The granularity of data is another important issue; the completeness and unambiguity of data will result in expansion of the domain knowledge realm. Handling of data in the military environment is more challenging and fraught with technical difficulties due to the magnitude of the data generated

by corresponding resources, continuous changes in the state of the resources and data, and volatility of the environments.[9] More efficient mechanisms on information search and retrieval, indexing query and information access will be required to address these issues.

- **Quality, Trust, and Reliability of Data**: The data, after observation and measurement, is provided by different sensory devices designed to perform a myriad operations. However, the quality of observations and measurements can change over time, for example, changes in the environment, faults in devices, or errors in device settings. As with any sensor, IoT enabled military sensors are not entirely impervious to inaccurate and erroneous measurements, thereby affecting the quality, viability and veracity of the data generated. Detection of anomalies, filtering out erroneous measurements and accepting data within the acceptable threshold can help in detecting errors and processing of data conferring to various operational requirements. Trustworthiness of these resources is another key issue which involves the capability of sensors to produce accurate and reliable data and its functioning in the changing environment condition. Sensors with high reliability attributes, environment independent functionality, fitted with robust feedback and verification mechanisms can bridge the trust deficit.
- **Interpretation and Perception of Data:** The data received from various sensors is a key enabler for developing situation-aware applications that can intelligently respond to corresponding changes in the operational conditions. Perception is the key to human intelligence and experience. Providing interpretation capabilities and analytics methods to sensors to process and elucidate changes in the battlefield will provide the military commanders with comprehension capabilities to take disjointed elements from the perception phase and understand their broader meaning and significance. However, sensor perception entails additional challenges such as: integration and fusion

of data from different sources, description of the events for cognitive understanding, risk threshold calculation, real-time processing of the data and the quality and dynamicity of outputs. The research is this field needs to develop solutions that can efficiently query and access the data from various sensors, geographically distributed with different assigned roles. The requirement of situation recognition, anomalies detection and pattern association with existing knowledge to create higher-level abstractions or new knowledge are some of the challenges which need to be tackled.[10]

- **Security and Privacy:** In the battlefield, the IoT enabled sensors will be used to describe the operational environment, the status of weapons, the location of mission critical assets,combatant deployment and other activities. This calls for mechanisms to provide and guarantee the security and privacy of data. While sharing and communicating IoT data, encryption and verification measures for meeting the desired security levels and privacy requirements are a must. As data is shared over the communication networks and can be shared among myriad users and devices, it is paramount to regulate access control through authentication and authorisation. Security and privacy imperatives in the IoT domain are central to the development and consolidation of reliable and efficient solutions in support of military operations.

Conclusion

Smart, connected military products will have a transformative effect on the quality, efficiency and effectiveness of military operations. Increased situational awareness, better understanding of equipment performance, improved maintenance practices, and better heathcare support to combatants will create opportunities for mission accomplishment, reduced attrition and casualty containment. The contours of future conflicts will be shaped in part by how these technological advances are assessed and adopted. Yet, in the context of warfare, technology is an enabler but does not govern it. It is not technology *per se*, but rather the organisation of technology that is important. What distinguishes the victors is their grasp of information—not only from the mundane standpoint of knowing how to find the enemy while keeping it in the dark, but also in doctrinal and organisational terms.[11] History demonstrates that changes of this magnitude do not occur without being accompanied by a fundamental change in the way war is conducted.[12] The forays made by IoT in the warfare realm are a culmination of advances in computerised information and telecommunications technologies. These advances, when married with related innovations in management and organisational theory, will inevitably have a profound impact on the means and ends of armed conflict.

Notes

1. Michael E. Potter and James E. Heppelmann, "How Smart, Connected Products Are Transforming Completion," *Harvard Business Review,* November 2014, p.64.
2. Neil Couch and Bill Robins, *Big Data For Defence And Security :Royal United Services Institute for Defence and Security Studies,* Occasional Paper, September 2013, p.1.
3. Clausewitz, *On War* (Project Gutenberg), Chapter II Section 24, Available online at http://www.gutenberg.org/ebooks/1946?msg=welcome_stranger. Accessed April 16, 2015.
4. Couch and Robins, *n.2,* p.10.
5. H. Sundmaeker, et al., "Vision and Challenges for Realizing the Internet of Things," IoT European Research Cluster (European Union, 2010).
6. Ibid.
7. Ibid.
8. Payam Barnaghi, Wei Wang, Cory Henson and Kerry Taylor, "Semantics for the Internet of Things: Early Progress and Back to the Future", p.16. Available online at http://knoesis.org/library/download/IJSWIS_SemIoT.pdf. Accessed April 17, 2015.
9. Ibid.
10. Ibid.
11. Peter L. Hays, Brenda J. Vallance and Alan R. Van Tassell, *American Defense Policy* (London: John Hopkins University Press, 1997), p.567.
12. Norman C. Davis, *In Athena's Camp: Preparing for Conflict in the Information Age* (RAND National Defence Research Institute, 1997), p.79.

11

Shaping The Cyber Zeitgeist in India: Challenges, Prospects and opportunities

"India is sitting on the cusp of a digital revolution; whether it is big metropolitan cities or small towns, a well-connected India has the potential to not only usher in economic and welfare opportunities for its citizens, but also the global economic order." This statement of Union Minister for Communications and IT, Mr. Ravi Shankar Prasad, on February 5, 2016[1] succinctly and effectively captures the essence of the cyber zeitgeist prevailing in India. It has fostered the efficient and inclusive governance structure, brought transformative improvements in the ways people live,interact, work and collaborate, and opened up new vistas of business, commercial and entrepreneurial opportunities.

With nearly 400 million Internet users,[2] India has embarked on the path of true transformation to a "Digital India", a visionary endeavour encompassing inclusive and equitable growth by tapping the potential of the digital revolution, promoting citizen-government interface by making the netizen an empowered citizen.[3] With one billion SIM card subscribers, a revolution in connectivity is sweeping India. India's future progress and growth is entwined with the expansion of the digital network and embedded in the security and sustainability of the digital ecosystem.

India has an enormous stake in a safe and secure cyber space, which has great strategic significance for its national security, political vitality, economic development and societal advancement.

India's national security environment is shaped primarily by regional imperatives and peripherally by global developments. Territorial disputes continue to strain India's relations with Pakistan and China. Unsettled **by the Indian economic growth, its vibrant democracy and expanding global geopolitical footprint, Pakistan has responded by** unleashing a sub-conventional proxy war against India with unremitting hostility. China views India as a military and economic competitor capable of restricting China's aspirational global and regional clout and its ascendance as a global hegemonic power. The Jammu and Kashmir (J&K) dispute and boundary issues are being raised by Pakistan and China at various international fora and during bilateral/ multilateral meetings, not for reaching mutually agreeable settlements but to keep the issues latent and simmering. The complicated and tenuous relationship which India has with its not so friendly neighbours has made India the target of a proxy cyber war, sometimes perpetuated by the states themselves, while, at other times outsourced to cyber mercenaries and terrorists.

Information technology has played a significant role in transforming India's image to that of a global player in providing IT solutions of the highest standards. The great strides made over the past years in information technology have not only brought economic well-being, enhanced employment opportunities and increased productivity,but have also underpinned the importance of securing, defending and protecting the cyber space. Slowly but surely, collective and conscious efforts were made to strengthen the cyber security and to prevent cyber misuse in all its forms and manifestations. The iconic Moore's Law of 1965, with unusual clairvoyance, predicted the ICTs' exponential pace and growth.[4] This growth has proportionally increased the cyber security challenges. The security policies, procedures, standards and guidelines need to evolve at a pace commensurate with the growing processing power, technical sophistication, widespread proliferation of ICT devices and strategic implications of cyber security breaches. Unfortunately, the untethered and explosive growth of new ICT technologies and the ubiquitous presence and penetration of the Internet saw the emergence of threats—far more insidious, far more formidable, and often hiding under a shroud of anonymity—which at times outpace the security responses of governmental agencies, and public and private users.

The cyber challenges are getting more complex, multifarious and unpredictable and are being perpetrated by actors—either independently or in collusion with others or on behalf of states—from geographically dispersed locations. This has created a completely new paradigm for national security, economic risk, individual privacy and, most of all cost implications in terms of sustainment of economic development, capability aggrandisement and societal coherence. The sustainment and maintenance of a secure, resilient and trusted cyber environment that supports India's national security, provides new impetus for the digital economy, promotes societal well-being, empowers citizens through information dissemination and enhances India's position as a leading provider of IT services, is a national priority and has been central to the national policy enunciation. The Indian government has a legitimate and necessary role in ensuring the maintenance and security of cyber space. The two primary roles for government are to develop, implement and enforce cyber security legislation, regulation and policy and to provide guidance, advice and operational capabilities to identify, prevent and detect cyber threats.[5] In addition, the government engages in bilateral and multilateral dialogues at various international fora, including the United Nations, for creating consciously holistic and mutually reinforcing agreements to promote coordination and cooperation in addressing cyber threats. The government,through its various agencies,also acts as an investigator of cyber crimes and as an enforcer of the enacted cyber laws. Some of the main challenges of the current cyber security zeitgeist are covered below.

Protection of Critical Information Infrastructure

In the Information Technology Act 2000, Critical Information

Infrastructure (CII)is defined as:"Critical Information Infrastructure means the computer resource, the incapacitation or destruction of which, shall have a debilitating impact on national security, economy, public health or safety".In one of the 2008 amendments to the IT Act, the central government granted itself the authority to "prescribe the information security practices and procedures for such protected system[s]." The transformative, emancipatory and empowering effects on critical sectors of digital and convergent communication technologies and their reliance on a consistent shared information system have made their Critical Information Infrastructures (CIIs) the lynchpins of their success. These CIIs are interconnected, interdependent, complex and distributed across various geographical locations.[6] The existence of cyber space vulnerabilities opens them up for exploitation by elements with hostile, malevolent and even conspiratorial intent, including state sponsored actors, terrorists, ideological and political extremists, data harvesters and financial scammers, disgruntled insiders, organised criminal groups, lone-wolf criminals and even by cyber-dilettantes. The CIIs of some of the Critical Infrastructures (CIs) are so inextricably interrelated and mutually interdependent that any disruption in a CI cascades across other CIs causing potentially multi-infrastructural collapse and catastrophic damage. Any delay, distortion or disruption in the functioning of these CIIs can easily lead to political, economic, social or national instability.

A central agency, responsible for mitigation, securitisation and protection of identified CIIs can effectively function when there is bottom-up, top-down and lateral sharing of key information garnered through qualitative analysis and study of the threats, vulnerabilities and criticality or consequence of an attack if it were to be carried out. The agency may also be entrusted with the responsibility to prevent classified or critical information from being compromised and timely dissemination of relevant and valid information to the authorised elements in each identified CII[7].

Cyber Terrorism

Terrorism in its many forms and manifestations has cost India not just loss of innocent and precious lives and unspeakable suffering to countless innocent people, but has resulted in diversion of substantive resources in the country's efforts to contain its spread. Terrorism—a scourge that transcends geographical borders and cuts across religious, sectarian and ethnic lines—evolves, propagates and retains its terror potency by permeating the public consciousness and infesting societies with fear. Terrorism thrives on publicity and cyber space facilitates terrorists to penetrate the collective consciousness and to vicariously expose the global community to the pain and suffering of the victims and their families. Besides, by propagating their convoluted ideological discourses with *pseudo-religious fervour,* the terrorist organisations partially succeed in bringing potential fence-sitters, sympathisers and ideologically aligned individuals into their fold.

Cyber space is used by terrorists as a key medium not only for coercion,enticement, indoctrination, proselytisation and propaganda but also for planning attacks after garnering information from cyber space about a potential target's location, security arrangements, and post attack impacts. Cyber terrorism is the convergence of terrorism and cyber space, perpetrated for the attainment of potential objectives such as damaging critical information infrastructure, disrupting vital networks, stealing trade secrets, provoking societal disharmony and radicalising groups along sectarian and religious faultlines.

Internet Governance

Since the time the Internet came into being and gingerly stepped into the public sphere, the term "**Internet governance**" has evolved. The term, at first, referred to the policy issues for its portability, operability, sustenance and reliability,and later encompassed the issues related to the management of domain names and IP addresses. As the Internet became ubiquitous, the definition also broadened considerably. In 2005, the UN-sponsored "World Summit on the Information Society" defined Internet governance as "the development and application by governments, the private sector and civil society, in their respective roles, of shared principles, norms, rules, decision-making procedures, and programs that shape the evolution and use of the Internet."[8] An equitable distribution of Internet resources, unfettered and multilingual access to all, and a stable and secure functioning of the Internet constitute the core of Internet governance.

The Internet may be a viable means of sharing information and for being socially relevant, but it is in its role as a source of power and domination that it is crucial for many nations for extracting greater political and economic mileage. The issues related to Internet governance have become highly contentious and political, and the stakes and challenges of Internet governance have become more complex and variegated. Preservation of national security, protection of economic interests, prevention of societal disharmony, and containment of internal dissident elements are some of the concerns, adding further complexities to the already tumultuous realm of Internet governance.

India is at pole position to swing the outcome of any debate on Internet governance. India's assertive role in this respect is highlighted by the opening statement made by the Indian representative at the NETmundial, "With a thriving and robust Internet ecosystem, India is well poised and willing to play an important and constructive role in evolving the global Internet governance ecosystem and in the process, make it more credible."[9]

On the issue of Internet governance, both the terms "multistakeholderism" and "multilateralism" have been used in many platforms by the Indian government. Both terms have evolved contextually in reference to the Internet governance ecosystem over the last decade. The multistakeholder approach is generally characterised by open participation and a bottom-up policy process that is consensus driven and usually produces outputs that are soft and non-binding. In contrast, the multilateral approach is generally characterised by participation which is limited to the member states and a top-down policy process that advocates voting for resolution and produces outputs that are more binding on its members.[10]

E-Governance

E-governance is the application of ICT for e-business in governance for the deliverance of government services, exchange of information communication transactions, integration of various stand-alone systems and services between the government and citizenry as well as interactions within the entire governmental framework.[11] In fact, good governance is an inclusive concept and practice which is possible with constructive interaction and collaborative work among the government, civil society and private sector. By encapsulating the finer points of good governance such as citizens' participatory engagement, citizen-centricity consensus orientation, accountability, transparency and responsive interactions, e-governance initiatives will ensure pragmatic application and 'empowering usage' of ICT innovations for delivering timely and efficient services to citizens. Various e-governance functions and their manifestations—in terms of citizens' access to government resources, online interactive transactions, SMS alerts, WAP applications and publishing—will ensure empowerment of the citizenry, more teeth to anti-corruption measures, and more transparent and accountable governance, and would be largely responsible for reduction of the spatial and temporal redundancy in government activities. Implementation of e-governance across the various arms of government at national, state and local levels, has the potential of enabling huge savings in costs through sharing of core and support infrastructure, enabling interoperability through standards compliance and presenting a seamless view of the government to the citizens. The successful realisation of this vision requires a massive nationwide infrastructure, reaching down to the remotest of villages, and large-scale digitisation of government records to enable easy, reliable access over the Internet. The ultimate objective is to bring public services closer home to the citizens.

Cyber Crime and Espionage

The Internet has created seemingly limitless opportunities for commerce, business, social interaction, entertainment and public discourse. The emergence of a hyper connected world,made possible by the digital revolution and the ubiquitous Internet, is a testament and celebration of freedom of speech and expression, of multiculturalism and social justice. The Internet has greatly enhanced the quality of life for many individuals and has helped in developing global consciousness on the basis of moral, social and political motivations, pre-conceptions and commitments. Individuals, corporations, public organisations, institutions and governments are using the Internet for propagation of their individual, commercial, ideological and political beliefs, notions and products, cutting across traditional boundaries of geography, communication and cultural identity.

There is historical evidence that any advancement in technology invariably finds its way into some criminal endeavour. The demographic transition during the Industrial Revolution saw the emergence of urban settlements with extremely high population densities. This created an environment in which street, predatory and organised criminals thrived. Similarly, the Information Revolution has created a domain conducive for both terrorist activities and criminal enterprises and an environment in which traditional criminals have joined hands with cyber criminals. Crimes against national security, crimes against the constitutionally established institutions, crimes against public peace, crimes against individuals, financial crimes, crimes against human rights, crimes against property, and terrorism – all are metastasising to the cyber domain .

India's cyber crime landscape has changed dramatically due to the proliferation of the Internet, ubiquitous connectivity, digital fluency, cloud computing, big data analytics, social networking and accelerated technology adaptation. The economic losses include financial loss due to cyber crime, theft of intellectual property, and industrial espionage. The potential threats of compromising and stealing classified information of government organisations have grave national security implications. The human costs in terms of reputations, livelihoods and financial distress caused by cyber criminal activities are enormous.

Cyber Warfare

The geopolitical situation and geographical imperatives have been the quintessential determinants in Indian domestic and foreign policies. Securing, protecting and promoting national interests—through political, economic and military means and through dynamic foreign policy enunciation and execution—will assure India's immunity from the causal and corrosive effects of a deteriorating security situation in its neighbourhood. Cyber space has created areas of concerns which potentially impinge on India's national sovereignty and national interests. There is proliferation of inimical individuals and groups and entities with anti-national, anti-democratic, and anti-societal intents and purposes who are leveraging cyber space with new tools of reconnaissance, surveillance, espionage and combat.

The numerous incidents of sensitive government and military computers being attacked and sensitive information being stolen are grim reminders of a multitude of insidious threats to national security. There is enough evidence to suggest that a substantial number of such cyber incidents are being perpetuated by nation-states or through proxies. The cyber realm presents a primary form of combat as well as an effective enabler and support provider for other domains of warfare. Many nations are putting in considerable efforts to develop, refine and consolidate cyber attack strategies and expand the repository of cyber weaponry. Today, cyber warfare is not an adjunct or afterthought to the national security strategy but rather an integral part of the national security framework.

Cyber Deterrence

Deterrence is a broad phenomenon that involves using threats of harm, usually to be inflicted by force to convince others not to do designated harmful things.[12] A credible deterrence posturing is designed and adopted by focussing on development of commensurate capabilities, their overt visibility, implicit influence and an explicit intent of using these. Deterrence uses both perception manipulation to subvert the adversary's motivation towards misadventure, and coercion and overt use of force, leveraging acquired deterrence capabilities, in the case of a military and strategic misadventure. However, the challenges of acquiring deterrence in cyber space have been complex and have persisted due to several reasons – the asymmetric nature, difficulties in accurate and timely attribution of hostile activities, level of threshold above which an inimical act warrants punitive reprisals, overarching dependence on technological prowess and a plethora of potential adversaries having the requisite intent and capabilities.

Cyber Policy Enactment

As part of the National Strategy to Secure Cyber Space, the creation and validation of a cyber security framework, followed by enunciation, and enactment of policy and strategy formulation and execution, provide coherence and direction to various government agencies, departments and individuals that have a role to play in national cyber security and resilience. The policy also needs to spell out the responsibilities of the private companies, organisations and individual citizens to bolster collective efforts aimed at strengthening the security and resilience of cyber space through greater vigilance, information sharing, cyber resource protection and adherence to instructions. The inherent dynamism and fluidity of cyber space will require updates, adjustments and amendments in terms of their temporal and spatial relevance. A pragmatic and carefully articulated national strategy will reduce national vulnerability to debilitating cyber attacks and speed up the amelioration of cyber risks. A viable and sound strategy with pragmatic directions and realistic action plans will contain the damage and will shorten the recovery time.

Social Media

The ubiquitous Internet and its spinoffs, most notably the social media,has allowed the citizenry to voice their opinions, expectations, demands and dissatisfactions, and to organise and rally around a shared affiliation regardless of the ethical, moral and legal underpinnings of a particular cause. The use of social media can both be causal and incidental in nature for many events, incidents and occurrences—initiated, instigated and directly or indirectly influenced—in the cyber realm.

The social media, apart from creating new social alignments and reconfiguring human behavioural patterns, is making it easier for inimical elements to assess information from new inferences and gain access to a large population. The social media has emerged as a chief platform with organisations like Al Qaeda and the Islamic State of Syria (ISIS) for propagation of an extremist ideology. Social platforms are being used for disseminating, engaging,recruiting and communicating for radicalisation of young people and sympathisers. Besides, social media can also be used to disseminate disinformation and spread misinformation, distort information to fit existing misconceptions, falsify information to fit vicious agendas or to weave a web of lies to deceive, misguide or mislead the unsuspecting victims. Social media can be used to stir up communal frenzy, to target innocent people and to inflame simmering tensions.

New Architecture for Defence Forces

India's complex and dense digital ecosystem poses a difficult strategic challenge. India's cyber space is incessantly being exploited, manipulated and subjected to attacks of varying intensity and frequency by internal and external threats. The integrity, functionality and safety of cyber space have emerged as key elements of India's strategic culture, and shape its strategic environment.

The breakthroughs in technology,and dependence on its potential in furtherance of present, future and aspirational military capabilities, new technology and its spinoffs are adopted, assimilated and integrated in one or the other domains of warfare. Cyber space contributes substantially to the economy of military operations, is a force multiplier and independently, or as part of other military operations, can unsettle, deceive, defeat or destroy an adversary. The "domain approach" is a logical evolution of military thinking and rationale to accrue strategic, operational and tactical advantages over potential adversaries. Defence Minister Manohar Parrikar recently remarked that the Indian armed forces, being vulnerable to cyber attacks, need to undertake technological enhancement of systems. He also said, "India's defence capabilities must be strengthened against disruptive and highly sophisticated cyber attacks.[13]

Countries around the world—based on their threat perception, acquired cyber capabilities and accorded levels of prioritisation to defence of cyber resources and capabilities – have adopted different approaches to developing a national cyber security capability and architecture. The US, for instance, pursues cyber threat management , mitigation and neutralisation strategies in the realm of military affairs and has established the United States Cyber Command (USCYBERCOM), with the following mission statement: "USCYBERCOM plans, coordinates, integrates, synchronises and conducts activities to direct the operations and defence of specified Department of Defence information networks and prepare to, and when directed, conduct full spectrum military cyber space operations in order to enable actions in all domains, ensuring US/ Allied freedom of action in cyber space, and deny the same to our adversaries".[14]

The overarching dependence of many societal, military, political and economic functions on cyber space has elevated it to a top national security concern. National security and the national interests of a sovereign nation are intricately linked and inextricably dependent upon its ability to maintain a strong cyber security posture, with proportionate emphasis on defensive strength and offensive capabilities. In all warfare domains, both defensive and offensive components add up and synergistically combine to provide comprehensive national security. Similarly, in cyber space, the serious external attacks can be repelled, deterred and effectively responded to by an operational organisational set-up with the mandate to monitor cyber threats, provide early warning of imminent threats of a serious nature with an arsenal of technical capabilities and a balanced force structure comprising capable and competent personnel.

Indian Cyber Strategy for Protection, Development and Utilisation of Cyber Resources, Capabilities and Assets

The Indian government, consistent in its commitment and approach to create, nurture and maintain a secure cyber ecosystem, set up the National Informatics Centre (NIC) as early as 1976, much before the World Wide Web made its foray into the public domain. The NIC has since emerged as a 'prime builder' of e-government/e-governance applications up to the grassroots level, as well as a promoter of digital opportunities for sustainable development.[15] To meet the demand for data communications at the national level, fledgling and rudimentary data communication networks were set up. Among the major public networks, three were set up between 1986 and 1988: the NIC Network (NICNET), INDONET and Education and Research Network (ERNET). NICNET is run by the National Informatics Centre (NIC) with its own nationwide satellite-based network serving primarily government agencies in 450 cities.[16] INDONET, run by CMC Limited, uses leased lines from the Department of Telecommunications (DoT) and is operated mainly for computer time leasing. INDONET, based on the Very Small Aperture Terminal (VSAT) is used by the public sector organisations as well as to connect the central government with the state governments and district administrations. ERNET serves the data communication needs of the academic and research communities.[17]

In order to bring in institutional and regulatory reforms and to give a fillip to indigenisation efforts, in 1984, the government set up the Centre for Development of Telematics (C-DoT) for providing an impetus to research in the switching and transmission segments.[18]In 1986, the Mahanagar Telephone Nigam Limited (MTNL) and the Videsh Sanchar Nigam Limited (VSNL) were set up under the Department of Telecommunications (DoT). VSNL was set up to plan,operate, develop, and accelerate international telecom services in India. Some of the regulatory reforms were conceived and implemented piecemeal without proper coordination and did not show any substantial signs of the predicted effects. The establishment of the Telecom Regulatory Authority of India (TRAI) in 1997 separated the regulatory function from the operational and other functions. Meanwhile, several technological changes and overlapping functional boundaries made it incumbent upon the government to view IT, telecom and broadcasting from the perspective of legislation, functional and operational interdependence,and effect policy formulation in a coherent and convergent fashion.

The monopolistic hold of VSNL as the sole Internet Service Provider (ISP) was eventually loosened by the government in November 1998 when private participation for ISPs was permitted. Initially, private operators had to use VSNL gateways, but the National Telecom Policy 1999 (NTP99) removed that constraint. Some of the operators set up their own gateways and were also permitted access to undersea wideband cable capacity with Fibre Optic Link around the Globe (FLAG)[19]and other similar carriers to have access to undersea bandwidth. This saw the Internet user base grow from 1.4 million in 1999 to over 15 million by 2003[20], and which is currently estimated to be 400 million.

In the initial stages, the pace of computerisation was relatively slow, however,its rapid growth has helped to offset the effects of the late start. With a vision and mission to have an inclusive governance structure with robust civil society participation, cyber space was used to extend government services to the citizenry,improve online interactions with government officials and for citizens; empowerment through access to information. The government's reliance on computerisation and Internet connectivity is a sincere attempt to bring the masses within the mainstream of political and social processes. Almost all the public and private sector undertakings have embarked on similar efforts for data communication, business transactions and to expand their public interactions across geographic, business, and functional boundaries.

The Indian ICT sector, driven by a strong performance in the service sector, innovation and a robust demand for products, is on a steady and upward trajectory,positioning India as a global hub of IT enabled services. The sector has proved its resilience on more than one occasion in tiding over the global recession and turbulent market conditions and has relentlessly pursued a double-digit growth. The industry clocked revenue of about US$ 146 billion with a growth rate of 13 per cent for FY 2015 and is likely to add revenues of US$ 20 billion to the existing industry revenues in the year 2016. Export revenues for FY 2016-17 are projected to grow by 12 to 14 percent and reach US$ 110-112 billion.[21] The IT-ITeS industry's contribution, relative to India's GDP, is set to touch an estimated 9.5 per cent and its share in total services' exports, more than 38 percent.[22] This steady and enviable growth stems from a combination of India's technological prowess, the government's thrust to create an environment conducive to stimulate greater innovation, availability of adequate and appropriate infrastructure and a large pool of IT professionals with a wide variety of skills.

The government, conscious of the onerous responsibility and far-reaching consequences of cyber exploits and attacks on critical infrastructures,has adopted a multipronged approach, including the use of diverse strategies and initiatives to underpin a nationwide cyber risk management, mitigation and prevention programme. The focal points of the government's efforts are as follows:

- Rapid identification, information exchange and prompt remediation to mitigate the consequences of malicious cyber space activity. Because no cyber security plan can be impervious to concerted and intelligent attacks, information systems must be able to operate while under attack and have the resilience to restore full operations quickly. A partnership on national and international levels between governments and industries to perform analyses, issue warnings, and coordinate response efforts will prevent, reduce, and ameliorate the consequential fallouts of cyber attacks.

- The vulnerabilities with exploitable potentials by cyber means exist, not only in the information assets of critical infrastructure, but also in external supporting structures, such as the networks and Internet. Vulnerabilities resulting from weaknesses in technology and its improper implementation need to be plugged across all the cyber assets and supporting infrastructures.
- Although the nation's critical infrastructure consists of both private and government-owned enterprises, the government, at all levels, performs essential services that depend upon cyber space for their sustainment, maintenance and operations such as food, water, public health, emergency services, defence, social welfare, information and telecommunications, energy, banking and finance, etc. Therefore,public undertakings have a great obligation and special responsibility to commit themselves to broad and sweeping measures across the whole range of cyber activities.
- Many cyber vulnerabilities exist because of a lack of cyber security awareness on the part of computer users, systems administrators and technology developers. Such vulnerabilities present serious risks to critical infrastructures and these risks are further exacerbated due to lack of cyber security awareness training and vague security policies and procedures. With sincere, result-oriented and meaningful efforts, the government is trying to close the gap between the imperatives of cyber security and availability of security-conscious and fully aware IT professionals, government officials, operators industry representatives, who are professionally trained in this aspect.
- Cyber space is a continuum rather than a series of discrete entities governed and controlled independently. India's cyber space is inextricably entwined with the global cyber space. Cyber attacks cross borders at the speed of light and discerning the source of the malicious activity is difficult. Safeguarding and defending

critical systems and networks in cyber space requires a system of international cooperation to facilitate information sharing, reduce vulnerabilities and deter malicious actors.

In order to build capabilities and capacities and lay down a framework which ensures a secure"cyber robust' and "defensible" information infrastructure, sincere efforts have been put in by the government by the enunciation and enactment of various policies, strategy formulations and their execution, and by the establishment of coherent milestones for various agencies, entities and individuals. Some of these are discussed below.

National Cyber Security Policy[23]

With an aim to monitor and protect information and strengthen defences from cyber attacks, the National Cyber Security Policy 2013 was released on July 2, 2013. The purpose of this was to ensure secure and resilient cyber space for citizens, businesses and the government. The mission statement of the policy is:

- To protect information and information infrastructure in cyber space.
- Build capabilities to prevent and respond to cyber threats.
- Reduce vulnerabilities and minimise damage from cyber incidents.

The policy highlights the significance of IT in driving the economic growth of the country and endorses the fact that IT has played a significant role in transforming India's image to that of a global player capable of providing IT solutions of the highest standards. The policy lays down the following strategic objectives:

- **A Secure Cyber Ecosystem:**[24] The Cyber Security Policy aims at protection of information infrastructure in cyber space, to reduce vulnerabilities, build capabilities to prevent and respond to cyber threats and minimise damage from cyber incidents through a combination of institutional structures, people, processes, technology and cooperation. The objective of this policy in broad terms is to create a secure cyber space ecosystem.

- **Strengthening the Regulatory Framework**: The policy stresses on creation of a dynamic legal framework as a deterrent for cyber criminals and aims to bring the perpetrators to book.
- **Protection and Resilience of Critical Information Infrastructure:**[25] A national and sectoral 24X7 mechanism has been envisaged to deal with cyber threats through the National Critical Information Infrastructure Protection Centre (NCIIPC).
- **Effective Public-Private Partnerships**: The policy calls for effective public-private partnerships and collaborative engagements through technical and operational cooperation.
- **Promotion of R & D in Cyber Security**: Research and development of trustworthy systems and their testing, collaboration with industry and academia, setting up of 'Centres of Excellence' in areas of strategic importance from the cyber point of view and R&D on cutting edge security technologies, are the hallmarks of this strategy as laid down in the policy.
- **Human Resource Development:** The policy also calls for developing the human resource through education and training programmes, establishing a cyber security training infrastructure through public-private partnership and establishing institutional mechanisms for capacity building for the law enforcement agencies.
- **Cyber Security Awareness:** The policy plans to promote and launch a comprehensive national awareness programme on security of cyber space through cyber security workshops, seminars and certifications to empower citizens to tackle the challenges of cyber security.

Critical Information Infrastructure (CII) Protection

Many of the critical services that are essential to the well-being of the citizenry, national economy and for national security are increasingly becoming dependent on cyber space. These need to be protected from cyber attacks in a way that is proportional to the threat perception. The Indian government has designated the "National Critical Information Infrastructure Protection Centre" (NCIIPC) of the National Technical Research Organisation (NTRO) as the national nodal agency for taking all measures across the entire spectrum of protection of CIIs in India.[26] To achieve its mission and vision, the NCIIPC engages in:

- Development of a mechanism to facilitate identification of CIIs through risk management.
- To lead and coordinate national programmes and policies on CII.
- Promote indigenous R & D relating to protection of CII, including modelling and simulation of complex CIIs.
- Development of a mechanism to facilitate sharing of information security breaches, incidents, cyber attacks, espionage among CII stakeholders.
- To facilitate capacity building towards creation of highly skilled manpower through engaging premier institutes.
- To develop a real-time warning system and facilitate information sharing on emerging threats and cyber attacks with CIsI.

Computer Emergency Response Team (CERT)[27]

CERT-In has been operational since January 2004 and is the national nodal agency for responding to computer security incidents as and when they occur. CERT-In also acts as the umbrella organisation for coordination of actions and operationalisation of sectoral CERTs. CERT-In envisages becoming the nation's most trusted referral agency for responding to computer security incidents as and when they occur. It enables all stakeholder entities to improve the security posture of IT services, enhance their ability to resist cyber attacks and recover within a reasonable time. In the Information Technology Amendments Act, 2008, CERT-In has been designated as the nodal agency for the following functions:

- Collection, analysis and dissemination of information on cyber incidents.

- Forecast and alerts about cyber security incidents.
- Emergency measures for handling cyber security incidents.
- Coordination of cyber incidents response activities.
- Issuance of guidelines, advisories, vulnerability notes and White Papers relating to information security practices, procedures, prevention, response to, and reporting of, cyber incidents.

Cyber Security Assurance Framework[28]

The Cyber Security Assurance Framework is a national framework for protection of critical information infrastructure. It aims to cater to the security assurance needs of the government and critical infrastructure organisations through "enabling and endorsing" actions. Enabling actions are essentially advisory in nature that can be seen and perceived as independent of bias and/or commercial interests. They involve publication of IT security guidelines and supporting documents to facilitate IT security implementation and compliance. Endorsing actions are essentially commercial in nature. These include:

- Mandatory compliance with the legal and regulatory framework.
- Compliance with Information Security Management Systems (ISMS) standards like ISO/IEC 27001/ IS 15150/ BS 7799, etc.
- Mandatory compliance verification through assessments, penetration testing, vulnerability assessment and application security testing
- Mandatory compliance reporting to CERT-In as a notified entity.

National Cyber Coordination Centre[29]

The National Cyber Coordination Centre (NCCC), which received in-principle approval in May 2013 from the Cabinet Committee on Security,is about to become a reality. Once established, this new body will come under the National Information Board and would be responsible for all forms of cyber intelligence and cyber security issues.

- The NCCC will be responsible for situational awareness of cyber space and for providing adequate early warning for cyber attacks.

- The NCCC is expected to screen all forms of metadata, ensure better coordination between various intelligence agencies and "streamline" intelligence gathering. To that end, it expands the charter of the Computer Emergency Response Team, India (CERT-IN).
- It is also the duty of the NCCC to alert all relevant agencies during a cyber attack and ensure better cyber intelligence sharing.
- The NCCC will also carry out'Flow Based Analysis' of Internet traffic in order to forecast and forewarn about DDoS attack build-up, virus/malware infections leading to abnormal traffic/network congestion, the possibilities of targeted attacks, etc.

Common Criteria Certificates in the Field of Information Technology Security[30]

The Common Criteria Certificates Arrangement is between government agencies in which IT products and protection profiles can be procured or used without the need for further evaluation. The main objectives of this arrangement are:

- To ensure that evaluations of IT products and protection profiles are performed to high and consistent standards which contribute significantly to security of those products and their profiles.
- To improve the availability of evaluated, security-enhanced IT products and protection profiles.
- To eliminate the burden of duplicating evaluations of IT products and protection profiles.
- To continuously improve the efficiency and cost-effectiveness of the evaluation and certification/validation process for IT products and protection profiles.

India's Stand on Internet Governance

India has participated in key activities of various fora and meetings organised for formulating the Internet governance structure and consensually agreed to consider it for global application. However,

India has supported one of the two models of Internet governance, i.e. 'multistakeholderism' and 'multilateralism', in many platforms. In 2011, India proposed the setting up of United Nations Committee for Internet Related Policies (CIRP) as the new institutional mechanism.[31] The CIRP would take inputs from the Internet Governance Forum (IGF) and would comprise 50 member states based on equitable geographic representation. CIRP was envisaged to have multistakeholder representation.[32]

In October 2012, India endorsed the status quo position of the ICANN-led Internet governance. The then Minister of State for Telecom, Mr. Sachin Pilot, who led the Indian delegation to the Budapest Cyber Space Conference, said that India would pursue enhanced cooperation with ICANN through a wider dialogue.[33]At the NETmundial on "International Telecommunication Union (ITU) Plenipotentiary" in November 2014, in São Paulo, Brazil, on April 23 and 24, 2014, the Indian submission proposed renaming the Internet as Equinet, a concept put forward by its then Minister of Communications and IT, Mr Kapil Sibal.[34]This appropriate **new neologism tries to articulate India's** rationale for making all nations equal stakeholders in Internet operations, thus, bringing in greater equity in the choice of standards, especially in areas such as cyber security, data protection and privacy.

In June 2015, at the opening conference of the ICANN in Argentina, Information Technology Minister Ravi Shankar Prasad unveiled an "Indian vision for the Internet", stating that "India recognises that all stakeholders are key and multistakeholderism is perhaps the only way to keep the system integrated, growing and expanding."[35] The endorsement of multistakeholderism allows India to engage substantively with Internet governance concerns at multiple fora. However, India did not endorse a particular multistakeholder model which was crucially timed to enhance ICANN's accountability to users outside the US, while ensuring that Indian internet users and businesses have an equitable say in the ownership of new and lucrative top-level domain names (like .kids, .books, .pharmacy).

The acceptance of the 'multistakeholder model' in principle will also facilitate a bottom-up approach on key Internet concerns such as net neutrality, freedom of speech and expression on the web. It is a step in the right direction to create democratic space for debating Internet policies to "sustain a future of equity, innovation, collaboration and inclusion", as articulated by Shri Ravi Shankar Prasad at the ICANN conference in Argentina.

Cyber Laws and Enforcement

The potential severity and consequent losses due to cyber crime necessitate revision of existing laws, and enactment of new legislations or amendments, wherever necessary. In the context of cyber laws and enforcement,the formal standards imposed by the law (*de jure* standards) are frequently impeded upon and *de facto* violations are not formally defined. To address this, the existing legislations and statutes are being reviewed to address the challenges that emerge out of *untethered proliferation of cyber attacks. The cyber law enforcement is a relatively new challenge for most enforcement agencies but these agencies have now gained sufficient competence and skills to deal with cyber crimes. Armed with enforceable laws, with provisions for imposition of a penalty or imprisonment on conviction, various agencies are now capable of combating sophisticated cyber crimes and unlawful conduct in cyber space and the Internet.* With an aim to provide a statutary framework for law enforcement activities in cyber space and to address privacy issues, jurisdiction issues and intellectual property rights issues, the "Information Technology Act, 2000" (ITA-2000) was enacted by the Parliament of India.[36] The above Act was further amended in the form of the IT Amendment Act, 2008 (ITAA-2008) to protect the interest of individuals, organisations and governments in cyber space from cyber crimes, with provisions for penalties and punishments.

Since the Internet is not a geographically or sovereignty bound entity, one of the United Nations agencies, the United Nations Commission on International Trade Law (UNCITRAL), proposed laws with a certain level of uniform interpretation, applicability and enforceability in all member countries.[37]With remarkable foresight, the Government of India initiated the process of enacting India's information technology legislation, soon after its adoption by the UN General Assembly. The Information Technology Act, 2000, is based on the UNCITRAL's Model Law on Electronic Commerce, which adopted an approach based on "functional equivalence".[38] The "functional equivalent approach" is based on an analysis of the purposes and functions of the traditional paper-based requirement and fulfilment of such purposes and functions through the electronic-commerce techniques. It also provides for equivalence on admissibility of the electronic record in a court of law, like a paper document. The different offences which are given under this part are as follows:

Table 11-1: Offence and Related Section under IT Act[39]

Offence	Section under IT Act
Publishing False Digital Signature Certificates	Section 73
Privacy and Confidentiality Breach	Section 72
Accessing Unauthorised Protected Systems	Section 70
Publishing Obscene Information	Section 67
Data Alteration and Hacking Computer Systems	Section 66
Tampering with Documents Sources with Computers	Section 65

Table 11-2: Computer Related Crimes Covered under IPC and Special Laws

Offence	Section under IT Act
Sales of Arms Online	Indian Arms Act 1959
Sales of Drugs Online	Narcotic Drugs and Psychotropic Substances Act, 1985
E-mail Abuse Section 500 of IPC Web Jacking	Section 420 of IPC
E-mail Spoofing	Section 463 of IPC
Cyber Frauds and Bogus Websites	Section 383 of IPC
Forging Electronic Records and Data	Section 463 of IPC
Sending Defamatory E-mail Messages	Section 499 of IPC
Sending Threatening E-mail Messages	Section 503 of IPC

Tri-Service Cyber Command for Defence Forces

The US' cyber threat perception, its consequences on national and individual security and proportionate response capabilities culminated in the establishment of the United States Cyber Command(USCYBERCOM), which reached full operational capability in October 2010.[40] A closer scrutiny of its role, operational capability and stated strategic objectives reflects its indelible universal viability and applicability across nations. Cyber attacks may take place without warning or provocation from a wide range of elusive adversaries (nation-states, non-state actors, cyber criminals and insiders)against targets distributed across the broad spectrum of social, political, military and economic institutions which have a direct bearing on national security and the individual lives of people. Any delay in responding meaningfully and effectively to cyber threats may prove costly and calamitous, taking a high toll in terms of financial loss, disruption of essential state functions, prosperity, interruption of essential services and jeopardising national security.

Cyber threats fall into four broad categories: espionage; warfare; terrorism; and crime. [41]In the Indian context, the defence forces have largely played a central role in dealing with threats and challenges emanating from activities falling under the categories of warfare, and an essential collaborative and supporting role in dealing with the threats of terrorism and espionage. Acts of physical and financial crimes are generally dealt with by law enforcement agencies. Given the high stakes and large uncertainties involved in dealing with cyber attacks, an institutional and organisational architecture, capable of defending cyber space, protecting critical infrastructure and identifying, anticipating and responding to new and emerging cyber threats is required to secure India's national interests domestically and overseas.

The Indian government is conscious and mindful of the possible consequences of cyber attacks, either independently or as an adjunct to kinetic attacks, and has, in principle, approved the setting up of a "Cyber Command" as part of the three new Tri-Service Commands being set up. It has been widely reported in the media that the defence minister has directed the Integrated Defence Staff (IDS)to "work out and fine-tune" the "basic structures" for the Cyber, Aerospace and Special Operations Commands.[42]

India's cyber warfare programme, from its nascent stage of development to some degree of consolidation, was neither overseen, nor intervened in, by the armed forces. The role of the armed forces in the overall cyber security architecture was limited to preventing breaches of cyber security within their own networks and protecting their own cyber resources. However, the institutional and doctrinal developments in the US' and China's cyber warfare programmes, which are being guided, steered and managed by their respective military departments, have made it absolutely and irrevocably mandatory for the Indian military leadership to charter its own path towards cyber warfare. With an aim to create and reinforce the credibility and effectiveness of strategic and operational plans and decision-making, the establishment of the Tri-Service Cyber Command will protect the national cyber space and practise the immutable precepts of warfare i.e. aggressive deterrence, active defence and proactive response against an enemy in cyber space.

Social Media Misuse and Indian Cyber Law

In a short span of time, the social media has proliferated in reach and capacity and has emerged as a vibrant platform for human interactions and communication. The ease of access and availability of various social media platforms, coupled with the human trait of sharing information which is deemed as emotionally arousing and profoundly sensational, has given rise to an entirely new set of social practices, without any consideration of their wider ramifications. A number of times, the contents that are posted on social media sites are inflammatory, inaccurate and unsupported,resulting in baseless accusations, false implications, slander and propagation of misplaced and convoluted ideas of race religion, politics, and history.

In order to check anti-social, anti-national and terrorist activities in cyber space and to prevent the advocacy of racial, ethnic or religious hatred enticing discrimination, hostility or violence[43] by the use of social media, the cyber laws and cyber jurisprudence have been developed, largely founded upon the Information Technology Act, 2000, as amended by the information Technology Act, 2008. The law categorically makes a person liable for the posting of any incriminating or illegal content or material on social media. The jurisprudence on social media misuse in India is only beginning to evolve and with more cases of social media misuse being registered, investigated and prosecuted, a clear message is put on the collective conscience of the citizenry that the social media do not comprise an unbridled and free-for-all arena, but one for restrained and responsible behaviour, and acts of violations and aberrations from normal acceptable social norms and divergence from legally binding rules will be punishable under the law.

Cyber space has now grown to become a domain of strategic significance and capacity-building and for accruing strategic leverage, economic advantage and legitimacy as a global power. The ubiquitous dependence of a nation on cyber space makes the disruption of cyber space a cause of grave concern and may have restrictive influence on its ability to function effectively in a crisis. The Internet has become a mass phenomenon, a catalyst for societal and economic development and improvement, a stimulus for political stability, a platform for propagating and sharing knowledge, a tool for realising entrepreneurial synergies, an instrument for social mobilisation and participation, and any trust deficit caused by the rampant cyber crimes, loss of privacy, acts of malicious intent and a deficient understanding of regulatory elements can cause serious economic and social harm to the nation and its citizenry. The conventional rules and legal norms associated with crime control and criminal justice are woefully inadequate for policing, regulating and enforcing the provisions of statutory laws in cyber space, while laws newly enacted or amendments made to existing laws are still lagging behind when it comes to regulation and governance of the conduct within the cyber domain. While this reflects the dynamism and vibrancy of cyber space of today, it can also cause instability and uncertainty about accountability. In cyber space, the blurring of boundaries and loss of distinction between the public and private dimensions of life increases the risk potential and risk impact over a larger population segment, from acts in cyber space, perpetrated, intentionally or by accident. In cyber space, the overriding imperative of national security needs to be consistent with the human rights obligations such as concerning freedom of expression,the right to privacy and the right to seek and share ideas.

The Indian government has taken a slew of measures to tackle cyber security violations and cyber crimes in the country.[44]While cyber threats have come to be considered as one of the quintessential security threats of the current 'zeitgeist', an overall legal and penal framework for tackling cyber crimes is still evolving and new laws /penalties are being added, amended or reenacted to deter cyber crime, prosecute offenders, reduce the risk of victimisation and empower people through legal rights, etc. The government's sincere and pragmatic efforts are not limited to cyber security, but instead cover the entire spectrum of cyber activities, including; but not limited to, the full range of impacts and mitigations measures; cyber resource management; dispute resolution and arbitration in cyber space; protection of legitimate online commercial interests; strengthening the defensive structure against cyber surveillance, espionage and hacking; all-inclusive support to the defence Services' demand for the establishment of a comprehensive tri-Services cyber security architecture; and protection of CIIs. The challenges are many and are of unique nature in terms of high disruptive potential, human and legal expectations, attribution of responsibility within the legal framework, new technology breakthroughs and their adoption without a corresponding regulating strategy, etc. However, sincere efforts are being made by the government in terms of policies and programmes to overcome some of these challenges.

Notes

1 NDTV, "India Sitting on Cusp of Digital Revolution: Ravi Shankar Prasad", http://www.ndtv.com/india-news/india-sitting-on-cusp-of-digital-revolution-ravi-shankar-prasad-1274353. Accessed April 23, 2016

2 "IAMAI: India's Internet User Base to hit 402 Million, Second-Highest in the World", *The Times of India*, http://timesofindia.indiatimes.com/tech/tech-news/IAMAI-Indias-internet-user-base-to-hit-402-million-second-highest-in-the-world/articleshow/49816190.cms. Accessed April 23, 2016

3 "India Offers to Set up IT Park in Sri Lanka", *The Hindu*, http://www.thehindu.com/news/international/india-offers-to-set-up-it-park-in-sri-lanka/article8202991.ece. Accessed April 23, 2016

4 Moore's Law, "How Overall Computing Power of Computers will Double Every Two Years," http://www.mooreslaw.org/. Accessed July 30, 2015

5 Chris Brookes, *Cyber Security: Time for an Integrated Whole-of-Nation Approach in Australia*, (Canberra : Centre for Defence and Strategic Studies, Australia, 2015), p.6.

6 National Technical Research Organisation Government of India, *Guidelines for Protection of National Critical Information Infrastructure*, Version 1.0, June 2013.

7 Ibid., p.9.

8 Château de Bossey, "Report of the Working Group on Internet Governance", June 2005, p.4.

9 "Statement by Mr Vinay Kwatra, Indian representative at the Global Multistakeholder Meeting on the Future of Internet Governance in Sao Paulo (April 23-24, 2014)",http://mea.gov.in/Speeches-Statements.htm? dtl/23246/Statement+by+Mr+Vinay+Kwatra+Indian+representative+at+the+Global+Multistakeholder+Meeting+on+the+Future+of+Internet+Governance+in+Sao+Paulo+April+2324+2014. Accessed April 23, 2016

10 Rekha Jain, *A Model for Internet Governance and Implications for India* (Ahmedabad: Indian Institute of Management, Ahmedabad, W.P. No. 2015-03-23), March 2015, p.31.

11 B. Saugata and R.R. Masud, *Implementing E-Governance Using OECD Model(Modified) and Gartner Model (Modified) Upon Agriculture of Bangladesh*. IEEE. 1-4244-1551-9/07.

12 Emanuel Adler and Vincent Pouliot, *International Practices : Cambridge Studies in International Relations* (Cambridge: Cambridge University Press, ,2011), p.141.

13 Hindu News Bureau, "Armed Forces Vulnerable to Cyber-Attacks, says Defence Minister," *The Hindu*, November 23, 2015, at http://www.thehindubusinessline.com/info-tech/armedforces-vulnerable-to-cyber-attacks-says-defence-minister/article7909315.ece. Accessed April 23, 2016.

14 US Department of Defence, "Cyber Command Fact Sheet", http://www.stratcom.mil/factsheets/Cyber_ Command, May 21, 2010. Accessed April 23, 2016.

15 National Informatics Centre, "About National Informatics Centre", http://www.nic.in/about-us. Accessed April 23, 2016.

16 Sebastian Morris and Rajiv Shekhar, *India Infrastructure Report 2001* (New Delhi: Oxford University Press, 2002), p.222.

17 Ibid.

18 Ibid., p.190.

19 Ibid., p.195.

20 IDSA Task Force Report, *India's Cyber Security Challenge* (New Delhi : Institute for Defence Studies and Analyses, 2012), p.13.

21 NASSCOM, The IT-BPM Sector in India Strategic Review 2015 (New Delhi: NASSCOM, 2015), http://www.nasscom.in/robust-growth-indian-itbpm-industry, p.6.

22 Ibid., p.4.

23 Ministry of Communications and Information Technology, Department of Electronics and Information Technology, *National Cyber Security Policy- 2013(NCSP-2013).*

24 Ibid.

25 Ibid.

26 n. 6.

27 Department of Electronics and Information Technology (DeitY), "Indian Computer Emergency Response Team (ICERT)", http://deity.gov.in/content/indian-computer-emergency-response-team-cert-dpl-rtoi. Accessed April 23, 2016.

28 Department of Electronics and Information Technology (DeitY), "Strategic Approach", http://deity.gov.in/content/strategic-approach. Accessed April 23, 2016.

29 NDTV, "National Cyber Coordination Centre to Be Set Up: Ravi Shankar Prasad", http://gadgets.ndtv.com/internet/news/national-cyber-coordination-centre-to-be-set-up-ravi-shankar-prasad-698967. Accessed April 23, 2016.

30 Common Criteria Portal of India, "Indian Common Criteria Certification Scheme(IC3S)", http://www.commoncriteria-india.gov.in/. Accessed April 23, 2016.

31 Jain, n.10, p.24.

32 Ibid.

33 Shalini Singh, "On Internet Rules, India Now More Willing to say ICANN", *The Hindu*, October 14, 2012, http://www.thehindu.com/news/national/on-internet-rules-india-now-more-willing-to-say-icann/ article3994985.ece. Accessed April 23, 2016.

34 BGR, "India Wants the Internet to Become Equinet", http://www.bgr.in/news/india-wants-the-internet-to-become-equinet/. Accessed April 23, 2016

35 Centre for Communication Governance (CCG) at National Law University, Delhi, "IT Minister Ravi Shankar Prasad's Remarks at ICANN53",https://ccgnludelhi.wordpress.com/2015/06/22/text-of-it-minister-ravi-shankar-prasads-remarks-at-icann53/. Accessed April 23, 2016.

36 The Information Technology Act, 2000 (No. 21 of 2000).

37 UNCITRAL, "Welcome to UNCITRAL",https://www.uncitral.org/. Accessed April 23, 2016.

38 n. 36.

39 Ibid.

40 US Department of Defence, *Establishment of a Subordinate Unified US Cyber Command Under US Strategic Command for Military Cyberspace Operations*, Memorandum for Secretaries of the Military Departments by the Secretary of Defence June 23, 2009, https://fas.org/irp/doddir/dod/secdef-cyber.pdf. Accessed April 23, 2016.

41 Arun Mohan Sukumar and Col. R.K. Sharma, *The Cyber Command: Upgrading India's National Security Architecture* (New Delhi: Observer Research Foundation, 2016), p.3.

42 Rajat Pandit, "Govt Gets Cracking on Three New tri-Service Commands", *The Times of India*, August 20, 2015, at http://timesofindia.indiatimes.com/india/Govt-gets-cracking-on-three-new-tri-Service-commands/articleshow/ 48550424. cms. Accessed April 23, 2016.

43 Talia Naamat, Dina Porat and Nina Osin, *Legislating for Equality: A Multinational Collection of Non-Discrimination* (Boston: Martinus Nijhoff Publishers, 2012), p.402.

44 Tech2," Indian Government has Taken a Slew of Measures to Tackle Cyber Attacks: IT Minister", http://tech.firstpost.com/news-analysis/indian-government-has-taken-a-slew-of-measures-to-tackle-online-scams-it-minister-243828.html. Accessed April 23, 2016.

Index

Outer Space: Law, Policy and Governance

G S Sachdeva

Rs 995

Cyber Warfare: The Power of the Unseen

M K Sharma

Rs 720